To Ba...

Best wishes

THE
GRAND TOUR
DIARIES

2018/19

Lionel Birnie

THE CYCLING
PODCAST

Published by Vision Sports Publishing Limited

Vision Sports Publishing Limited
19-23 High Street
Kingston upon Thames
Surrey
KT1 1LL
www.visionsp.co.uk

ISBN: 978–1–909534–99–5

Cover and text design: David Hicks Design
Photography: Simon Gill

Printed in the UK by CPI Group

CONTENTS

To all our listeners and
Friends of the Podcast

CONTRIBUTORS

Lionel Birnie co-presents *The Cycling Podcast* having covered the sport since the late nineties. He co-founded *The Cycling Anthology* and ghost-wrote Sean Kelly's autobiography, *Hunger*.

Daniel Friebe co-presents *The Cycling Podcast* having written about cycling since the early 2000s. He is the author of *Mountain High, Mountain Higher* and *Cannibal*, a biography of Eddy Merckx.

Richard Moore co-presents *The Cycling Podcast* and *The Cycling Podcast Féminin* and is the author of seven books, including *In Search of Robert Millar, Slaying the Badger* and *Étape*.

François Thomazeau is the former head of sport at Reuters France, the author of several novels and non-fiction books, a musician (recording and performing as Sauveur Merlan), and the owner of a bookshop in Paris. He first reported on the Tour de France in 1986.

Orla Chennaoui is the presenter of Eurosport's Grand Tour coverage and co-hosts *The Cycling Podcast Féminin*.

Simon Gill is *The Cycling Podcast*'s official photographer and his work has also appeared in the *Guardian, Rouleur* and *Procycling* magazine.

INTRODUCTION

In 2013, when we started a podcast on the eve of the Tour de France, it didn't occur to us that we'd continue beyond that year's race, far less that we'd still be doing it six years later.

We could never have imagined that it would spawn T-shirts, mugs, live events and books, or that our original team of three – Lionel Birnie, Daniel Friebe and Richard Moore – would be bolstered by François Thomazeau, Orla Chennaoui and Ciro Scognamiglio, to name a few of our regulars.

Yet here we are with our second book, telling, in diary form, the stories behind the stories from the three Grand Tours and the Women's Tour of the 2018 and 2019 seasons, illustrated with the stunning images of our photographer, Simon Gill.

And in case you're wondering, or perhaps confused, the picture on the jacket, one of Simon's, is from the most remarkable and dramatic day of the 2019 Tour de France, when hailstones and a landslide forced the cancellation of stage 19 (the image shows Mitchelton–Scott sports director Matt White, a regular on the podcast, at the summit of the Col de l'Iseran shortly after the stage was stopped).

We began covering all three Grand Tours – the Giro d'Italia, Tour de France and Vuelta a España – in 2016. Each of these races is a three-week adventure for us as well as the 180 or so riders: we travel thousands of kilometres, stay in a different hotel each night and encounter a rich assortment of places, people and food.

The diaries weave the races and these experiences together. They include stories of traffic jams, wrong turnings and detours across the desert; of delicious meals in remote Pyrenean *haciendas* and service station sandwiches on the autoroute; of roasting in the heat of southern Spain, being pelted by hailstones in Andorra and narrowly avoiding landslides in the Alps.

Listeners to the podcast will be familiar with François's bullshit detector, Daniel's policing of pronunciation and cappuccino, Richard's wine-tasting notes and Lionel's aversion to *andouillette* and addiction to *cassoulet*. This is the meat and drink of *The Cycling Podcast*, quite literally, so why a book?

Over the past six years we have happily surfed the podcasting wave, our audience growing as more and more people discovered this fantastic but very simple and old-fashioned medium. Podcasts are, after all, just radio shows that you can listen to whenever you want, helping to pass the time while driving, commuting or travelling, walking the dog or washing the dishes.

Although we all share a background in print, we have fallen in love with audio. We have learned that there are things you can do using sounds and the spoken word that you can't do so easily in print. And in a sport as complex and mysterious as cycling, where so much of the action still happens beyond the gaze of the cameras and even most of the protagonists, the depth and breadth of audio can feel like a great luxury.

But of course there remain things you can do better and more easily in writing, which is why we will always be drawn back to our first love, books.

Although we cover the Grand Tours as a team, there are experiences and stories that are sometimes more easily shared via pen and page or keyboard and computer screen. While the best moments in the podcast tend to come from the unpredictability and spontaneity of a conversation, writing is more individual and personal. And you can take your time to get it right on the page. So while we strive for 60 per cent accuracy on the podcast, in this book it could be as high as 80 per cent.*

In any case, we hope that *The Grand Tour Diaries 2018 & 2019*, our second book after *A Journey Through The Cycling Year*, complements the podcast, offering something different but in broadly the same irreverent, and occasionally informative, style.

---

* *Not a guarantee*

2018 GIRO D'ITALIA

by Lionel Birnie

Thursday, 3 May

The *Grande Partenza* is going to be dominated by two questions. Should the Giro d'Italia be in Israel? And should Chris Froome be in the Giro d'Italia?

I have spent weeks reading extensively on both subjects and as I board the EasyJet flight to Tel Aviv I still don't know the answer to either question.

I used to be a very nervous flyer, to the extent where I would arrange alternative travel if it was at all possible. Although I'm OK now, it's still a bit of a shock when, half an hour into the flight, the captain comes on talking in that peculiar, upper-middle-class drawl they all have. It's as if the whole business of conversing with anyone who can't actually fly a plane themselves is a whole lot of unnecessary bother. I suppose in a way it's quite reassuring.

'Good afternoon, *laydeez-un-gennermen*, I'm afraid there's a problem with the flight.'

In the past this would have had me gripping the arm rest, but this time I think, 'Oh well, if anything goes really badly wrong at least I won't have to decide whether or not Chris Froome should be riding the Giro.'

It turns out they've forgotten to empty the plane's toilet tank at Luton Airport and as it is now nearly full we have a choice. We can either all avoid using the toilet unless it is absolutely necessary, or we can divert to an airport somewhere *en route*, adding hours to our journey time, missing our landing slot in Tel Aviv, and generally causing a lot of inconvenience.

Immediately I'm bursting for the toilet, but I'm assured by the steward that number ones are not the problem. This turns out to be a relief in more than one way.

Already, I can sense my general ignorance of one of the major religions is going to catch me out this weekend. I used to be a fairly committed atheist in the Richard Dawkins/Ricky Gervais/Stephen Fry mould, but I've softened a bit as I've got older. I still don't believe there's a lucrative round of post-Tour crits waiting for me after life's final stage, but I'm no longer dismissive of those who do.

In terms of geopolitics, I'd count myself as curious and reasonably well-informed. But the more I've read about Israel, the more confused and conflicted I've become. I can see both sides of the argument, but I'm already realising that this is not enough. Every time we've talked about the Giro's decision to start the race in Israel, we've had criticism from both sides.

As journalists, we often tell ourselves that if people on both sides of a debate or dispute are critical then we probably got the balance just about right. But to receive emails accusing us of antisemitism and of caring not a jot for the plight of the Palestinian people, doesn't give me any reassurance that we're getting anything right.

What I cannot understand is the accusation that by covering the Giro in Israel, we're legitimising Israel. I also see no sense in boycotting the Israeli stages because our job is to cover the bike race, report what we see and hear, and add context if we get the sense we're not seeing the whole picture.

As we drive out of the airport and through Tel Aviv, I see offices and bill-boards for some of the world's biggest companies. I think back to the times the England or Chelsea football teams have played against Israeli opponents in competition. During the Classics I watched adverts during Eurosport's cycling coverage encouraging people to holiday in Israel. It seems peculiar to me it's the Giro d'Italia that's seen to be giving Israel legitimacy, when Israel already hosts businesses and holidaymakers all year round.

After checking into our own hotel, we walk down the road to the American Colony Hotel, where we can get dinner. The past guests, according to its website, include Lawrence of Arabia, Winston Churchill, Bob Dylan, Uma Thurman, Richard Gere, Giorgio Armani, Tony Blair and Mikhail Gorbachev. And now *The Cycling Podcast*. As I write this, six months have elapsed and it's disappointing to note the hotel has not updated its website accordingly.

The courtyard is shrouded by a canopy formed of trees, plants and shrubs, so it feels a little bit like being indoors outdoors. We order the *meze* and a buffet of Middle Eastern snacks arrive – hummus, pita bread, smoky baba ganoush, feta salad, stuffed vine leaves, little lamb kebabs and other delights that are less familiar but equally tasty. With the plates and dishes covering the table, my hands dart left and right and cross over like a one-man band reaching for half a dozen instruments in quick succession.

Richard asks for the wine list and orders something local. 'Good choice,' says the waiter. It arrives and the waiter is not wrong – it's delicious.

After a while I say, 'How much was the wine, Richard?' 'I don't know,' says Richard. 'It was near the bottom of the list of reds.'

Reaching for the wine list, I note that the wines are not listed in price order, so being at the bottom of the list does not indicate that it's one of the cheaper ones. I compare the wine list with the label on the bottle and feel my eyes widen slightly when I see the price – 420 shekels. That sounds expensive.

I glance at the food menu again. Each of our delicious dishes range from three to nine shekels. So, a quick calculation tells me that either the wine is horrendously expensive, or the food is impossibly cheap.

'Did you work out the exchange rate, Rich?'

'No' he replies – sipping wine from the glass held in one hand while reaching for the last lamb kebab with his other, probably.

The currency converter on my phone tells me the bottle of wine is around £90. 'Richard, that bottle of wine is around £90,' I say.

He pauses chewing momentarily. 'Oh well,' he says. 'We can't send it back now.'

'Bloody hell, Buffalo, that's the equivalent of six friends of the podcast.'

Now, we don't make a habit of such extravagant spending, except when François is with us, but to all of our friends of the podcast I say, 'Cheers, I hope you've enjoyed our coverage this year as much as we enjoyed that Israeli wine. Thank you very much for your support.'

Friday, 4 May

Stage 1: Jerusalem time trial, 9.7 km
Stage winner: Tom Dumoulin
Pink jersey: Tom Dumoulin

After breakfast at our hotel, Richard, Tom Cary from *The Telegraph* and I take a taxi to Jerusalem's Old City and enter the Muslim Quarter via the Damascus Gate. It's busy. The streets are narrow, warm and dark. There are little shops selling food, clothes and toys, including a surprising number of plastic toy guns.

Another stall has frankincense and myrrh, and what I think must be chocolates covered in gold foil. 'Are we all right for myrrh, Rich,' I say – confident that *The Cycling Podcast*'s frankincense supplies are sufficient to see us through to Rome.

As we reach a junction there are four armed police in bullet-proof vests holding large machine guns. Mounted high on the ancient crumbling limestone walls, I count three CCTV cameras. I take a photo of this jarring juxtaposition of the past and present, and one of the officers calmly motions at me to put my phone away.

We move on and meet the Via Dolorosa just as a group carrying a wooden cross approaches. This is a weekly ritual. They're following in the footsteps of Jesus, who was forced to carry the heavy wooden cross to his own crucifixion. There's a solemnity to the procession, but I feel the air has tightened up a bit. If there are flashpoints in the Old City during tense times, they're more likely to happen on Fridays because it's a day of worship for everyone.

Tempers have frayed lately, especially since US president Donald Trump declared Jerusalem to be the capital of Israel and made a pledge to move the US embassy to the city. This had upset Palestinians and Muslims across the Middle East.

As we cross from the Muslim Quarter into the Christian Quarter, there's a security checkpoint, and we have to go through an airport style X-ray machine and have all our bags searched. The man confiscates our recording equipment and tells us we can collect it later.

We head to the Western Wall. There are a couple of dozen Hasidic Jews praying at the Wall. Inside there's a library of religious texts and some wooden chairs and tables. The ancient stone and dark make for a cool and peaceful place for people to pray.

On the other side of the wall shines the golden dome of Temple Mount. It's then that it hits me – with an almost bewildering force – that three of the world's major religions all converge on this small patch of earth. Of course, I knew this to be the case beforehand, but to witness it is something else.

We walk up to the church that stands on the site where Jesus is said to have been crucified. And even an atheist like me understands the significance of the place.

As we pop out of the Old City at the Jaffa Gate, which sits between the Christian Quarter and the Armenian Quarter, I feel the same way I do when I emerge blinking from a particularly engrossing art gallery or museum. I realise I've been concentrating so hard on taking it all in that I'm left with only a superficial impression of the place.

I've seen bits of wall and pavement that date back more than 2,000 years, but there's a sense that it seems almost unreal somehow. I get the significance of being in a place that means so much to so many but there's also a nagging sense of regret – or is it guilt? – that it doesn't move me on a spiritual level.

It's less than 10 minutes' walk to an altogether more familiar world. There are barriers and pink balloons and cars covered in the logos of bicycle manufacturers. Then comes the familiar stiff swish of carbon fibre time trial bikes as the riders begin their warm-ups. We could be in Italy. In fact, we could be anywhere in the world.

During lunch, we hear the news that Chris Froome has crashed while checking out the time trial route. Within minutes there's footage of the crash on the Internet. We watch as Froome pedals softly through a slightly downhill right-hand bend, and his front wheel slips from under him.

I wonder out loud how much the salbutamol case is hanging over his head. It's still to be decided one way or the other, and Froome's participation in this Giro has been under intense scrutiny. The case is complicated. He maintains he did not take more than the permitted dose, but nevertheless stands to be stripped of his Vuelta a España title and suspended if he cannot prove it.

The Giro picks up where it left off last year with Tom Dumoulin in the pink jersey. The Dutchman beats Rohan Dennis's time by just two seconds. I wait for the BMC Racing team car to return, and when it does Max Sciandri and Marco Pinotti sit with shoulders slumped in their own separate worlds of disappointment.

Eventually, Sciandri gets out of the car, crosses the street, and takes a deep breath. 'There's no real words,' he says. 'We're analysing in our heads where we could have gained a couple of seconds. The plan was good – he executed it good. But Dumoulin won, so there's nothing you can really say. The dream was to get the jersey and take it to Italy to honour Andy.'

He's referring to BMC Racing team's benefactor and biggest fan Andy Rihs, who passed away a couple of weeks ago. Meanwhile, Froome has lost 37 seconds – a huge amount of time in the circumstances.

Back at the pressroom, Dumoulin's press conference is wrapped up in double-quick time. Shabbat, the Jewish day of rest, starts at sundown and it's getting decidedly gloomy outside. The organisers promised everything would be done and dusted in time. With the light fading, I've never seen the Giro d'Italia officials move so fast.

Saturday, 5 May

Stage 2: Haifa–Tel Aviv, 167 km
Stage winner: Elia Viviani
Pink jersey: Rohan Dennis

Our drive to the start in Haifa takes us parallel to the partition and occasionally right alongside it. Over the fence and razor wire we see Palestinian flags flying.

We're making an episode of *Kilometre 0* about the *Grande Partenza*, and our job this morning is to ask the riders and team staff their thoughts about coming to Israel. The one group we can't ask is the Palestinians. But a listener called Stephen Tunstall, who is on a ride with some Palestinian cyclists, records some comments for us.

The stage start takes place outside the Sammy Ofer Stadium, the space-age looking home to both Maccabi Haifa and Hapoel Haifa football clubs. When we wrap up, we head back to the car. I pat my pockets and realise I can't easily locate the car key.

'You've got the car key, haven't you Rich?'

'No', he replies firmly. 'You have.'

I pat my pockets again but can't find them anywhere. I speed up to a fast walk, scanning the pavement in case I dropped them earlier. When I arrive at the car, I see the keys sticking out of the car boot lock.

'Not a problem,' I say confidently. As I always say, a Grand Tour has not truly started until I've mislaid my wallet, my phone or the car keys somewhere. So, the Giro is officially underway.

The stage is won by Elia Viviani. Much of it is uneventful, but there are two standout moments.

One is the size of the crowd on the final climb of the day. The other is the way BMC Racing led out Rohan Dennis for the second intermediate sprint so he could net a time bonus and take the pink jersey.

Usually our accreditation passes get us into the compound at the back of the podium but after the finish I find our access seems to be more tightly restricted here in Israel. When I try to get in after the post-stage presentations, I'm stopped by a man in uniform.

I'd like to talk to Sylvan Adams, the Israeli–Canadian billionaire and the driving force behind the Giro coming to Israel. He's also the owner of the Israel Cycling Academy team.

I see him coming down the steps from the podium with the broad smile and twinkling eyes of a man who's loving being in the limelight. He can barely take a step without being shaken warmly by the hand or slapped heartily on the back.

After about 20 minutes or so, I manage to slip into the backstage area and hover near Mr Adams until there's an opportunity to introduce myself. He's charismatic, energetic and, as a world masters champion on the track, he clearly loves cycling, so he's thrilled the Giro is in Tel Aviv.

'Magic, absolutely magic, taken it up a notch again today with the crowd here in Tel Aviv,' he says.

He asks me whether I've visited Israel before and what I make of it. It's always slightly disarming when interviewees turn the question back on me.

'It's not what I was expecting,' I say. 'But I'm not sure what I was expecting.'

'The Giro has,' he says, 'helped show people around the world that Israel is beautiful, democratic, free and safe. The second goal is to develop the sport of cycling in Israel.'

I have to ask him about the partition because there are people who can't come freely to Israel. His expression changes quite abruptly.

'Actually, that's not true. Anyone can come to Israel. Who can't come to Israel?' he says.

'I'm thinking about the wall that separates the Palestinians. I mean, I'm learning about this all the time, but what's your take on that situation?'

He says that the Palestinians have very bad leadership, that Israel is within its rights to keep out people who want to harm its citizens, and finishes by saying that the whole point of the Giro was to show the world the best that Israel has to offer.

As I walk away, I'm even less sure what I think about the whole thing. I'm still thinking about it hours later when we sit down for dinner and a beer on the sea front.

Saturday night in Tel Aviv feels familiar. There's a busy road between the bustling bars and restaurants and the beach, and in between the road and the beach there's a pedestrianised promenade running the full length of the front. As the sun finally goes down, people go past on foot, on bikes or on rollerblades. We could be in Nice, if a matter of kilometres away from Nice there were a fence of razor wire keeping certain people from visiting.

Sunday, 6 May

Stage 3: Be'er Sheva–Eilat, 229 km
Stage winner: Elia Viviani
Pink jersey: Rohan Dennis

The start is in Be'er Sheva in the Negev Desert, and so we face a drive of around an hour and a half just to get there. On the way we pass several of the Bedouin villages that are unrecognised by the Israeli state. They are little more than shanty towns populated by people who have no official stake in the country.

Just as we realise we're cutting it fine, Be'er Sheva appears on the horizon. The details in the Giro's roadbook are scant, the road signs unfamiliar, the maps on our phones aren't working.

'We're cutting this fine,' I say helpfully. I'm driving, which at least spares me the responsibility of having to navigate. Tom is in the back, which leaves it to the Buffalo to give directions.

Missing the start of the stage would not normally be the end of the world, but on this particular day there is just one road between the start in Be'er Sheva and the finish in Eilat, meaning that if we were to arrive late we'd have to trundle along behind the peloton all day.

'I'm not sure we want to drive 229 kilometres at an average speed of 45 kilometres an hour behind the peloton, do we?' I ask rhetorically.

We try to get onto the course where the road is blocked by barriers, but the police are having none of it – even though our car bears official stickers that should permit access and there is still an hour before the race starts.

I do a U-turn and follow another of Richard's cut-throughs. We join the back of a very long traffic jam. 'That's blown it,' I say helpfully. 'We'll not make it now.'

I notice cars ahead of us are turning off the road and driving across the rocky wasteland in all directions. I look at Richard and notice his eyes are following one of the cars towards the brow of the hill to who-knows-where.

'We're not going cross country,' I say firmly.

'Why not?' he says.

'Because... because... we don't even know where it goes,' I say, scarcely believing I have to explain.

'These people seem to think it will be all right.'

I turn to Tom in the back seat. 'What do you think, Tom? Because I think this is a bad idea. What do you think?'

'I think that if we sit in this traffic jam we're going to miss the stage entirely,' he says, volleying responsibility firmly over the headrest to Richard and me.

'What if we hit a rock or something and get a puncture? We'll be stuck in the middle of nowhere,' I say.

'Just follow that car', says Richard.

Against my better judgement, I turn the steering wheel and follow across extremely rocky ground. I bump and bounce our way towards the brow of the hill, grind through some deep gravel, slalom past some craters and pop out on a rough road that passes underneath the traffic jam we've just left behind.

Another couple of turns and we have clear road to the start of Stage 3 of the Giro d'Italia. We see the race route ahead and this time we're allowed onto the course and make our way to Eilat.

'Easy,' says Richard. 'Nothing to worry about.'

'Well, we're not going to be able to speak to any riders or do any work this morning though, are we?' I reply.

The wind is blowing in Eilat. The stage is, again, uneventful. And Viviani again wins. He's in sparkling form at the post-race press conference, after which I head back to the pressroom to wait for the Giro organisers to sort out the boarding passes for everyone who has a seat on one of the four charter flights to Sicily tomorrow.

It's a long wait. No one seems to know what's happening. Earlier in the afternoon, they said boarding passes would be ready at three, then four; then it was five, then six-thirty, then eight.

Our hotel is 15 kilometres away. The Buffalo is stamping his hooves because it's his birthday tomorrow and he wants to have a nice celebratory meal tonight.

We pop across the road from the pressroom and record the podcast on a hotel terrace. By the time I get back, the boarding passes are only 20 minutes from being ready. That turns into 45 minutes by the time I have mine in my hand.

And so by the time we reach the restaurant, all the balloons we've definitely arranged in advance for the Buffalo's birthday have deflated. The bubbly has gone flat, and the candles on the cake have burned down to waxy stumps. So the best we can do is order a round of beers and wish him many happy returns for tomorrow.

by Richard Moore

Sunday, 6 May

The improvisation required to make it to the start of this stage was definitely the right call. As I said to Lionel just before we veered off the road and headed into the rough desert, 'Even if this doesn't work out, what a story!'

As our stay in Israel draws to a close we begin to reflect on it. As well as nightly episodes, we have been making an episode of *Kilometre 0* on the Giro's three days here, speaking to some of the riders about their impressions as well as local people and Sylvan Adams, the driving force behind the Giro's Israel *Grande Partenza*, or 'big start' as they say in Italy.

It's fair to say that we were quite apprehensive ahead of our visit here, not so much from a personal safety perspective but more because we weren't sure how we should cover it. Sports and politics are intertwined, but to what extent do our listeners want to hear about the politics? Some do. Some don't. But we had a taste of what to expect last winter when we tried to cover the Giro's announcement that it would start in Israel from both sides – and then got criticism from both sides. We're used to emotive, divisive debates in cycling, but this was – unsurprisingly – on another level.

In our *Kilometre 0* we keep any views we have out of it, because the last thing anyone needs is more uninformed opinion. We are interested to hear some local perspectives. One of the most interesting is Elliott, a cycling fan living in Jerusalem. He is quite pessimistic. 'There seems to be no solution at the moment because the political sides are too far apart to come together any more,' he says. 'People in the middle are feeling a sense of hopelessness.'

It's a pity that the people in the middle – the vast majority in any population – so often go unheard.

I like to think that I learned a lot from reading about Israel before coming and then spending these few days here but, as Lionel has said a few times, the more he reads, the more complicated it seems. For us as journalists we revert to first principles – and to remind myself what these are I reread the British sports writer Paul Hayward's appreciation of the late Christopher Martin-Jenkins. 'A finer label than *journalist* is *reporter*,' wrote Hayward, 'because the correspondent who sets out to record and describe is more valuable than the one who wants only to preach. You would never know this from studying the modern media, where reporting is being annihilated by opinion.'

My more frivolous impressions of Israel include being struck by the number of e-bikes whizzing around. In Jerusalem and Tel Aviv in particular, the bikes all seem to have little motors in them; it all feels very futuristic, which provides a strange juxtaposition with all that history in Jerusalem.

The racing over the three days is largely inconsequential, though Chris Froome's crash before the time trial seems ominous for his chances: I say on the podcast that there are shades of the 2014 Tour, where it all went wrong for him. They don't call me Mystic Moore for… well, they don't call me that at all actually.

One of the lasting memories of Israel comes from Stage 3. We hear about the Israelis and the Palestinians but tend to overlook the many other groups of people with claims to this relatively small piece of land. As we head out into the desert on the long, straight road to Eilat, there are smallish clumps of rudimentary buildings at various intervals. Around them people stand and watch the convoy of vehicles, including our media car, that precede the Giro.

They are the Negev Bedouin, who live in what the Israeli government calls *dispersals* and what the rest of the international community calls *unrecognised villages*. They have no electricity, running water or any other services. The desert is empty and bleak. I wonder what they will make of the race when it goes past; I also wonder how they survive out here.

But the Bedouin people have been surviving out here for about 7,000 years.

Monday, 7 May

Rest day: Eilat

Of all my 30-plus birthdays, this is perhaps the strangest. With everyone leaving early for Italy, I have the full day in Eilat before an evening flight home. So I book what I think is a nice beachside hotel. But, well, let's just say that I'm sure there are nicer beachside hotels in Eilat. Much of it resembles a building site. But at least there is a beach.

I spend most of the day snorkelling, watching beautiful fish nibbling at coral. At one point I follow a leopard-patterned sea snake as it slithers across the ocean floor, an experience I relate to my brother, who knows about these things, in a WhatsApp message. He replies by telling me that (a) sea snakes are deadly and I shouldn't have gone anywhere near it and (b) there are no sea snakes in the Red Sea. (I look this up later. There's a popular story about a sea snake in the Red Sea killing 320 tourists, including 120 divers. But it's a hoax. Apparently there *are* no sea snakes in the Red Sea. But here's the thing: I definitely saw one.)

All in all, though, it is a strange, solitary but also enjoyable way to spend my birthday.

Less enjoyable is my departure from Israel. At tiny Eilat Airport I queue for my 'exit interview'. My passport is taken away. Ten minutes pass, 20 minutes, 30 minutes. I start to get slightly anxious about my flight to Tel Aviv, and my connecting flight to London.

I am asked if anyone asked me to carry anything. 'No,' I say, aware that I am sounding defensive, though I'm not sure why. Then my exit interviewer asks whether my bags have been out of sight at all. 'No,' I say.

'Because someone might have put something, maybe a bomb, in your bag if you couldn't see it,' she points out.

Oh, right.

I am asked why I have been in Israel ('to report on a bike race'), why five years earlier I went to Qatar ('to report on a bike race') and Oman ('to report on a bike race'). It feels as though the onus is on me to prove that there wasn't some sinister explanation for my visits to places that I'm perfectly entitled to visit. But then I also think, not for the first time on this visit, about Israel being surrounded by countries it regards as enemies (and who regard Israel as an enemy). With our British passports allowing us free and easy movement we are very fortunate and take so much for granted. For the moment, at least.

I get my passport back just before the final call for boarding. Farewell, Israel. I'm not sure when, or if, I'll see you again.

by Lionel Birnie

Monday, 7 May

Rest day: transfer from Israel to Sicily

The email from the Giro organisers said something about the charter flights to Sicily leaving from a brand-new airport in Eilat that's not yet open to the public.

My journey starts by taking a taxi to a hotel in the centre of town to board a coach that's been laid on to take us to the airport. We drive for an hour into rockier, dustier country and arrive at what looks suspiciously like a military airport in the middle of the desert.

There's a good reason for this – because we're at Ovda Airport, a military airfield in the middle of the desert. The giant lettering on the front of the building – and when I say *building* I mean corrugated iron shed – is cracked and broken. The top of the *O* has fallen off, so it actually reads *Uvda*.

As I get off the coach, I'm almost blown off my feet and dust hits me in my eyes. I can feel the nervous flyer in me awakening. The prospect of taking off from a run-down military facility in a dusty, near-gale force wind is not terribly appealing.

My nerves are eased slightly by the fact that I'm on the fourth of four planes, along with Team Sky, Mitchelton–Scott, BMC Racing, Team Sunweb, EF Education First and UAE Team Emirates. 'If this plane goes down,' I think, 'I'm not even going to get a mention'.

I take my seat next to the window. Vegard Stake Laengen of the UAE Team Emirates team sits down next to me. He's reading a book – *The Subtle Art of Not Giving a Fuck*.

It's an uneventful, quiet flight. I don't know what I'd expected on a plane full of pro riders. Perhaps I'd wanted to imagine these air transfers have the same atmosphere as a school trip, with chatter and banter and Chris Froome and Tom Dumoulin arm-wrestling for the right to sit by the window. Actually. everyone puts on their headphones and retreats into their own world for a few hours.

At the other end, the carousel takes ages to whirr into life, so half the Giro peloton is left hanging around at baggage reclaim. I have a chat with BMC Racing's Max Sciandri, who explains how he convinced Rohan Dennis that getting the whole team to bring the bunch together so he could win the time bonus sprint to take the pink jersey was a good idea.

'The thing is in cycling,' he says, 'it's too easy to just sit back and think it's not worth trying something in case it doesn't work and people laugh at you. The guys were prepared to look stupid if it didn't work.'

But it did work. And Dennis brought the pink jersey back to Italy and in doing so he and his team honoured Andy Rihs, BMC Racing's late benefactor.

After the usual faff picking up the hire car, I check into my hotel, go for a quick run – and when I say *quick*, I mean short – then head back to the airport to pick up Daniel, who is flying in from the Tour de Yorkshire.

In the evening, we head into Catania where I order *pasta alla Norma*, a Sicilian speciality I've been looking forward to. It should be a bright, summery dish with aubergines, tomatoes and basil. Unfortunately, this is lacklustre – I can make better at home.

Tuesday, 8 May

Stage 4: Catania–Caltagirone, 202 km
Stage winner: Tim Wellens
Pink jersey: Rohan Dennis

The hire car has a soft tyre. The roads in Sicily are in poor condition and the hire car is a bit of a turkey, so it's hard to know if it was already soft when I picked it up or if I damaged it hitting one of the many potholes.

Catania is scruffy but vibrant. As we head to the centre of town for the stage start, a scooter weaves across the front of our bumper, then a bus pulls out on us – the driver is presumably thinking that if it comes down to a straight fight between us and him, he'll be all right. Then I get honked at for waiting a nanosecond at a junction. Ah Sicily, it's good to be back.

Our next *Kilometre 0* episode is on *Il Garibaldi* – the Giro's roadbook which contains maps and profiles of the stages and other information the riders need.

I ask a few riders whether in these days of GPS tracking and Google Street View the roadbook's relevant any more. In the old days, the road-book sometimes seemed almost designed to fool the riders – perhaps by failing to highlight the difficulty of a particular climb by leaving it uncategorised. But now there's information overload. Technology can help the riders look in much more detail at the roads but it seems the physical road-book is still a valuable companion.

Max Sciandri is amusing on the subject. 'The *Garibaldi* is our bible. You always have to read it. I always read about the dishes of the area because I like that stuff,' he says, a man after my own heart. 'On a good day, I'll get on the radio and say, "Hey guys, it's pasta with sardines tonight."'

In Caltagirone, the buffet in the pressroom is spectacular, but the soft car tyre is nagging at me, so I restrict myself to just one plate before going in search of a petrol station to put some air in it before the stage finishes.

The finish itself is a thriller and the final climb catches out a few – perhaps they've not read enough in the roadbook or checked out the roads on Google. Tim Wellens of Lotto–Soudal gets it just right, surging clear to win.

At our hotel, there are a couple of guys in Giro d'Italia polo shirts at the next table. It turns out that they are travelling round Italy selling cuddly wolves to the fans. Lupo, a cartoonish wolf, is the official mascot of the Giro and is very popular with children.

The two men are part of a team of people driving Transit vans of cuddly toy wolves around Italy for three weeks. I do a quick calculation and work out that between them they will sell more than a quarter of a million euros worth of wolf by the time they reach Rome.

Wednesday, 9 May

Stage 5: Agrigento–Santa Ninfa, 153 km
Stage winner: Enrico Battaglin
Pink jersey: Rohan Dennis

The Chris Froome story has rumbled on, but it's fair to say it's slipped off the radar a bit while the focus has been on the Giro's long weekend in Israel.

On Monday, *The Times* published an article headlined 'Study raises doubts about Chris Froome's salbutamol test'. A research paper published last week in the *British Journal of Clinical Pharmacology* claimed that the World Anti-Doping Agency's test for salbutamol was unreliable and in need of a rethink. This, it seems, will form the cornerstone of Froome's defence.

The whole case seems to hinge on proving the unprovable. The rule regarding salbutamol hinges on the limit of the amount taken in a 24-hour period. A case is only considered if the amount of the substance in a urine test exceeds a certain threshold. Froome is well over that threshold but that doesn't prove he exceeded the permitted dose.

There doesn't seem to be enough of a body of evidence on salbutamol absorption rates and whether a high trace in the sample is definitively indicative of exceeding the dose. Froome insists he did not take more than the permitted amount that day at the Vuelta a España. The problem is we all want to reach for simple solutions in cases like this. Innocent or guilty? Case closed.

I've seen Froome's case compared to the drink-driving limit, but that's completely the opposite way round. The law is based on the concentration of alcohol present in the system, not the amount that's been drunk.

I head to the Team Sky bus to speak to Dave Brailsford, the team's boss. He's standing by Froome because he believes him when he says that he did not exceed the dose.

I don't know what to think but it would be a terrible miscarriage of justice if Froome had indeed not exceeded the dose and was stripped of his Vuelta title and suspended.

But, on the other hand, the rule is clear and it does seem to be developing into a pattern that Team Sky mobilise an army of experts and lawyers to challenge these things when they blunder into the anti-doping tripwire. Brailsford sometimes doesn't help his cause either. The sceptics might warm to him more if he dropped the management speak once in a while.

I ask him about the Froome case for the podcast and by the time he's finished I feel I've gone almost cross-eyed trying to keep track of the clauses and sub-clauses. Even the straightest of questions gets a convoluted answer. But, giving Brailsford the benefit of the doubt, the case is not as straightforward as some have made out.

When the recorder is switched off, we chat informally for a few minutes. Brailsford talks about his few days in Israel and tells me about a training ride he took to Bethlehem. He talks engagingly about what it was like to cycle in the West Bank. I asked him if he wanted to talk about it on the tape. He thinks for a moment but says no. It's a shame, because there's a side to Brailsford that he rarely allows people to see, or in this case, hear.

After the stage Daniel and I stop in Menfi, birthplace of Team Sky's Salvatore Puccio, to record the podcast. We discuss Enrico Battaglin's stage win and clarify that he is no relation of Giovanni Battaglin who won the Vuelta and Giro within weeks of one another in 1981.

All is going well until Daniel springs an exciting new segment of the podcast on me. It's called 'Lionel Learns Italian'. I'm game for anything within reason and so I agree. What follows is the biggest stitch-up in cycling since Stephen Roche promised to give Roberto Visentini a hand on the climbs in the 1987 Giro.

Daniel hands me his laptop and in the text window on the screen there are about 300 words of complex Italian on the historical and cultural significance of Mount Etna. I thought we'd start with something simple, like how to order a nice afternoon cappuccino.

Against my better judgement I give it a go and stutter and stumble my way through it. The reaction on Twitter once the episode has gone out is no surprise to me. Hearing me pass the beautiful Italian language through a broken mangle has delighted precisely no one.

'We're not doing that again,' I tell Daniel.

Our *agriturismo* in the remote countryside does not have a restaurant, so we follow some rather vague directions from the owner in search of a place he says is open. We drive round and round the village – including up the same dead end twice – in search of this place. We use a combination of Google Maps and Trip Advisor to try to find it with no luck. Daniel's becoming convinced the place doesn't exist.

'Is it a front for the Mafia?' I ask conspiratorially.

We end up in an ice cream parlour and attempt to quash our hunger with a local beer before heading back to the B&B to go to bed with no dinner.

Thursday, 10 May

Stage 6: Caltanissetta–Mount Etna, 169 km
Stage winner: Esteban Chaves
Pink jersey: Simon Yates

Last night, we were presented with a quirky system for ordering breakfast by the owner of the *agriturismo*. We could choose four items from the list, but only four. This morning two trays have been left on the table on the terrace outside our rooms. I've opted for two croissants, a coffee and a yoghurt.

Daniel – controversially – has gone for two cappuccinos. I joke that if he was a sports director selecting a team for the Giro, he's the sort of man who'd pick two sprinters. As I finish my cappuccino, which is at least 60 per cent froth, in one small gulp, I have to accept Daniel's selection policy was the best.

Our day is an adrenaline-packed dash. After the start, we take a small detour to Catania Airport to swap our car with its soft tyre for a far superior model. We just about make it to Mount Etna before the police close the roads. And then, after Esteban Chaves and Simon Yates have done the old one-two to take the stage and pink jersey for Mitchelton–Scott, we dash down the mountain on foot to where the team buses are parked.

The pair of them are looking formidable already in this Giro, but the fact that they've taken 26 seconds from the likes of Pinot, Pozzovivo, López, Dumoulin, Aru and Froome, who collectively had no real response to their eruption on the volcano, is still a little surprising.

There's a real sense of urgency after the finish. No one wants to hang around too long because we all remember how long it took to get the ferry across to the mainland last year. So it's not long before we're in the peloton of Giro traffic heading to the port. The queue to get on the boat is just as chaotic as it was last year, but somehow the Giro traffic seems to have priority boarding this time, so it works out much better.

If the Giro organisers decide to host stages in Sicily for each of the next five years, I reckon they'll have improved the logistics to 'just about OK' by then.

On the ferry we see Matt White, the effervescent Mitchelton–Scott sports director with a couple of other staff members. He has a case of Sicilian beers under his arm. 'These are for the boys,' he says, 'but they've all stayed on the bus, so there might not be any left for them after we've finished with them.'

On the other side, we face a bit of a drive to our B&B. When we arrive, the owner suggests we head down to the coastal town of Bagnara Calabra to find a restaurant. As the crow flies, the coast is about 200 metres below us. By road it's about nine kilometres snaking backwards and forwards. It's getting late and I'm starting to fear we're going to miss dinner for the second day in a row.

We park up in town close to the hotel where Team Sky are staying. By now it's a couple of minutes before eleven. Just as we're scanning the streets for signs of an open restaurant we see Chris Froome walking across the road towards the hotel, having just completed his transfer from Sicily.

We're relieved to find a pizzeria is still open, and after ordering we check Twitter and see some film of Dave Brailsford getting into a helicopter at the top of Mount Etna. He looks a bit like a Bond villain whose dastardly plan has just been foiled. It later turns out that Sky had hired the helicopter from the race organisers to fly Froome across so he could avoid sitting in the traffic jam waiting for the ferry.

Sky weren't the only team to do this, by the way – UAE Team Emirates hired a chopper for Fabio Aru too. Unfortunately, Froome took two hours to produce a urine sample for the anti-doping test after the stage, so the helicopter went without him.

When I see Brailsford the next morning, he's in surprisingly good humour. 'We're always telling the riders how important it is to stay hydrated', he says.

Friday, 11 May

Stage 7: Pizzo–Praia a Mare, 159 km
Stage winner: Sam Bennett
Pink jersey: Simon Yates

Today's stage is the closest I think I'll come to covering an old-school Giro d'Italia, when the riders used to pootle along at an easy pace until the last hour when they raced all out to the line. We drive more or less the whole route ahead of the peloton on the course. We stop for a quick lunch, then a coffee, and arrive in Praia a Mare in time to see the action at the finish.

Sam Bennett of Ireland wins the stage. Bennett's an interesting character. Born in Belgium because his father was a lower-division footballer over there, he grew up in Carrick-on-Suir, where comparisons to the great Sean Kelly could have smothered a promising career before it got going.

I detect a sensitive soul and quite a self-critical personality in Bennett. Beaten twice by Viviani in Israel, and with a string of top-three places in the Giro both this year and last, I was starting to fear he might not make the breakthrough.

In Eilat in Israel, he was really harsh on the mistakes he made in the final kilometre, and I think back to the 2016 Tour de France when he crashed, smashed himself up and rode through the pain barrier just to finish in last place – the *lanterne rouge* – and yet he was critical of his performance.

I wait at the BMC Racing team bus for Nicolas Roche. When he rolls in, I step forward and ask if he has a moment. 'Do you know Sam Bennett well?', I ask.

It's a stupid question, but I want to be sure, because although Roche is a good talker who always has something interesting to say on almost any subject, he also doesn't suffer fools too happily, and can volley a loose question into the top corner of the net. If I'd assumed he knew Bennett well, I could imagine him saying something like 'You think I know him just because he's Irish?'

But he says, 'Of course I do', and he's happy to talk. Roche talks about his friend Bennett, about the self-doubt, and Roche's own efforts to encourage Bennett to believe in himself a bit more. It turns out to be a good angle for the podcast, which we record outside a noisy bar in Praia a Mare. The easiest day ever is wrapped up by eight o'clock.

We drive a short way to our hotel and we're seated at a table at our restaurant, La Rondinella in Scalea, by nine.

The *antipasto* is wonderful, especially the artichoke and aubergine in olive oil. Then we have *chicche*, which are little pea-sized balls of potato and pasta, a bit like shrunken gnocchi. It's served with sausage. After that is *baccala*, which is salted cod and chickpeas. I'm so full after that I can't manage dessert, but the waitress insists I try the cheese.

Just as we're finishing up, Ciro and the crew from *La Gazzetta dello Sport* arrive. They featured La Rondinella in that day's paper as the place to eat on the Giro route. So, they get a very warm reception, and we get a complimentary grappa. Thanks Ciro.

Saturday, 12 May

Stage 8: Praia a Mare–Montevergine di Mercogliano, 209 km
Stage winner: Richard Carapaz
Pink jersey: Simon Yates

We take one of Daniel's detours off the beaten track to the Zoncolan of the south. On the way, he tells me of a story of a minor Internet hoax that made its way into the press a few years back. Fake news before Donald Trump made the phrase ubiquitous.

Back at the start of the 2000s, some users on a cycling Internet forum started talking about a mythical climb at Rifugio Calvanico near Salerno. It was, according to the forum, harder than the Zoncolan, and so revered by local riders that the Giro organisers had taken notice and were thinking of including it in the route.

The rumour got picked up by a cycling website, and then a newspaper, then another, and before anyone could actually verify the existence of the climb the Giro organisers were being asked about it. The only problem was there was no such climb. The Zoncolan of the south was a myth. The road that climbs ahead of us to the wooded hilltop looks challenging enough, but it's no Monte Zoncolan.

We record a segment for the podcast about it, and afterwards I lament the loss of a cycling media tradition even older than repeating unverified nonsense from the Internet without checking it – that of bestowing nick-names on the riders. The Eagle of Toledo. The Badger. The Peacock of Sandrigo. The Ferret of Firenze. OK, I possibly made that last one up. The cogs in my mind start to turn over.

'Daniel, what's black pudding in Italian?' I ask later that afternoon in the pressroom.

As we record the podcast over artisan beer at yet another stunning rural retreat, I ask whether we can give Simon Yates a nickname and get it into the Italian press. Yates is from Bury, which as everyone knows is famous for its black pudding. A delicious, healthy sausage made from pig's blood and cubes of fat stuffed inside a thick skin. In France, it's called *boudin noir*. In Spain, it's *morcilla*. In Italy, it's *sanguinaccio*.

Daniel winces, but no one can hear a wince in a podcast, so I press on with this and *Il Sanguinaccio Volante* is born. Simon Yates is the Flying Black Pudding. I ponder whether the Italian media might pick up it up and run with it.

We do also talk about the cycling. In the wet, Chris Froome's front wheel slipped from under him on a hairpin bend on the final climb and although he didn't lose any time to any of the main contenders, he did slip to ninth overall behind the stage winner, Richard Carapaz. The Eagle of Ecuador.

Sunday, 13 May

Stage 9: Pesco Sannita–Gran Sasso, 225 km
Stage winner: Simon Yates
Pink jersey: Simon Yates

I take the cable car up to the summit of Gran Sasso with Ciro. As a man who lives to see the sea, if there's one thing he hates more than being in the mountains, it's being in a cable car in the mountains. He tells me that the riders are expected to take the cable car back down the mountain after the stage.

'Just imagine if the cable broke,' he says.

There's a pause that reveals an impressive sense of comic timing.

'It would be a disaster for the podcast.'

This is the highest point in the Apennines. I can tell that Daniel is already fed up with me asking whether this is the Dolomites, so instead I ask him whether it's the Alps.

It's a long stage and it takes a while to warm up, but when it does it's almost enough to make me forget about the cold wind whipping around my ears. We watch on the big screen as the leading group hits the climb. Visually, it's stunning. Beautiful, gentle mountains with just the right balance of soft greenery and jagged rock. Banks of snow are dotted across the landscape having stubbornly resisted the weak early summer sun's insistence that they melt.

The road looks like a thin strip of grey satin draped delicately across the grass taking the riders wherever it happens to have landed. And the lake is sublime. It's on days like this that the Giro lives up to its marketing hype of being the best race in the most beautiful place.

But what about the race? It's a slow burner as I said. The breakaway has some firepower in it, Gianluca Brambilla, Tim Wellens and Giovanni Visconti included. The last man standing is Androni Sidermec's Fausto Masnada. I can almost hear the Silver Fox, Gianni Savio, sigh when Masnada is caught with about two and a half kilometres to go.

One rider who is red hot is Simon Yates, who sits and waits until the perfect moment to jump and wins his first stage and crucially takes the time bonus.

Tom Dumoulin loses a dozen seconds and the narrative of the race is set. It's the punchy little climber versus the lithe time trialling machine. Can Yates cover himself in enough insulation to offer a protection for the time trial at the start of the third week? His lead over the defending champion is now 38 seconds, but, just like last year, the Dutchman looks like he's climbing more than well enough.

In contrast, the good ship Froome has sprung a leak and is taking on water at an alarming rate. Another minute and seven seconds lost today means he's almost two and a half down overall. The Giro is as good as lost.

As they cross the line, the riders are rapidly shown into a building to put on warm clothes. There's confusion among the media waiting to speak to them because, other than Ciro, who seems to have some sort of magic pass enabling him to reach parts the rest of us cannot, we're not allowed in.

I decide to wander over to another building – the one where people are queuing to get the cable car – and I find a back door. I peer through the window and show my pass to the man on the other side of the door, and – although he's not sure whether he should or not – he lets me in.

Others see me slip inside and try the same trick, but the man – perhaps realising he's made a mistake – is adamant. No entry. Inside stand half the peloton, wrapped in their team tracksuits and warm hats. Some of them have their bikes with them. It's chaos – Giro style.

I pick off a few interviews, including Hugh Carthy, who was in the break, and Dumoulin's teammate Sam Oomen, and then watch as the riders from the *gruppetto* begin to arrive, swelling the tail back further. At a push I reckon 30 or so people can safely get into each of the cable car cabins, so this backlog is going to take a while to clear.

I hear a tap on the window and turn to see Daniel with the Eurosport crew – Sean Kelly, Rob Hatch and Carlton Kirby – standing outside. After some gesticulating by Kelly, they're let in too and so we stand squashed like sardines for almost two hours waiting to shuffle forwards until it's our turn to get in the cable car.

'Ridiculous,' says Kelly. 'The riders should go on strike,' he adds, not entirely seriously, but not entirely jokingly either.

At half past six there's a commotion and a little figure in a pink jersey is marched through the crowd, which parts to let him through. It's Simon Yates, of course, and right on his wheel is Ciro, using his magic pass again.

For us, there's another hour's wait, and then 10 minutes or so flying down the mountain, during which I hope Italy's health-and-safety regulations and the cable car's recent maintenance schedule are up to scratch.

Monday, 14 May

Rest day: Penne

Sometimes, Daniel's penchant for booking the remotest *agriturismo* gets on my nerves. Last night was one of those times. It had taken absolutely ages to get down from Gran Sasso in the cable car. Then we made a mess of recording the podcast.

We made an educated gamble and opted to get on the road in the hope we could find a decent restaurant en route to our hotel where we could chew over the day's stage while digesting a good meal.

Google Maps was not our ally. It tried to direct us to a restaurant in the middle of nowhere, and it took us three laps of the village to find the place. By the time we'd recorded the episode and had something to eat it was well past eleven and there was still a good 45 minutes to drive. I know, dear listener, I know. The lengths we go to for *The Cycling Podcast*.

Google Maps let us down for a second time when we tried to find our B&B for the night. We went up and down the same stretch of country lane three or four times trying to find the place. Dogs were barking in the dark night. I won't lie, I was biting through my tongue at this stage. I thought, 'Why can't we just stay in a town every now and again?'

Daniel claims it's because parking can be an issue, but I know that's not the real reason. I know that the man-of-the-natural-world side of him wants to wake up somewhere remote so he can enjoy a peaceful morning run.

My frustration is eased considerably by a very friendly welcome from our Dutch hosts at the Dolce Far Niente near Penne. They offer us a beer and we sit in the moonlight and bring the curtain down on the first phase of the Giro in style. The following morning's breakfast is remarkable – easily the best of the Giro. The views are stunning too. On one side sits the town on the hill, on the other is a lovely lake.

Daniel decides to head off to Team Sky's press conference and I take the executive decision that one of us ought to stay behind and go through all the questions our listeners have sent in for our debut *Press Conference* episode.

I sit on the terrace with a cappuccino and spend the morning working lightly with my eyes closing every now and then.

The B&B's owners offer to do all my laundry – not something I'm going to turn down. I go for a run down by the lake. Daniel returns in the early evening and before dinner we answer as many of the questions as we can for the podcast, and then head into town. It's the most restful rest day I can ever remember.

We find a restaurant, where we're told that there's a set menu to celebrate the Giro. The place is almost empty, which strikes me as a bad sign. When the waitress brings us a beer and a plastic glass, a paper plate and plastic cutlery, Daniel and I exchange glances. Next, we are presented with some pretty average ham, cheese and bread to put on our paper plates.

Daniel asks the waitress what's for the pasta course. A paper plate of ravioli, it seems. We decide to make our apologies and see if we can do better somewhere else. There's an awkward negotiation over how much we should pay for our thimble of beer and slice of cheese and ham. We end up handing over an extortionate 20 euros.

The next place we find is rammed. Judging by the number of men sitting at the long trestle table drinking pints, it appears that the Giro's logistical workforce are here. After a hard day putting up barriers they deserve a beer, but it means there's a backlog in the kitchen. We end up waiting more than an hour for some pretty average pasta, but at least the wine is served in proper glasses.

Tuesday, 15 May

Stage 10: Penne–Gualdo Tadino, 244 km
Stage winner: Matej Mohorič
Pink jersey: Simon Yates

The 'Flying Black Pudding' nickname has caught on, but not in quite the way I'd hoped. Ciro Scognamiglio and *La Gazzetta dello Sport* have ignored it, but the Belgian newspaper *Het Laatste Nieuws* ran a headline yesterday calling Yates 'De Vliegende Bloedworst'.

The *Evening Standard* in London has attributed the nickname to 'the Italian press' and both *BBC Breakfast* and *Sky Sports News* mention 'the Flying Black Pudding' on air, although the latter was courtesy of *The Cycling Podcast*'s agent on the inside, Orla Chennaoui.

It's only been a few days but already the origins of the nickname have been lost. It sort of proves my point that once something's been said it is repeated without too much of a second thought. It's how the great myths of the sport grew to become legend, such as the one about Bernard Hinault calling Paris–Roubaix a circus, winning it, and then never taking part again, which is not true.

A few of our listeners have been critical, saying it's disrespectful to a brilliant athlete to compare him to a sausage, but really I feel that misses the point. No one seriously thinks Simon Yates is a flying black pudding.

Others do take it in the spirit in which it was intended. Listeners send us artwork, one or two of which are alarmingly phallic, although one is an elegant ring of delicious looking black pudding flanked by angelic wings. It could almost be an album cover for a 1990s grunge band.

A long stage of 244 kilometres turns into a nightmare for Esteban Chaves, who was lying second overall, 32 seconds behind his Mitchelton–Scott teammate Yates this morning. No one in the team is quite sure what has gone wrong for the Colombian, but he was in trouble early on and has lost 25 minutes.

In the press conference, I ask Yates whether the fact his teammate has slipped so dramatically out of the picture helps or hinders his chances. Both Yates brothers are often criticised for their monosyllabic answers when interviewed on television, but here Simon appears to be growing into the role of a race leader.

He's not naturally outgoing, I don't think, but he engages thoughtfully with each question and gives considered answers. In the false setting of a press conference, you can't really ask for more than that.

There's still the hint of a ruthless streak, though, and I'm left with the impression that he's not particularly bothered that Chaves is out of the picture. In fact, it may well simplify things for him and the team in the second half of the Giro because the hierarchy is now established.

As he reaches the end of his answer to my last question, he says 'I'm not too sure about that nickname by the way.' Fortunately, he laughs a little as he says it. Perhaps he hasn't seen the phallic artwork.

In the evening, we head down into Assisi for dinner at a restaurant that had been recommended to us by our hosts at the hotel. I enjoy a little dish of spaghetti with local smoked ham, followed by a fillet steak with black truffle that is so soft it could have been tenderised by being used as a makeshift chamois leather in Fausto Coppi's shorts during a particularly long Giro stage.

Wednesday, 16 May

Stage 11: Assisi–Osimo, 156 km
Stage winner: Simon Yates
Pink jersey: Simon Yates

The view of the rolling Umbrian hillside as I step outside my room is enough to take my breath away. The gravel path gives a satisfying crunch as I head to breakfast. Daniel certainly knows how to pick a relaxing rural hideaway.

In the hotel's small reception area sit three large men in suits. They eye me suspiciously. There's an atmosphere. I head down the steps towards the breakfast room and the owner – a wiry woman in her late 60s with darting eyes – heads me off. I don't think she realises I'm a guest in the hotel.

'Colazione?' I ask hesitantly.

'Mangare?'

She looks from side to side and reluctantly shows me to a table at one end of the room.

At the other end of the room sit two men, the younger of whom checked us in last night and is the son of the older woman, who has now disappeared into the kitchen.

The conversation is hushed, intense and peppered with gesticulations. I don't need to understand Italian to know that the younger man is in trouble for some reason or other and the older man is going to make him pay for it.

There's no sign of anything to eat. I wait for a good 10 minutes and finally the woman returns with a cup of coffee and a slice of dry cake I've not ordered. Italian breakfast is rarely a sumptuous buffet, but this is ridiculous. Daniel isn't back from his run yet. I send him a text. 'There's a bit of an atmosphere at breakfast. Something is going on.'

When Daniel arrives, the older man approaches us and he and Daniel talk in quite an animated fashion for a few minutes. When they finish, I ask Daniel for a summary of things. It turns out the older man is a policeman, as are the three heavies in the foyer, and the younger man is indeed in trouble.

The policeman asked Daniel what time we arrived last night. 'About eight,' he said.

'No, it wasn't,' said the policeman. 'It was 8.20. We watched you arrive.'

It turns out the hotel is under investigation for failing to register guests or declare its income for tax purposes. The police had pounced early in the morning while I was still asleep and Daniel was out on his run. We're asked if we heard anyone throwing mobile phones out of an upstairs window. We say we didn't hear anything.

A lawyer arrives in such stereotypical attire I begin to wonder if we're actually part of some hilarious hidden camera programme being made for Italian TV. He wears a dark suit with pinstripes wider than a second-hand Ferrari salesman who's doing some too-good-to-be-true deals. His shoes are so pointy I'm worried he'll have my eye out when he walks down the stairs towards me.

'This is,' Daniel says, 'Italian justice in microcosm.' The lawyer and the policeman are laughing and joking over a cigarette outside, and the suspects – the mother and son – are furtively rummaging in the drawers of a cabinet, searching for papers. Or perhaps hiding them.

One of the heavies comes in to take evidence. He writes so incredibly slowly it's painful to watch. When he's finished, Daniel's diligence in translating my statement is none too reassuring. 'What's it say?' I ask.

'Oh, you arrived just after eight and stayed the night and so on.'

'No, no. What exactly does it say? I'm not signing a police statement I can't understand.'

Eventually, we're allowed to go. It's been the most exciting police raid at the Giro d'Italia since Vini Caldirola rider Giuseppe Di Grande jumped out of a hotel window in Sanremo in 2001.

In the afternoon, we stop in Filottrano, where Michele Scarponi lived until he was killed by a vehicle while out training in April 2017.

We arrive just as the publicity caravan does and the blaring techno music is slightly discombobulating, especially when we go into the café Scarponi used to visit every day after training, and Daniel speaks to some of the regulars. I can't follow exactly what's being said, but their sadness is obvious and affecting.

Scarponi's career encompassed all of the ups and downs associated with the era. He inherited a Giro d'Italia title when Alberto Contador was stripped of it in 2011, and at various times Scarponi was a client of the two most notorious blood doping doctors in cycling, Eufemiano Fuentes and Michele Ferrari.

But from what I can gather, Scarponi was universally well liked, and could brighten even the darkest day. Once the music fades, it's apparent the impact his death has had on those who knew him.

At the finish, Simon Yates again shows his desire to gain time wherever possible by winning the stage and another time bonus.

The narrow streets and steep finish are tailor-made for him. In the podcast we record while sheltering from a sudden torrential rainstorm, Daniel makes the slightly controversial point that all Yates has really done so far in this Giro is win an edition of Tirreno–Adriatico. The real mountains are still to come. At first, I think it's a harsh observation but later, as I flick through the road-book and look at the stages remaining, I think he may have a point.

One thing we can say with certainty is that Froome is definitely out of this Giro. Another 40 seconds squandered today, so his overall deficit stands at three minutes 20 seconds. They could climb Monte Zoncolan three times in the final week and he'd not take that back.

Thursday, 17 May

Stage 12: Osimo–Imola, 214 km
Stage winner: Sam Bennett
Pink jersey: Simon Yates

The idea of holding bicycle races on motor racing circuits often sounds better than it is. The riders are too small and the curves that look so dynamic when racing cars or motorbikes sweep through them lose something when tackled at less than a quarter of that speed.

This is almost an exception.

Torrential rain and a mishap for Elia Viviani on the approach to Imola make for an exciting finish. Sam Bennett and his Bora–Hansgrohe team do a remarkable job in the final 25 kilometres. Bennett climbs the tricky little hill on the run-in like a Liège–Bastogne–Liège-winning Sean Kelly.

Bora–Hansgrohe's black-and-green jerseys are all over the front of the peloton as they reach the circuit and then, with Matej Mohorič and Carlos Betancur still up the road, Bennett launches his sprint so early it's either a show of supreme confidence or a terrible misjudgement provoked by panic.

As Bennett later explains, his team had done so much work for him bringing the breakaway riders back within reach, he knew he had to be decisive and take responsibility from so far out.

By quirk of fate, the Bora–Hansgrohe and Quick-Step buses are parked next to each other in the paddock outside the motor-racing circuit's grand-stand, and the contrast in moods outside each could not be starker.

Bennett's teammates are close to tears at what they've pulled off. A testament to the Irishman's popularity, certainly, but there's also the feeling that the Bora–Hansgrohe riders want to be recognised as more than just Peter Sagan's teammates. This Giro is giving them that opportunity.

Next door, the inquest is already underway and the accusations are flying about. A Belgian team with a strong Italian contingent means there's some world-class finger pointing and shoulder shrugging going on.

Viviani returns and throws his bike against the bus. He's had the proverbial shocker. Caught in the second half when the bunch split, then dragged back to the main peloton just as they reached the motor racing circuit only to slip off the back again, the question is who's to blame. Viviani for putting on his rain jacket or for taking it off at the wrong time? His teammates for not being nearby when he needed help? Or the sports directors for not ensuring the plan was clearer? No one's quite sure.

For the third day in a row, Simon Yates is asked about his nickname in the press conference. This time he flatly denies any knowledge of it, and so I sink down a little in my seat to avoid his gaze. It's not the last time I'm shifting awkwardly in my seat today.

Dinner is at a restaurant at the end of the driveway to our impressive B&B. It's getting late and I'm still faffing about uploading files for the morning's *Kilometre 0* episode, so Daniel heads off to get a table before the kitchen closes. As I make my way to join him, he sends a text. 'There's a singer on tonight,' it says. My heart sinks.

There are eight people dining in the large restaurant: a group of four men drinking beers and avoiding eye contact with the band, a couple who look like they're glad of the opportunity not to have to talk to each other, and Daniel and me.

Dinner is strange and very un-Italian. We make our way through four fussy, complicated dishes with little enthusiasm. When the cover band strike up Culture Club's *Karma Chameleon*, I finish my dessert in three bites and ask for the bill. As soon as the bill arrives, the band call it a night. So, we stay for a *digestif*, which we enjoy in peace and quiet.

Friday, 18 May

Stage 13: Ferrarra–Nervesa della Battaglia, 180 km
Stage winner: Elia Viviani
Pink jersey: Simon Yates

'Dr Ferrari lives in Ferrara,' says Daniel at breakfast. 'We should go and visit him.'

'Do you know exactly where, though?' I ask, keen to avoid a wild-goose chase.

'His address was in some court documents I read. I've had a look on Google Street View, so I'm pretty sure I can find it.'

On the way, Daniel and I recall Dr Michele Ferrari's greatest hits. He is, of course, one of the most notorious blood doping doctors in cycling's rich history of such things.

It all started off so innocently, or so it seemed. He was the boffin in big glasses who masterminded Francesco Moser's successful attempt to break Eddy Merckx's hour record in 1984. Dr Ferrari was bringing the laser precision of science to cycling.

A decade on, he was the team doctor for the Gewiss team when three of their riders pedalled away from the rest to finish first, second and third at La Flèche Wallonne. Eyebrows were raised so high that day they were practically round the back of some people's heads.

EPO had been rumoured to have been as much a part of the peloton as handlebar tape and chamois cream since the start of the 1990s but the drug was placed firmly in the public domain by Doctor Ferrari the day after that edition of La Flèche Wallonne.

Not only did Gewiss take the top three places but nine of the top 10 rode for Italian teams. In fact, eight of the top 10 were Italian riders, and the French newspaper *L'Equipe* smelled a rat.

They asked Dr Ferrari about the dangers of EPO use. The drug was, of course, undetectable at the time. Dr Ferrari said that drinking 10 litres of orange juice was also dangerous – the implication being that EPO was perfectly safe if it was used under medical supervision.

Ferrari was the man Lance Armstrong later turned to, and together they won the Tour de France seven times. It was, of course, all fuelled by blood doping – just as most of that era was – and in 2012 Dr Ferrari was given a lifetime ban from sport by the World Anti-Doping Agency.

'That's it,' says Daniel, as we pass a red-bricked villa that could best be described as shabby-chic. It's set back off the busy single-carriageway road, and I pull in at the next opportunity – perhaps 300 metres down the road – and we get out of the car to walk back.

We're about halfway to the house when we see a small figure on a bike pull out of the driveway and pedal off down the road.

'Is that him?' I ask.

'I think that's him,' says Daniel.

'Shall we run back to the car and try to follow him?' I ask. But I already know the answer to that question. By the time we manage to pull out onto the road, Dr Ferrari will be long gone. He's a difficult man to catch.

We decide instead to ring on the buzzer at the gates. A woman answers and tells Daniel that Dr Ferrari is out training. We assume the woman is his wife, but we can't be sure. Daniel asks if he might be heading to the start of the Giro stage in Ferrara.

'No,' comes the reply. 'The Giro d'Italia does not interest us.'

I wonder out loud what we'd have done if we'd have arrived three minutes earlier and had been there just as Dr Ferrari pulled out of the driveway.

The purpose of going to his house wasn't to doorstep him, though, and we play the segment in this evening's podcast. I suppose it was a light hearted diversion that illustrates the complexity and sometimes absurdity of Italian cycling.

'Did you notice,' I say, 'Dr Ferrari wasn't wearing a helmet?'

'Well,' replies Daniel, 'old Michele always did like to live on the edge.'

Later, Daniel's magical mystery tour takes us to Treviso, which is a very well-healed town. The last time I was here was for the world championships in 1999. The road races were held in Verona just down the road, but the time trials were all here in Treviso. Fabian Cancellara won the men's junior time trial that week. I reflect on the fact that he's now retired and think about how quickly time passes.

We're here for part one of *The Cycling Podcast*'s tiramisu taste test. Treviso and nearby Tolmezzo are fierce rivals who contested the Tiramisu World Cup that ended in controversy earlier in the year.

Just like the great rivalries in Italian cycling, there are claims and counter-claims about who has the best recipe and method. Disputes over the origins and authenticity of the recipes rage. It's up to Daniel and me to decide which tiramisu is Francesco Moser and which is Giuseppe Saronni. Or Coppi and Bartoli, or Pantani and Gotti depending on your vintage.

Treviso's tiramisu is rich, creamy and more solid, more brick-like than I'd imagined. It's a formidable opponent and I can't see it being beaten. But we shall have to wait until tomorrow to taste Tolmezzo's offering because as we head to our hotel, I hear the sound of hooves. The Buffalo is approaching. And, equally formidably, the Zoncolan is looming.

by Richard Moore

Saturday, 19 May

Stage 14: San Vito al Tagliamento–Monte Zoncolan, 186 km
Stage winner: Chris Froome
Pink jersey: Simon Yates

There appears to be some mistake. Flying into Venice last night I thought I was returning to the Giro d'Italia. I seem to have landed instead at the Tiramisu World Cup.

Today – finishing on top of Monte Zoncolan, for heaven's sake – the priority of my esteemed colleagues Daniel and Lionel is to find a place in Tolmezzo called Albergo Roma, who were runners-up in the recent World Cup in Bologna and who claim to have invented tiramisu in 1953. Eventually we locate the place and sit down. I ask for a menu. They don't have menus. They only serve tiramisu.

I have some. I mean, it's fine – it tastes of tiramisu. Then I stomp off in search of proper food.

With a full belly, I am ready to take on the Zoncolan. It means a chairlift ride and then a hike for Lionel and me – Daniel makes up some excuse to stay in the pressroom, I presume so that he can watch the wedding of Prince Harry and Meghan Markle. The not inconsiderable effort to reach the top is worth it as we crest the hill and survey the amphitheatre beneath us. With the road curling around, and contained on both sides by the steep slopes of the mountain, it's a spectacular setting, packed with people, including a man with a tent and four children under the age of 10. He is surprisingly chipper.

There's a wonderful atmosphere – a 'crackle in the air', as Lionel says on the podcast – and a great sense of camaraderie up here, with Mexican waves and everything. The first rider we see is none other than Chris Froome, rising like Lazarus after all his travails of the opening two weeks. Behind him is the pink jersey, Simon Yates – closing fast, almost catching Froome and consolidating his lead. But it sets up a fascinating final week. Dave Brailsford is positively giddy. 'Chris has turned this situation around,' says Brailsford, and laughs off the rumours that Froome was poised to head home. Adding fuel to the rumours was the fact that Tim Kerrison, his coach, has left the Giro for Tenerife. But this is logical, says

Brailsford, with the Tour de France team, headed by Geraint Thomas, training on the island.

The prospect of Froome hauling himself back into contention inevitably brings back to the surface all the controversy of his participation in the Giro with his salbutamol case unresolved. It's an interesting but not surprising phenomenon: that his participation is only controversial if there's a chance of him winning.

Sunday, 20 May

Stage 15: Tolmezzo–Sappada, 176 km
Winner: Simon Yates
Pink jersey: Simon Yates

It's *arrivederci* to Lionel after today's stage. He's in spiky form on the podcast, which he puts down to catching the sun while eating a very nice lunch on the terrace of a restaurant in the outskirts of Sappada. Daniel has hopped across the border into Austria to interview Marco Haller, so we take advantage of his absence by ordering a cappuccino after a dessert that isn't tiramisu.

Sappada is a place I only know as the location of Stephen Roche's heist at the 1987 Giro.

When the race was here 31 years ago Roche's teammate Roberto Visentini was in the pink jersey; Roche dropped him on the descent at Sappada, laying the foundations for his win, though he insisted, when I interviewed him for a friends special last year, that he didn't actually *attack* Visentini. I must have looked sceptical when Roche said that, because, with a twinkle in his eye, he insisted, 'It wasn't an attack, because I didn't get out the saddle. How can you attack someone if you don't get out the saddle?'

Hmmm. Sure.

Simon Yates looks as ruthless in 2018 as Roche undoubtedly was in 1987. He wins his third stage in the pink jersey and as Daniel says, he might have had five, gifting the win on Etna to Esteban Chaves and almost catching Froome on Zoncolan. Today Yates looks to have wrestled the Giro to the ground and put his foot on its throat. There's carnage behind him, Dumoulin being dropped by the chasing group and Froome losing more ground, perhaps paying for his Zoncolan exploits.

Speaking to Yates's DS Matt White at the finish I expect him to be happy but am struck by just how bullish he is. He dismisses the idea that

Yates could run out of steam. 'What if his form deserts him in the final week?' I ask. 'Where's it going to go?' asks White. In the podcast I say that my impression was that Yates's team think victory is almost within touching distance. 'Touching distance?' asks an incredulous Lionel. 'What, touching distance for someone with incredibly long arms? Mr Tickle, maybe?'

Tomorrow's a rest day and Daniel and I will be spending it in the out-skirts of Trento, home to some fine wines. I'm hoping we can sample one of the Chardonnays, perhaps the Moser 2012, which opens with enticing scents of Alpine wildflower, pear, flint and a whiff of pastry. I've heard it has an airy, weightless character, doling out ripe apple, creamy white peach, minerals and a dollop of vanilla before a dry, juicy finish.

Or maybe a glass of Pinot Nero – a 2009 bottle of Ferrari, perhaps, with its aromas of toasted bread, chamomile and dried aromatic herb, with a hazelnut note lingering on the finish.

Yes, that would be nice.

by Daniel Friebe

Monday, 21 May

Rest day: Trento

Half of the rest day is spent driving to Trento from our overnight billet in Niederdorf in the South Tyrol, the predominantly German-speaking part of Italy. I sense a melancholic air in the podcast convoy, which for the last couple of days, since the Buff's arrival with our sponsorship Svengali, Dave the Deal, has consisted of two cars. One reason for the sombreness is Napalm's impending departure.

Another, at least as far as I'm concerned, is that the journey funnels us through and swiftly out of Dolomite valleys that, if I had my way or could arrange a hit on Mauro Vegni, the Giro would colonise for the last few days of every edition. Trying to convey the beauty of these mountains is, to steal an aphorism once used about music-writing, like dancing about architec-ture. Or, maybe, podcasting about cycling. You get the idea.

It's largely pointless, though many still try. Alexander Robertson made one of the better stabs in his *Through the Dolomites* of 1896, writing, 'What Venice is among cities, these Dolomites are among mountains. In line and colour, form and behaviour, they are unlike other mountains. They resemble reefs, over which may have broken, throughout long ages, the billows of an angry ocean.'

Robertson was by all accounts an interesting chap. Born in Edinburgh, like our own Buffalo, and later a prolific contributor to *The Scotsman*, like our own Buffalo, Robertson – I discover now – built and established a protestant church in, of all places, Sanremo in 1881. He later moved to Venice and lived there as a recognised Church of Scotland minister until his death in 1933.

This evening, at our beautiful guesthouse overlooking the owner's vineyards above Trento, I'm reminded that Scotland still sends forth into the world men of rare cultural sophistication and impeccable linguistic dexterity. The Buff proves this when our young host kindly offers us a *degustazione* of the property's latest vintages. 'Hmmm, that's nice,' says the Buff, downing the first glass, a Traminer. Wine number two, a Chardonnay, is also unceremoniously dispatched. The Buff's tasting notes for this one: 'Mmmm, nice too.'

I look to the heavens, wondering if I can see Napalm's plane, or maybe call it back.

Tuesday, 22 May

Stage 16: Trento–Rovereto time trial, 34.2 km
Winner: Rohan Dennis
Pink jersey: Simon Yates

The long-awaited time trial gives us less information about who's going to win this Giro than we'd hoped. Warming down outside his team camper van, Tom Dumoulin looks perky enough about the minute and 15 seconds he's gained on Simon Yates – but is making downbeat noises into the microphones and dictaphones hovering in front of his face.

Dumoulin is now more or less telling us that he needs a miracle, a total capitulation by Yates, in order to win the Giro. The climb to Pratonevoso in two days will be a sort of third time trial – a single, 40-minute effort not unlike the one to Oropa that Dumoulin aced twelve months ago. Speaking to him, his coach and his *directeurs*, you get the feeling they have it earmarked as his last chance.

Sky's team vehicles are parked 50 metres or so away from Sunweb's but the moods in the two camps, it seems to me, are further apart. Froome's fifth place today is his worst result in an individual time trial of over 10 kilometres in a Grand Tour since the 2014 Vuelta. 'Chris', as the Italian newspapers have taken to calling him in his diminished, deweaponised current state, is still nearly four minutes down on Yates and, I sense tonight, turning his thoughts towards the Tour.

His team boss, Dave Brailsford, has already hinted to me more than once during the Giro that the UCI's doping case against Froome is falling apart and could even be shut down before the *Grand Départ* in six weeks' time. Consequently, any notion of Froome sitting this one out, even as a diplomatic move or bowing to ASO pressure, may soon become redundant.

Brailsford also concedes that he and Froome have already been thinking ahead in the last few hours. He tells me that, last night, he presented him with a list of bullet points – as he puts it, 'things Froomey really needs to address and resolve before the Tour'. One of the issues is a particularly painful saddle sore that has hampered him throughout the Giro, but which Sky have kept secret. The team has come up with a short-term solution that will supposedly help Froome over the coming days, especially on the gravel section of the Colle delle Finestre.

Wednesday, 23 May

Stage 17: Riva del Garda–Iseo, 149 km
Winner: Elia Viviani
Pink jersey: Simon Yates

A relatively uneventful stage won, as widely predicted, by Elia Viviani, takes us from the biggest and perhaps most famous of the Italian lakes, Garda, to one that hardly anyone outside Italy has heard of, Iseo.

I've been here a handful of times and, to be honest, never found it particularly appealing. The classic ingredients are all in place – the encircling mountains and vineyards reflected in the shimmering water, the lilting rhythm of walks along the promenades and *imbarcaderi* (jetties) – and yet there is also something about the Lago d'Iseo that makes me uneasy that I can't quite place. Or, rather, I can't work out whether I feel this way just because the only person I know from here is Mattia Gavazzi – and Mattia's story, which he told me in great detail on a rest day during the 2013 Giro, is ultimately quite a sad one.

Many cycling fans will know the name and the bare bones: once touted as the most talented Italian sprinter of his generation, Mattia ultimately lost his career to a cocaine addiction which resulted in four positive tests, the first when he was a junior and the last in 2016. His version of how, when and where the problems started – in the June of 2000, down by the waterside, when a group of pot-smoking friends passed around a bag of white powder – has stuck in my memory.

So too did his account of his first race as a professional, the Étoile de Bessèges, when Frank Vandenbroucke came onto the LPR team bus to see old friends after one stage, told Gavazzi he liked the cut of his jib and the arc of his pedal stroke, then asked where he was from. 'Near Brescia,' Gavazzi told him, to which Vandenbroucke replied thoughtfully, 'Brescia, eh? Good coke there…' – and Gavazzi knew exactly what he meant.

I haven't spoken to Mattia for a couple of years, but send him a message today to ask if he'll be at the finish. When he replies in the affirmative, we arrange to meet by the team buses after the stage. Our catch-up takes place under a tree as rain hammers down all around us, but Mattia doesn't seem particularly fazed. He tells me today's been tough – not least because, not wanting to sound immodest, he knows he was as gifted a sprinter as Viviani and is still only 33. That could have been him collecting the bouquet on the podium.

He shrugs. Everyone has their crosses to bear – and Mattia knows that his battle will be much longer, with much higher stakes, than a Giro d'Italia. He now runs a building company and says he's 'almost become a normal person again'. The 'almost' worries me and, I pick up from his darting eyes and stiffening shoulders, it worries him too. We part with a handshake and promise to stay in touch. We agree it's been good to see each other again, even if, last time, five years ago, I'd gone away and written a happy ending which has turned out to be rather premature.

Thursday, 24 May

Stage 18: Abbiategrasso–Pratonevoso, 196 km
Winner: Maximilian Schachmann
Pink jersey: Simon Yates

I think Simon Yates might be toast in this Giro – and I know exactly how he feels. Ten years ago I had to ride up to Pratonevoso for a *Procycling* magazine feature, and my legs deserted me in the last couple of kilometres too. It's a real shame Strava wasn't around then, so we can't compare our times...

All delusional tomfoolery aside, I do agree with those who have said there is blood in the water tonight. When, from dominating a major tour, a rider suddenly starts losing his rivals' wheels as Yates did in the finale today, that's usually a sign of shifting momentum and sometimes an irreversible trend.

Admittedly, the steady climb today suited a rider like Dumoulin, who's more snowplough in the mountains than Yates's ski lift, but the glimpse of vulnerability, added to Yates's inexperience, multiplied by his team's brittleness with Esteban Chaves still struggling, make me fear the worst for Yates with two big days in the Alps to ride.

Our hotel for the night is a wonderful *agriturismo* back down in the Po Valley, better known here as the *Pianura Padana*. *Agriturismi* are now a mainstay of Italian tourism and, every year, of our Giro. They are farms also offering accommodation and meals made with home-grown or home-reared ingredients. For 60 or 70 euros a night you usually get a fairly luxurious room, often in an old grange or barn restored and decorated with typical Italian *eleganza*, and sometimes even a swimming pool.

The breakfasts can be sparse, as they often are in Italy, the home of the national heresy they call *fette biscottate*, literally 'baked slices' and which I know and loathe as desiccated sawdust tiles. Or they can be multicourse banquets like the one that'll be served tomorrow morning, laden with farm-to-fork cheeses, meats, breads, jams and juices.

Like I said, I fear Yates may be toast. Better, at least, than being a *fetta biscottata*.

Friday, 25 May

Stage 19: Venaria Reale–Bardonecchia-Jafferau, 185 km
Winner: Chris Froome
Pink jersey: Chris Froome

There's a rather crude Italian expression, similar to our 'mutton dressed as lamb', which goes that someone is *dietro liceo, davanti museo* – literally 'high school at the back, museum at the front'. It bears absolutely no relevance to the Giro but it keeps popping into my head this afternoon. Professional cycling becomes ever more slick and academic, yet there are many aspects of this sport that belong less in a museum and more at an archaeological dig.

Chris Froome, the robot created by Team Sky boffins, storming the Giro and dethroning Simon Yates with an old-school attack on an anachronistic gravel track to the Colle Delle Finestre underlines what I'm talking about. So too does the way in which Sky's chief rocket scientist, Dave Brailsford, watches this little piece of cycling history unfold.

The Buff and I have committed logistical suicide by trying to walk two kilo-metres from the pressroom, over a motorway, under a railway bridge and back up the race route to the team buses – and probably get what we deserve when a policeman stops us on a roundabout at the foot of the final climb. It's there that we see Brailsford. He's on his own, wheeling Vasil Kiryienka's bike – the Belorussian having abandoned it earlier in the stage – and, most perversely, Brailsford is watching the stage on a dodgy stream on his mobile phone.

For a second, I try to imagine an equivalent scenario in another sport – say, José Mourinho locked out of Old Trafford, with one ear pressed against the portable radio he's borrowed from Stan the Burger Van Man – but the image is just too preposterous. Yet in cycling this kind of *ad hoc*, antediluvian – albeit 4G-powered – dilettantism abounds. In a minute Brailsford will be scrolling through photos on said phone and showing us pictures of the mas-terplan – a grid scrawled in blue biro on a scrap of paper, tabulating how, all being equal, Froome would lose weight over the course of the final week. He would then smash everything up in Stage 19, ie today.

There's even something so very old-fashioned about Simon Yates's col-lapse. He loses 39 minutes – the sort of time gap Fausto Coppi and Charly Gaul used to inflict on their rivals. Froome could have listened to the whole of *What's Going On*, *Illmatic* or *A Hard Day's Night*, or started watching *Back to the Future*, and seen Marty go back to 1955, by the time Yates has finished.

'I think we'll talk about this day for a long time,' Thibaut Pinot, who may now finish the Giro on the podium, tells me as he climbs aboard his team bus after a cable-car ride down the mountain. I think old Thibaut might be right.

Saturday, 26 May

Stage 20: Susa–Cervinia, 214 km
Winner: Mikel Nieve
Pink jersey: Chris Froome

To me, the Valle d'Aosta, where the Giro takes us today, has always been a bit like *Kill Bill: Volume I* – we had a moment in 2003, I initially liked what I saw and the repeated disappointments of subsequent viewings have never quite been able to edge out that first, favourable impression. In the film's case, the selective amnesia could be explained by a rare pathology that we'll refer to here as yellow-leather syndrome. In Aosta, today, I saw no samurai swords, no Uma Thurman and definitely no Beatrix Kiddo outfits – and yet I was reminded once again why memory and reality don't quite match up in this particular, idiosyncratic corner of north-west Italy.

Aosta has mountains, many mountains – and I love mountains. The Gran Paradiso is among the highest and handsomest mountains in the Alps. It is Aosta's talisman. It's not the peaks that bother me here. My beef is with the valleys – or rather the one from which the region takes its name. Again, the problem lies in a chasm created by the mind, between the glistening Eden criss-crossed by babbling brooks and overlooked by thatched-roof cottages that I'd want it to be and the exhaust pipe dominated by the A5 motorway that it really is.

On that first visit in 2003 I was 10 days into a six-week trek across the Italian Alpine chain, from Sanremo to Trieste, and possibly didn't have the physical or mental energy to challenge my sugar-coated preconceptions. Now I learn that the Valle d'Aosta has by far the highest suicide rate of any Italian region – and, more bizarrely, according to a survey carried out by an organisation that calls itself Happy, the highest proportion of negative tweets per inhabitant. Frankly, I'm not all that surprised.

Today's stage should have been, to paraphrase something Christian Prudhomme once said about the Tour de France in Yorkshire, the grandest of *Grande Finales* – and yet it falls short. RCS could scarcely have chosen a more grandiose finish line: the Matterhorn, Europe's most recognisable pinnacle, pokes out over our heads and the peloton's like the giant hat of a white wizard.

The magic, however, was apparently all used up yesterday by Froome's Houdini act on the Colle delle Finestre. The pretenders and particularly Tom Dumoulin try with a flurry of late attacks, but the slope is too gentle and the legs – everyone's legs – are too tired. There will be no repeat of the 1997 Giro stage to the same location, when the traitorous Ivan Gotti ousted my hero then and possibly even now, the mighty Pavel Tonkov.

The anticlimax makes it feel like a mountain stage too many – and that's certainly the case for Thibaut Pinot. I'm waiting at the team parking area a kilometre from the finish when a lightning storm starts rolling in and with it murmurs of Pinot having suffered a terrible collapse. Mauro Vegni, the race director and a man with a scowl worthy of a weather warning, disappears into the café–restaurant commandeered as a changing room looking even more grim-faced than usual. Apparently the two events are linked. Later, we'll learn that, having finished in the *gruppetto* and kissed goodbye to his podium chances, Pinot has been rushed to hospital and treated for dehydration and exhaustion. Needless to say, he won't finish the Giro tomorrow in Rome.

The Buffalo and I are also ducking, or in his case stampeding, out tonight. With him behind the wheel, the car journey down to the valley is punctuated by my squawks of disbelief as I read tweets reacting to what George Bennett told me in Susa this morning about what he said at Bardonecchia last night – namely that by 'doing a Landis' of course he didn't mean Froome had 'railed a bunch of gear'.

People online think Bennett has been called to order by his team overnight, and that I'm somehow facilitating the cover-up. Any fool could tell from the tone of Bennett's voice that he's not reciting a prepared statement and, failing that, they could consider for a second that it was LottoNL–Jumbo's own camera crew that filmed and posted the first, offending clip. But that's not how social media works. Hence tonight, Matthew, on Twitter, I'm being compared to Baghdad Bob, Saddam Hussein's Information Minister.

'People are fucking mental,' I tell the Buff, meaning of course people who aren't friends of the podcast.

Sunday, 27 May

Stage 21: Rome, 115 km
Winner: Sam Bennett
Pink jersey: Chris Froome

If yesterday lacked drama then today, when we're not even going to the race, is hot out of the blocks. The Buff and I are both flying out of Milan Malpensa – him to London, me to Berlin – and have agreed on a nine o' clock departure from our (charmless) hotel in Saint-Vincent. I have the keys so walk across the street to the pavement on which we dropped anchor last night, put her in reverse and turn into the hotel driveway.

It's then that a group of guests dragging their luggage out of reception start pointing urgently at the bottom of the car. The Buff has now also appeared, and is looking where they're looking and smiling – but it's not a good smile. I would even go so far as to say it's a wry, ominous 'Oh, look what Bad Santa has left under the tree' sort of smile – an expression that says, 'Ohh fuck, there's a massive nail in one of the tyres.'

Within a few minutes, our mild panic has escalated somewhat after we've established the car rental company has supplied us with the wrong wheel spanner. No one we or the hotel manager can find in reception or the breakfast room has the right one either. The time's ticking, the current best case of a local mechanic getting here in an hour won't get us to the airport on time, and Buff's demob-jauntiness has gone the way of Simon Yates's pink jersey.

It's while these pennies are dropping that a somewhat senior gentleman hobbles out of nowhere and onto the set of our unfolding nightmare. I don't think we even have time to tell him what's wrong; I've barely opened my mouth before he's producing a miracle-tool out of his pocket, squatting by the wheel, and prodding and gouging at the bolts. Within about four minutes the spare is on and, with a flamboyant swoosh of his right arm, our new friend the wheel whisperer is waving us out of the pits. Malpensa is 145 kilometres away and we've got just over an hour to get there. With one tyre whose recommended maximum speed is 80kph.

We don't make it in time for my baggage drop-off but, as we arrive at the airport, inspiration strikes, practically poleaxing the Buff: I'll head straight to the gate with just hand luggage and he'll take my big suitcase and get it to my girlfriend, who's visiting me in a few days. 'Brilliant. Thanks, Buff,' I call over my shoulder as I sprint towards the terminal. 'If you get stopped and searched at customs, just try to make sure they don't lift up the insole of the New Balance trainers. OK?'

He suddenly looks even paler than usual, bless him.

2018 WOMEN'S TOUR

by Orla Chennaoui

Wednesday, 13 June

Stage 1: Framlingham–Southwold, 129.7 km
Stage winner: Jolien D'hoore
Green jersey: Jolien D'hoore

Stage 1 of the Women's Tour started in the shadows of the rather wonderful Framlingham Castle, in Suffolk, with the team buses and minivans making use of the castle car park as their paddock. Despite the setting, there was little sense of grandeur among the women's teams. Even for the start of a race as prestigious as the Women's Tour, the atmosphere was remarkably relaxed. Not that nerves were absent, but with most buses lacking the luxury of the men's peloton, there isn't really anywhere for the riders to hide, with most pinning on race numbers and getting their final leg rubs in full view of the wandering, curious public.

Plus, there's something very levelling about the top riders in the world having to share public conveniences before one of the biggest races in the calendar. As we walked down the hill to the start line just before the roll-out, we saw last year's winner, Kasia Niewiadoma, and teammate Pauline Ferrand-Prévot clumping awkwardly out of a pub. At least I presume they'd been to the ladies. They could just as easily have been enjoying a quick nerve-settling stiffener. I trust not. They'd definitely need the toilet after that.

If the atmosphere at the castle was of a relaxed touristy vibe, the energy and excitement of the race grew in proximity to the start line. The roads into town were lined with barriers and people, the crowds next to the stage some half-a-dozen deep. A wave and a smile from Canyon–SRAM DS Barry Austin, and all around, that freshly polished anticipation of a race whose possibilities were as yet infinite. That's how I interpreted the atmosphere at the time.

It later transpired that at least some of that excitement had absolutely nothing to do with the race. A basic Google search of Framlingham will tell you the pop star Ed Sheeran is a local lad, and the castle on the hill is the *Castle on the Hill* from his international hit song. It turns out there had been a rumour doing the rounds that Sheeran was to be at the start line to wave the race on its way. I was told on good authority that the entire Mitchelton–Scott team had believed the speculation, and going by the slightly disappointed looks on the faces of a few of my colleagues, I suspect they weren't the only ones.

Our little travelling convoy had the next best thing, however. In keeping with our intention of bringing the start and finish towns to life for our listeners, I had compiled a playlist in keeping with various culturally relevant themes. As we drove out of Framlingham, I ignored the collective protests from Richard and Tom Cary, our colleague from *The Telegraph* and travelling companion for the race, and started what I had planned would be our Ed Sheeran stage.

Despite forewarning, I sang alone. Both Richard and Tom had ignored my instructions to learn the lyrics to *Castle on the Hill* so that we could enjoy 'driving at 90 down those country lanes, singing to *Tiny Dancer*'. I had been practising, so was unperturbed by any attempt to drown me out with the Smiths. A few weeks later, Tom and I received an email from Richard querying who had been driving the car when we were clocked by a speed camera. Turned out it was Richard. He'd rather enjoyed driving at 90 down those country lanes after all.

Having made it to the finish line in Southwold in remarkably good time, we found an incredibly pretty seaside town sitting sleepily on the North Sea coast. Southwold is dominated by a lighthouse in the middle of the town, which is surrounded by brightly coloured Victorian terraces. For the riders, the seaside setting would mean little more than the threat of crosswinds, which rarely combine with a sprint finish without incident.

We had noted on our own drive along the route that there were a number of potential course hazards in the final few kilometres, offshore winds notwithstanding.

A 90-degree left-hander at 2 kilometres to go led onto a less-than-polished stretch of uneven road, before a sharp right-hand turn became the upward drag along the promenade to the finish. Given the false flat and impressive crowds, it was difficult to get a vantage point of the final few hundred metres, so we stood on a wall, necks craned and thumbs cramped from the constant Twitter refreshing. The last social media update before the sprint itself gave no indication of anything other than a straightforward, fully upright charge to the line.

That relative silence would have led you to believe that all the drama belonged to Jolien D'hoore, the Belgian national champion who had just returned to racing after breaking her collarbone a few weeks earlier and triumphantly took the stage win.

But as the riders caught their breath and the media pack briefly lost theirs in the short dash to become entangled in the immediate aftermath of the race, it became clear not all had been as straightforward as we had been led to believe. As Wiggle High5 rider Katie Archibald put it, 'Everything was fine until it wasn't.'

The last 10 kilometres were marred by a number of crashes, with several of Archibald's teammates caught up at various stages, though all, including Archibald – who herself had just returned from a broken collarbone – were able to resume the race. Things looked more serious for another rider, who came down closer to the finish line.

'Abi's down – it looks really bad', I overheard an almost-crying Alice Barnes say to her parents at the finish line. It turned out her close friend, the Trek–Drops rider Abi Van Twisk, had fallen on the very stretch of road we had identified before the final, the nervy right-hander onto the finish line, coming off on a pothole according to Barnes's teammate Kasia Niewiadoma.

Van Twisk was completely immobile as the peloton raced past. In the immediate aftermath there was some confusion. Team boss Bob Varney said he'd been to see Abi and said several times including on the podcast that she had lost consciousness, but that she was now alert and being checked out by doctors. By the time we began our podcast later that evening, we knew her injuries were potentially race-threatening, but not medically serious.

To bring balance to a day that had begun with an Ed Sheeran overload, and to bring calm to an otherwise hectic race report, I played out the podcast episode with Elgar's *Nimrod* from *Enigma Variations* since he, too, was a local. Sitting in the sunlit, chilly courtyard of Adnam's brewery, it was one of those rare moments in the middle of the race chaos when all is still, when the podcast itself can be a bridge between the cultural history of an area and the sporting madness it finds itself in.

Except Elgar wasn't a local to Stage 1: he was from Stage 4. I had mixed up my cultural notes. We should have been playing Benjamin Britten's *Young Person's Guide to the Orchestra*. My admitted smugness having dissipated, I gave up on any cultural pretensions on the drive to the hotel. We played Dolly Parton at full blast instead. *Jolene* was our clumsy attempt at a homage to the stage winner Jolien D'hoore. No, it wasn't quite right, but it was close enough. It had been a long day already.

Thursday, 14 June

Stage 2: Rushden–Daventry, 143.9 km
Stage winner: Coryn Rivera
Green jersey: Coryn Rivera

If the start of Stage 1 saw riders use the nearest pub to answer a pre-race call of nature and nerves, Stage 2's race start, in the middle of a lush, open park created more of a challenge. It's one the women's peloton seems well used to. I spotted two Trek–Drops riders waddling off into the bushes, sensibly choosing the opposite side of the team paddock clearing to the finish line, and return a few minutes later looking unbothered by the inconvenience and distinctly less waddly.

The lack of obvious facilities at the race start got us thinking – as did a chat Richard had with Tim Harris, the driver of the *chief commissarie*'s car at the race, who noticed that roadside nature breaks were becoming more common in women's racing. While the men's peloton can, and frequently does stop by the side of the road once a breakaway has been established, the particular way in which women's clothing needs to be removed (I'm thinking of the spectacular indignity of a desperate Tom Dumoulin as he was caught squatting mid-2017 Giro d'Italia – welcome to our world, Tom), inspired us to produce a special 'water feature' for the podcast.

The increased length of women's stages, from 135 to 160 kilometres, as well as better nutritional education, means it's no longer practical for the riders to not stop at some stage during a race. One male DS suggested to Rose Manley, our co-presenter on *The Cycling Podcast Féminin*, that the peloton could perhaps schedule its collective nature break for a spot where they might be able to have some privacy. I suspect this was more to spare the perceived blushes of the public than the riders, but clearly queueing at a public convenience mid-race is a non-starter whatever the thinking.

I was surprised by the riders' honesty when we started asking about their mid-race toilet habits and the lack of any obvious embarrassment. But then, pulling down your bib shorts to expose your arse in front of dozens of your colleagues probably dispenses with a lot of unnecessary timidity. For us non-racers it's difficult to imagine. Even in my drinking days, I would rarely dare to expose my bum on a roadside. Rarely.

'There was one time I remember I was on the side of the road in a race,' Marianne Vos told me. 'I had my bike there, leaning against the tree, when the mechanic came running towards me with wheels. I was like "Er, sorry, I'm here!" So yeah, he turned around and went back. He doesn't do that any more.'

Wiggle High5's Annette Edmondson's rule of thumb is that 'Generally you have to take everything off, and then go as fast as you can. Then you jump back on and try to use the small group of you to get back to the group.

'There's also another way to do it', she said. 'Some people are actually able to put their hands up the side of their knicks and pull them over to the side. Some people can do that quite skilfully. I haven't mastered that technique so I'm not going to try it again.' I'm desperately curious to find out what happened the first time she tried it. But I think I can hazard a guess, and it was probably quite messy.

Canyon–SRAM's Kasia Niewadima tells us she used to race with just one brace so that it was easier to stretch her bib shorts when the moment required, but that she has since been taught a revolutionary technique by her teammate Alena Amialiusik. She didn't share details of the technique in question, only that it's 'much better and easier' and apparently doesn't require the removal of race radio.

Perhaps in an era of marginal gains this is the biggest area for potential improvement in women's racing. Just imagine the men's teams discovering an entirely legal tactic that could save them either minutes in a stage race or a considerable amount of valuable energy trying to chase back onto the bunch. Yes, I've decided this is where the future of women's racing lies. In developing the whizziest whiz in the peloton. Don't tell me we aren't tackling the issues that matter on *The Cycling Podcast Féminin*.

Friday, 15 June

Stage 3: Atherstone–Royal Leamington Spa, 151 km
Stage winner: Sarah Roy
Green jersey: Coryn Rivera

By Stage 3, the race casualties were starting to build. Or fall, I should say. Abi Van Twisk, who'd raced heavily bandaged the previous day after her horrific crash on Stage 1, didn't make it to the race sign-on. Instead, her day started with a lift to the train station with Richard, Tom and me, before the solo journey back to London. The speed with which a rider is spat out of the race bubble always seems brutal to me.

One day, Abi's very visible heroics are being applauded and supported, with a team of riders and coaches doing everything they can to reinforce and make comfortable her race cocoon; the next, she's swamped by rushed, stressed commuters in suits, sloshing takeaway coffee and running to catch the train. Still in her team kit and shorts, Abi's slight frame and heavy bandaging make her look younger and more vulnerable than she is on the station platform. It takes a certain kind of mental toughness not just to be a racer, but to deal with the moments when you're suddenly not.

Trek–Drops had other worries on the team. Hannah Payton had been up sick through the night and was simply hoping to survive the day. She and the remaining riders would be working for Eva Burman, who was sitting eighth on GC. I was to spend the day with the team boss Bob Varney and his mechanic Mikey in the race car. This was to be the longest day of racing of the Women's World Tour calendar. It wasn't a day to be without one rider and struggling to hold onto another. But as Bob would discover, there was much worse to come.

Just 25 kilometres in, race radio issued a call for the Trek–Drops car to make its way up through the race caravan. One of their riders needed help.

An ambulance, already on the scene, showed us where we needed to be. The British riders Hayley Simmonds of WNT and Trek–Drops' own Manon Lloyd were being given the once-over by race medical staff. Simmonds climbed into the back of the ambulance, but Lloyd, mindful of her dwindling team and precious top-10 position to help protect, got back on her bike after several, long, agonising minutes.

The crash and decision to continue racing was only the beginning of Manon's battles, however. By the time she and the Trek–Drops car got back on the move, they had already been left in the sweeping wake of the tour convoy. The swell of traffic, cyclists and fans, temporarily stilled and parted to allow the race through, were flooding back onto the reopened roads, threatening to drown Manon in her attempts to reach the invisible elastic that would allow her to pull herself back through the convoy.

A police escort led the way. The buffer of physical protection in front and Bob's regular, measured words of encouragement from the team car behind, were all she had to distract from the physical pain and mental suffering of racing as hard as the others, but with no race in sight. 'Come on Manon, we can do this. Trust me. Sit on the bumper, sit in the middle, and we'll take you back, nice and controlled. We'll give you as many instructions as we can. If you feel unwell at any point, just let me know.'

Bob then turned to his mechanic in the back seat. 'Right Mike, I need some pretty cool directional changes please.' An indeterminate number of minutes later, with still no race in sight and a realisation there wouldn't be for some time: 'You have to believe this is going to be cool, Manon. Come on, let's go deep. Come on, keep your rhythm…'

After some 10 kilometres, we briefly heard the crackly static of race radio in the team car. I hadn't realised we'd lost it. It only served to make us realise how isolated from the race we were. Manon had no peloton to follow, no teammates to draft behind, no lines to swoop into in the wake of the others. A wrong turn now would be a blow to both the psyche and the time deficit, a recovery from which would be difficult to imagine.

'OK, Manon, we have a series of roundabouts coming up now,' said Bob. 'Which exit, Mikey? Third exit, Manon. I may speed up then wait for you on the other side. 'Go, go, go.'

The quirk of geography and signalling mast positions which allowed us to receive race radio failed us just as quickly, and we continued for another 20 kilometres in the racing wilderness. We knew, however, that we were getting closer to the back of the race when we began reaching stretches of road where the fans were only just starting to pack up. On hearing the police siren and seeing a rider in team kit, clearly still racing, the crowds turned back to the road, shouting encouragement, delighted to still have something of a race to cheer.

Finally, 52 kilometres into the stage, and almost 30 km after the crash, Manon Lloyd was back in the race bubble. From there, she still had a full day of full-gas racing to simply hang on. But she had made it this far, at least.

Time now for Bob to deal with the rest of the team, who had been out of contact with their DS for much of the day. A voice over the team radio: 'Bob, Hannah's in the back of the ambulance.' Hannah Payton hadn't survived. One rider saved, another down. 'You look after yourself, Hannah. It wasn't meant to be – there are other bike races.'

Another voice. This time Eva Burman's. 'Bob, can you hear me now?' 'Give me one minute, Eva, and I'll give you an update… While I'm here does anyone need any water? We're down to four riders now. Eat, drink and recover.'

Anyone watching the TV highlights later that day would have remained oblivious to these minutiae of the racing day. The official drama was being performed a considerable distance up the road by a highly impressive break of two riders, who had managed to stay out front for nearly 70 kilometres: Ann-Sophie Duyck of Cervélo–Bigla and Vita Heine of Hitec Products—Birk Sport.

Only a privileged few ever get to witness the hidden battles of bike racing, played out in the thick of or, indeed, at the back of the bunch. Yet the beauty of the sport lies precisely in the myriad different race stories on any given, single day. I had just witnessed one of the most brutal.

Tomorrow was to bring a DNS for Manon Lloyd. Unable to take to the start line for Stage 4, she never did get to race in front of her home Welsh crowd. A scan a few days later revealed the rider had suffered a fractured pelvis but had battled on for 125 kilometres regardless. As for the rest of Trek–Drops, they finished in Colwyn Bay with just half of their team still intact, but a top-10 place secured nonetheless. Eva Buurman finished eighth. Bob made sure to thank the whole team at the end of the race – Abby-Mae Parkinson, Lizzie Holden, the injured Abi Van Twisk, the ill Hannah Payton and, of course, the indomitable Manon Lloyd for their part in what was a supreme team performance.

Saturday, 16 June

Stage 4: Evesham–Worcester, 131.5 km
Stage winner: Amalie Dideriksen
Green jersey: Coryn Rivera

An unexpected element of covering the Women's Tour, perhaps due to naivety on our part, was the incredibly sparse live coverage given to the race, despite its prominence on the women's calendar.

We've become almost blasé about being able to immerse ourselves in every move, every break, every flick of the elbow in a race. As journalists, we can suffer from information and armchair analysis overload, but it's what we've become used to.

Women's racing rarely has the luxury of the live TV cameras needed to facilitate such indulgence. For the Women's Tour, there was a very good daily highlights programme on ITV, and plenty of print journalists at the race each day, but for the podcast's aim of being the first outlet to have a comprehensive reaction to the day's racing, as well as full race reports with some sort of coherent narrative and extra colour thrown in for good measure, we were largely operating in the dark.

Mostly, we had only the official race Twitter feed to go on. Here is a sample of tweets from Stage 1:

'Km 20: It's been a cagey start to the stage with the riders waiting for each other to make the first move. Race all together.'

'Km 35: Despite a split in the bunch at the QOM at Christchurch Park, the bunch is now all back together.'

'Km 57: The race is heating up with action at the front of the peloton, however no moves have managed to stick.'

Not a single name, not a flourish of detail. Nothing to help colour the race beyond the general outlines of vagueness.

Then, a moment of tension.

'We're currently experiencing a loss of signal in the race convoy – we'll be bringing live text updates again once we get it back.'

Could this be the part of the race where we would have been given the key details we'd been craving? Was the stage blowing itself apart and we just didn't know it? I can't stand it! I need to know what's going on!

'Km 80: We've just passed the 50-to-go marker!' (Phew, we're back.) 'The bunch is currently all together despite several attempts to get away.' (Really? That's what we missed?)

And for the geeks among us who just love a bit of detail: 'The pace is high in the peloton, which is strung out in a long line.'

To stand in this information void is to be completely unaware of whether what has happened on the road was worthy of our soon-to-be projected excitement on the podcast or not. Sure, we know the winner, but was the racing any good? Did it really all stay together until the final few kilometres, or was there any indication of alliances formed and broken, team rivalries exploited and strained, key protagonists showing moments of weakness?

Strangely, it became quite liberating to go about piecing together the day's events from scratch. It felt like a throwback to the, shall we say, more creative days of sports journalism when moments of greatness were shaped in the public mind by the imagination, flair and, to a certain extent at least, journalistic skill of the stringers and reporters ringing in their copy.

It may be self-indulgent to borrow a perceived romanticism and transpose it onto your own actions, but certainly every race finish involved a dash around as many riders as possible to get their take on the day's action, with little or no prior indication of what had happened during the stage, painting the picture with as broad a brush stroke or as fine a detail as only our conversations could allow.

On Stage 4, as it happened, there was plenty of excitement to report: an early crash with five abandonees, a temporary neutralisation, a disagreement between the three escapees, Charlotte Becker, Cecilie Uttrup Ludwig and Audrey Cordon-Ragot, a crash in the final 3 kilometres and an eventual win for former world champion Amalie Dideriksen, which was her first Women's World Tour victory in over a year.

So no shortage of drama to discuss on that evening's podcast. Or at least, that was our take on it. And few will have been in a position to contradict.

Sunday, 17 June

Stage 5: Dolgellau–Colwyn Bay, 122.6 km
Stage winner: Lotta Lepistö
Green jersey: Coryn Rivera

To read the race reports of this year's Women's Tour would be to get the impression that the result was something of a procession for race winner Coryn Rivera. Indeed, every stage after the race opener in Southwold ended with the American in the leader's green jersey, and her increasingly customary winner's press conference. She had already laid out earlier in the week that she no longer saw herself as just a sprinter, but was hoping to emerge through the course of the race as something of a GC rider as well.

To have described Rivera as 'just' a sprinter would have been a little harsh anyway, given the 72 US national titles she had amassed from road to crit, cyclo-cross to track. Rivera had certainly restrung her bow through the course of the week of racing, and it would have taken a huge upset to defeat her and her well-drilled Sunweb team on the final day into Wales. In the end, however, the final stage did have something of a processionary feel after all.

That was largely because the peloton had been warned all week and indeed long before to fear the Welsh climb of Nant Gwynant. The entire race played out in expectation of this mythical beast that was to split the race on the final day and provide a strategic launch pad for any teams with well-timed ambitions on GC. As it was, the battering of a fairly typical Welsh summer's day aside, there was little to trouble the race as it made its way through Snowdonia, and the expectation of the climb neutralised any of its potential impact. The riders looked somewhat surprised to have reached the summit as soon as they did, many only warming up for what they understood would be a brutal day of racing.

As the lead riders reached our stop-off vantage point, just beyond the final queen of the mountains banner of the week, they were followed disappointingly closely by the rest of the bunch, all zipping up their rain jackets earlier than expected, with little or no hope now of the planned attacks on the climb to come. From here it would be an unsophisticated, relatively uneventful charge to the line in Colwyn Bay on the Welsh coast, and a first win of the year for Cervélo–Bigla's Lotta Lepistö.

Coryn Rivera did indeed take her first stage race win, with the Women's Tour's first ever winner Marianne Vos in second, and a heavily bandaged Dani Rowe, not so fresh from a bad fall before the finish line the day before, finishing with her best ever finish on the road on the third step of the podium, and the title of Best British Rider.

The slightly disappointing race finish aside, the week's racing had been a huge success. Once again, the Women's Tour had shown that with the right investment, commitment and energy, not only did the crowds turn out in their noisy droves, but women's racing as a whole was able to make a stir in the sports pages and beyond. We'd had our fair share of crashes, injuries and dramas to provide a narrative away from the racing, and *The Cycling Podcast Féminin* had survived its first equivalent of a Grand Tour on the road together.

I'd even managed to rope the whole crew, Tom Cary included, into a few hours of car karaoke on the road to Wales and discovered a mean talent for air guitar that I never would have suspected in Rose. The listeners, too, proved there was an appetite for proper coverage of the race, and we all left craving more. We'll certainly be back next year. We're told there will even be some serious climbing thrown then in for good measure.

2018 TOUR DE FRANCE

by Lionel Birnie

Saturday, 7 July

Stage 1: Noirmoutier-en-l'Île–Fontenay-le-Comte, 201 km
Stage winner: Fernando Gaviria
Yellow jersey: Fernando Gaviria

The Tour de France is a strange beast. In most towns it takes over and creates an atmosphere of its own. But in the *Vendée* it seems a little bit lost in all this space. It's tempting to think of this start as the *Petit Départ* rather than the *Grand Départ* because the towns that are hosting the stages are small and spread all over, so there's no real focal point.

That's not to say it's without its charm, though. The greenery, the *chateaux* and the white stone walls are all attractive and this stretch of the Atlantic coast is all relatively unspoilt.

We're up very early because the road to Noirmoutier is to be closed to traffic, even accredited vehicles, at eight o'clock. We drive to the start in bleary-eyed silence before sitting in a traffic jam to get into the little seaside town. It means we have quite a lot of time to kill in the Tour's village while we wait for the team buses to arrive.

The pop-up village is reassuringly familiar because it hasn't changed for years. For those who've never visited the Tour, the village is a little tented area for VIPs and people working on the race. You can get a cup of coffee, a copy of *L'Equipe* and a bite to eat if you can elbow your way past the mayor's friends in the queue for a piece of bread and ham. But it has to be said it's all starting to feel a bit quaint and tired these days – a bit like a village fête that needs an injection of fresh ideas into the organising committee.

As Richard, François and I sit and drink our coffee, I ponder the three weeks ahead. There's a jumble of feelings. It's difficult to separate the tingle of excitement from the pang of homesickness. I see familiar faces, people I only ever see at bike races, and it hits me that this is my life for the next three weeks.

I watch the world go by: five-time winner Eddy Merckx walks past being five-time winner Eddy Merckx. It's a responsibility he bears with impressive fortitude. How must it feel to be asked on a daily basis to assess the current peloton through the prism of his late 1960s and 1970s prime?

I remember when the Tour was in Ypres a few years ago I watched as journalist after journalist asked him the same questions about the race hitting the cobbles and he answered with a glassy-eyed stare. When it was my turn, I too asked the obvious one before saying 'And finally, Eddy, who's the second best cyclist of all time?' It struck me that he didn't smile too often at questions, but he did at that one.

Next to wander into view is Raymond Poulidor, who famously never wore the yellow jersey despite finishing on the podium eight times. He's 82 now but a fixture at the Tour, working for Crédit Lyonnais, the bank that has sponsored the yellow jersey since the late 1980s. Every day he pulls on his sponsor's yellow polo shirt and I wonder if anybody in the Crédit Lyonnais marketing department ever got the irony of asking a man who never wore the *maillot jaune* to be their best-known ambassador. Perhaps that was the whole point.

The Tour has started with a road stage several times in recent years. Some have been spectacular – Corsica and Yorkshire stick in the mind – while others have felt, well, a bit flat. The course today is flat – there's just one fourth-category climb between Noirmoutier and the finish and so the talk is of a shoot-out between the sprinters, which has the added spice of knowing the yellow jersey is also up for grabs.

The list of contenders is considerable – Sagan, Kittel, Kristoff, Groenewegen, Cavendish – but as I stand by the Quick-Step bus I sense there's a crackle of anticipation. Their Colombian, Fernando Gaviria, is making his Tour de France debut, but is one of the strongest favourites. I ask Brian Holm how Gaviria feels this morning. 'He's nervous, eh?' Holm says. 'But he should be nervous, this is the Tour de France.' That's close to being the first 'The Tour is the Tour' of the race.

At the finish, Gaviria wins the sprint and the yellow jersey, and a listener asks us a pub quiz-style question that has us stumped. Who was the last rider to win a road stage – not a time trial – on their very first day of the Tour de France? I have to admit defeat and look up all the opening-day stage winners on the Internet. It turns out the answer is the Belgian Edward Sels, who won the opening stage of the 1964 Tour.

It takes us a little longer to digest the drama of the day, a series of crashes in the final 10 kilometres that do some damage. Richie Porte and Adam Yates lose 51 seconds, so too does Chris Froome after he runs onto the grass verge and ends up going head over heels. Nairo Quintana breaks both his wheels after running into a traffic island and he loses even more time. There's no such thing as a gentle introduction to the Tour de France.

Our hotel is a sumptuous *chateau* in the countryside owned by a Swedish man who seems none too bothered that England have knocked Sweden out of the World Cup. The Buffalo from Edinburgh, on the other hand, is simmering at the prospect of England reaching the semi-finals, but more of that later.

Sunday, 8 July

Stage 2: Mouilleron-Saint-Germain–La Roche-sur-Yon, 182 km
Stage winner: Peter Sagan
Yellow jersey: Peter Sagan

A funny day, during which it feels like everything is trying to go wrong. We get lost on the way to the start because our satnav is trying to be too smart. It knows that the roads around the start are closed to public traffic because of the Tour so it keeps trying to send us on a long detour.

We arrive with enough time to get a couple of things done. I join the scrum around Lawson Craddock, the EF Education First rider who crashed heavily during the opening stage, rode half of the 201 kilometres on his own, and finished last almost eight minutes behind.

He looks like he's gone a dozen rounds in the boxing ring and has a nasty wound above his left eye. He's also fractured his scapula, which is likely to give him much more of a problem on the bike. He talks eloquently about the crash, about how uncomfortable his night's sleep has been, and about how much harder his Tour de France has become.

He mentions that every day he survives in the Tour he will donate $100 to the velodrome in his home city of Houston, Texas, which was damaged by Hurricane Harvey last year. He asks for his supporters to donate too, and with that Craddock and the team have turned a bad situation into a positive one.

However, I feel slightly uneasy about the fetishisation of pain at the Tour. It's too easy to get sucked into liking and sharing posts on social media that compare a footballer rolling around on the floor after the slightest contact with a rider pressing on with blood dripping from his face and broken bones.

Cycling is beginning to take the issue of concussion seriously, though, and after we've spoken to some of the EF Education First medical and support staff, I'm confident enough to say they're not allowing Craddock to put himself in danger.

But in how many other sports do people carry on with serious injuries. I'm struggling to think of any. Is it brave or is it foolish? In smaller races riders will pull out with injuries as bad as Craddock's, but the Tour is the Tour [that's two – ed.], and they will push as close to the pain barrier as they can tolerate just to get through the day.

As I walk back to the car, I put Craddock's chances of finishing the stage at no more than 50/50 – I give him even less chance of getting through tomorrow's team time trial. It shows what I know, because Craddock does finish the stage, and the team time trial, and the Tour, albeit in last place, and in the process he raises almost a quarter of a million for that velodrome in Houston.

In the Tour you can be up one minute, down the next. Fernando Gaviria's hopes of winning for a second day in a row are ended in a crash two kilometres from the finish – which also means there's a much-reduced group to contest the sprint.

We record the podcast at a bar near the finish line and them temporarily say goodbye to François. He's going to spend the team time trial day working for ASO's press team, providing live updates for the Tour's website, and so he'll be staying with them tonight.

Richard and I drive out of town and decide not to take a short detour to fill up the car, gambling that we'll find somewhere else on the way. It nearly turns out to be a terrible decision, because the needle on the petrol gauge descends towards zero faster than one of the heaviest sprinters plummeting down the Tourmalet.

The distance to our hotel is 50 kilometres, the car has 46 kilometres' worth of fuel in the tank and Google Maps tells me there are no open petrol stations in the vicinity. We stop at a petrol station despite the fact the Internet tells us it is closed. Richard manages to work out that the pumps are self-service and we fill up the tank. Disaster averted.

Our B&B is a curious place – we're basically staying in someone's house. A big white dog stalks the dining room and there are children's toys everywhere. It's comfortable enough but it's a bit odd and not terribly relaxing.

We head to a little *crêperie* and pizzeria in town which turns out to be the only place that's open. After being shown to a table quickly, we pick up the vibe that the owners are struggling to keep up. At every table sit diners staring into space, suggesting that they are not yet diners. We're warned it may take an hour before we get anything to eat. In the end it's well over that, but it's better to get something than nothing at the Tour.

Monday, 9 July

Stage 3: Cholet team time trial, 35.5 km
Stage winners: BMC Racing
Yellow jersey: Greg Van Avermaet

I'm up early to ride the Cholet team time trial course with Tom Cary from *The Telegraph*. We drive up to a village on the course, buy ourselves a croissant and coffee for breakfast and then get rolling. Our plan is to follow the road back into Cholet, covering the final 10 kilometres of the team time trial route, then cross town to the start line and ride the first 25 kilometres of the course, arriving back at the car.

When we reach the start line at Cholet, a quick wave of my Tour de France accreditation gets us onto the course and just as we're weaving past the people who are organising the barriers and putting down the timing mat, we see a Mitchelton–Scott team car.

As I roll alongside, sports director Matt White winds down the window. 'Go in front of us and we'll get a read off your lines through the corners,' he says, laughing. It strikes me that the last thing Mitchelton–Scott need is to know how a rotund man who corners like a 50-pence piece that's been rolled across a highly polished dining table takes the corners.

They speed off and leave Tom and me to a very pleasant rolling ride. The crowds are already out – some clap enthusiastically, some shout 'Allez, allez, allez'; others chortle slightly.

It reminds me of the time I rode the time trial course around the lake and into the hills at Annecy in 2009. It was the year Cadel Evans was having a bit of a shocker on the climbs. As I huffed and puffed up the climb, a young Frenchman broke into a light jog alongside me and, laughing a bit too much for my liking, shouted back to his friends, 'C'est Evans!'

On the undulating roads around Cholet, I have a sudden sense of *déjà-vu*, which is not uncommon at the Tour – it happens frequently that you're driving down a particular road and you know you've been there before.

In this case it reminds me that I've actually ridden this course before. The 2008 individual time trial, which was won by Stefan Schumacher before he tested positive for a blood-doping product and the race result was later reassigned to Kim Kirchen, was held on more or less the same course as this. The difference is that there's the inclusion of a short, sharp hill on the run in to Cholet this time.

It's clear that the race will be between BMC Racing, Sky and Quick-Step, and so it proves later on – although Mitchelton–Scott and Sunweb are right on their tails. Movistar have a relative shocker, losing 49 seconds to Sky.

I always find the idea of a team time trial more appealing than the reality. One positive is that it means a pretty short day because the first team does not set off until mid-afternoon. But on the other hand, a team time trial usually comes early in the race when we're still feeling fresh and not in need of a relatively easy day.

We arrive in Cholet an hour or so before the first team is off and I head into the *zone technique*, a maze of trucks, trailers and camper vans where the TV crews live with the generators and satellite dishes and thousands of metres of cables linking everything up. This is the hub from which they beam the Tour around the world. It's a world of its own in there and often you see the logistical staff, the people responsible for building up and breaking down this town within a town, dozing in the shade before their day's work resumes once everyone is off air.

I head to Eurosport's double-decker studio to meet the Australian rider Adam Hansen, who's not riding this Tour. His record-breaking run of 20 consecutive Grand Tours – a run stretching back to the 2011 Vuelta a España – has come to an end. I spend a very enjoyable half-hour or so listening to him talk about observing the Tour from the other side of the fence, so to speak, for the first time. The conversation makes a great episode of *Kilometre 0*.

Reunited with François, we record the podcast and then head back to our B&B before finding that every restaurant, even the *crêperie*-cum-pizzeria from last night, is closed tonight. We drive to the next town and everything is closed. 'Monday night in France is the new Sunday night', says François dryly from his nest in the back of the car.

Tom and I hit the phones but everything within touching distance seems to be closed. 'There's a pizza place in the next town,' says Tom. We follow Tom's directions. 'It's just down here on the right,' he says. We see what looks like a garden shed with a sign on the roof that says 'Au Feu de Bois'. As we pull up, François says with an almost childlike wonder, 'It's a pizza machine.' He gets out and goes to investigate.

'We can do better than takeaway pizza,' says Richard. François gets back in the car, answering a question that hasn't been asked. 'So, you put your money in, choose your pizza, and then the machine makes it.' He sounds delighted with the ingenuity of the whole thing.

There's a couple outside the shed waiting for their pizza and they tell François it's pretty good. We decide to take our chances and drive onto the next town, Clisson, on the basis that if there's nothing good there we'll come back to the 24-hour pizza machine.

'This place has really good reviews,' says Richard. On the main road into town, we ignore signs telling us the road ahead is closed. We slalom past two trees that have been chopped down and left overnight, and we accidentally drive the wrong way up a one-way street. 'Something is telling us to go back to the pizza machine, guys,' says François.

I'm glad we press on because the meal we end up enjoying is wonderful. The restaurant is called Le Kilbus and it is the top-rated restaurant in Clisson on Trip Advisor. The decor is modern, fresh, and clearly chosen by people who know what they're doing. The staff are young, switched on and efficient, and the menu is reassuringly short and precise. There are no gimmicks here, nor a slavish but misguided interpretation of Escoffier. Everything we have is excellent.

I start with a pea soup with *ricotta* that is so light and summery that it puts a smile on my face. Then comes *filet mignon* of pork, which is served pink and is delicious. That's followed by some carefully curated cheese. We head back to the B&B later on in contented silence, broken only by François. 'I wonder what the pizza from the machines are like,' he says. He's joking, of course.

Tuesday, 10 July

Stage 4: La Baule-Escoublac–Sarzeau, 195 km
Stage winner: Fernando Gaviria
Yellow jersey: Greg Van Avermaet

People often ask how we cover the Tour, or what a typical day is like. And today's stage is about as typical as they come, although there is a longer than usual drive from our B&B to the start at La Baule.

Over coffee and croissants we study the Tour's roadbook so we know what lies ahead. The roadbook gives detailed descriptions of each day's stage. There are maps that show the race route and the deviation designed for those of us who want to get from the start to the finish as quickly as possible. There's information that is useful for the riders – but rudimentary in the days of Google Maps and other apps – such as the length and gradient of the climbs. The roadbook tells us how to get into the Tour 'bubble' via the PPO – the *Point de Passage Obligatoire* – where to park and where the pressroom is.

When I get the roadbook, I always look for three things. How long is the drive to the start from our hotel? How long is the route we must drive from the start to finish? And how far is the pressroom from the finish line and the team buses? These three things can make or break a day.

The Tour means spending hours in the car each day. Richard and I share the driving, and François settles into his nest in the back, claiming that although he can drive, after years of living in Paris and Marseille, he has no need for a car, and doesn't feel the Tour de France is the place to do his only driving of the year. It's a fair point. But it does mean we ferry him around like royalty. Which he is really, having first covered the Tour in 1986.

We pass the time talking about the race, planning the podcast and listening to music or other podcasts. Richard is in charge of the playlist and although I joke about being subjected to Radio Buffalo for three weeks, I secretly quite like it, and by the end of the Tour I will have built up a Spotify playlist to transport me back to July in France at a later date when the mood takes me.

Sometimes we put on a podcast. Our staples are the BBC's *Desert Island Discs* or *From Our Own Correspondent* or *The Media Show*. Or we'll listen to *Freakonomics Radio*, Malcom Gladwell's *Revisionist History* or long-form interviews by the likes of James O'Brien or Adam Buxton. We'll even put on Lance Armstrong's podcast, *The Move*, which is always entertaining, even if

I find the view of a retired quarterback who's not been at the race for eight years a little out of touch sometimes. Controversial, I know.

We sit in a lot of traffic jams. On days like today when the start is in a small town, the queue can start as soon as we meet the PPO.

We try to arrive around an hour and a half before the start. That gives us time to speak to a handful of riders and team staff and grab a coffee in the village. My strategy is always to try and get something we can use today and something we can use a few days down the line. And I'm often working on something in advance for an episode of *Kilometre 0*. At the moment, we're asking people about Sunday's cobbled stage.

Once the race has rolled out of town, we follow the signs for the *hors course* – the route designated by organisers to take us to the finish quickly and without getting tangled up with the race route.

We are allowed to drive on the course ahead of the race and once a week or so we do choose to do this, even though it takes us much longer. Driving the course always reminds me that the Tour is a living, breathing spectacle. We see the crowds and the leisure cyclists riding the route and we get a feel for the course and notice details that may inform our analysis of the race later on. So I like to do it every now and again.

When we arrive at the finish, we park up and walk to the pressroom. Sometimes we're in time for the buffet laid on for the media. The quality varies greatly. As we're heading for Brittany, I'm hopeful of a good spread, but I'm disappointed as it's meagre fare today.

No disappointment will be greater than the time I'd decided to buy a sandwich at a service station on the route only to arrive at the pressroom to find the buffet consisted of fat Breton sausages wrapped in pancake. I tried to force one down but found I was too full to enjoy it.

So it's a daily gamble whether to eat on the way or wait for the buffet, and sometimes we'll ask François to call ahead to our colleagues who arrive early and get a verdict on the spread that awaits.

There's usually time to sit in the pressroom and catch up with emails and podcast-related admin while watching the race on TV.

Today I have some links to record for a couple of episodes of *Kilometre 0*. It's at times like this that I realise just how vast, busy and noisy the Tour is. Trying to find a quiet place to record away from the din of the commentary at the finish line, or the sound of vehicles beeping as they reverse, or people shouting for no obvious reason whatsoever, can be a challenge, and I always think 'Why didn't I do this earlier, in the peace and quiet at the hotel?' But the answer is there's rarely time to do things earlier on the Tour.

On a routine stage like today, we'll head out to the finish line when the race has about 20 kilometres to go. Sometimes I'll watch on the TV in the little tent reserved for press and team staff near the finish, but usually I'll wait near the team buses.

A couple of the teams – Lotto–Soudal are one – have big TVs embedded in the side of their buses and you can stand there and watch the finish, although the bright sun often makes it hard to see what's happening. These days I can also watch the race on my phone now that data-roaming costs in the EU are no more expensive than at home.

Then we wait for the peloton to roll in and past us like the tide. It's a matter of identifying a target and dashing after them, or waiting while they complete their warm-down or post-race shower.

Richard, François and I will compare notes and aim not to go for the same riders or staff. What we're generally looking for is some reaction that we can use in the podcast, but also information that can tell us what was going on in the race – stuff that we couldn't see on TV. Once back at the pressroom, we'll have a brief editorial meeting and plan the podcast running order, but not so much that it becomes scripted.

Usually, we try to find a bar or a pleasant outside space to record, but today we decide to get on the road and drive to Vannes, where we're staying for the night. France are playing Belgium in the World Cup semi-final and François has booked a table with a view of the TV so we can watch the match.

We record the podcast as the town begins to fill up with people and the place is buzzing. This makes for a good episode because we have to compete with background noise and we all raise our game a bit.

With the podcast in the can, it's over to our producer back at home to edit, polish and tweak, and get the episode online, while we relax, enjoy a dinner of fish and a glass of wine while Groupama–FDJ beat Lotto–Soudal in the football. The celebrations are late and noisy. Excited people of all ages fill the road, blocking the traffic, and singing *Allez les Bleus* and *La Marseillaise*.

It's all very good-natured and quite stirring. At one point we see our colleagues Sam Dansie and Sophie Hurcom from *Procycling* magazine run the gauntlet. They drive out of a nearby car park and across the roundabout just as a young Frenchman slides across their bonnet in celebration. They manage to get clear just before the crowd fills the road again.

We decide to wait and toast French success before walking to our hotel.

Wednesday, 11 July

Stage 5: Lorient–Quimper, 204 km
Stage winner: Peter Sagan
Yellow jersey: Greg Van Avermaet

Have you heard the one about the Englishman, the Frenchman and the Scotsman who tried to cover the Tour de France on the day England were due to play Croatia in the World Cup semi-final? It nearly didn't end well.

Tension crackles in the podcar all day. The bickering begins during the hour's drive to the start in Lorient.

'I don't get it', Richard says. 'I thought you were Irish now?'

'I still support the England team,' I reply.

'But I thought you disliked the England team.'

'It depends who's playing and who the manager is. I'm finding Gareth Southgate and his boys quite likeable.'

My breezy response causes Richard to grip the steering wheel that little bit harder and his bottom lip juts out. I think the fact that I can take it or leave it where the England team is concerned irritates him even more.

The tension has been rumbling away ever since I picked him up at Ashford International Station before the Tour. I swung into the car park with Baddiel and Skinner's *Three Lions* blasting out of the speakers.

'You can turn that off for a start,' he said.

Even a burst of Scotland's 1978 World Cup anthem *Ally's Tartan Army* a few days ago failed to raise much of a smile, although Richard did sing the line 'England cannae dae it, 'cause they didnae qualify' with particular gusto.

François awakens from his nest in the back seat, relishing the opportunity to stir things up a bit.

'Don't worry, Richard, even if England win tonight they'll lose to France in the final.'

'I don't want them to reach the final', Richard says. 'They'll be unbearable'.

We drive on in silence.

The stage itself is a beauty. The Breton countryside looks magnificent. The narrow roads and punchy climbs of the Finistère region give it a spring Classic feel.

With the Mûr-de-Bretagne to come tomorrow, it's strange to see Lilian Calmejane in the break with Toms Skujiņš and others. Calmejane and

Skujiņš are the last two standing, but they're caught on the final hill before a hair-raising run to the finish.

The top 10 here reads like the top 10 in the Amstel Gold Race, if not Liège–Bastogne–Liège. Sagan wins it, of course, but there's a spirited second place for Sonny Colbrelli. Gilbert, Valverde, Alaphilippe, Dan Martin and the yellow jersey Greg Van Avermaet come next.

Afterwards, we drive to our base for the night in the pretty riverside town Châteaulin. François has called ahead to reserve a table with a view of the TV at a bistro. It turns out to be more of a bar than a bistro and as we record the podcast a number of customers who have clearly spent the best part of the afternoon and early evening drinking try to interrupt.

We wrap up the episode a few minutes before kick-off, but I still need to record a couple of links for tomorrow's episode of *Kilometre 0*, so I step outside the bar. By the time I return, the game has kicked off and England have taken the lead. I'm not sure if Richard is fuming that England are ahead or smirking because I've missed the goal.

Tom and I enjoy the match until Croatia equalise and then inevitably score the winner in extra time. It's usually impossible to get annoyed at François but this evening is the exception.

'It's a shame England didn't manage to win,' he says, enjoying the opportunity to sound incredibly patronising.

'Oh come off it, François, you've spent the last half an hour hoping Croatia would score,' I say.

'I was going to say I was looking forward to beating you in the final.'

By now, the bickering has an edge to it. I'm not sure what proves to be the final straw but suddenly Richard responds to a point I don't think has been made. 'Why don't you get over yourselves?' he says to Tom and me. 'Your sense of entitlement is amazing.'

As if to demonstrate my sense of entitlement, I get up and stomp out.

Our B&B is just round the corner, but I get halfway there before realising my suitcase is in the car and Richard has the car key. I turn back and see the others walking along the pavement towards me. I hold my palms out by my side in an apologetic gesture. We head across the river and have a beer while the air clears, and we end the night friends again.

'It's a good job we don't get so chauvinistic about the Tour, isn't it?' says François.

I thought about saying, 'Well François, it's nearly 32 years since you last won it,' but I think better of it.

Thursday, 12 July

Stage 6: Brest–Mûr-de-Bretagne, 181 km
Stage winner: Dan Martin
Yellow jersey: Greg Van Avermaet

The morning after the night before. On the way to the start in Brest, we discuss the fallout with a sense of perspective that was perhaps missing last night.

I wander into the village and see Jonathan Vaughters, the team boss of EF Education First. He's queuing for some *frites*. We chat about the BMC Racing Team's search for a replacement sponsor and the rumours that the Polish CCC team might be about to make a takeover bid.

After winning the team time trial and with Van Avermaet in the yellow jersey, the team has positioned itself front and centre in the shop window. But cycling's a funny sport. Vaughters knows what it is like to try and save a team. He lost a sponsorship deal at short notice last autumn and had to scramble to cover the funding gap. This included launching a successful crowdfunding bid.

'If anyone can do it, Jim can,' says Vaughters with a slightly wry tone. BMC Racing's boss is Jim Ochowicz, one of cycling's great survivors. He's been in the sport for more than 30 years, first as *directeur sportif* of the pioneering 7-Eleven squad – the first American team to ride the Tour de France, in 1986.

They later became Motorola and helped launch Lance Armstrong's career. Ochowicz was briefly involved as a consultant for Andy Rihs's Phonak team when Floyd Landis won the 2006 Tour de France, only to be stripped of the title for failing a dope test. Ochowicz doesn't mention that so much. He returned to the sport at a high level as team manager of BMC Racing not long afterwards, and he's been there ever since.

The stage is the best of the Tour so far. Dan Martin is brilliant on the Mûr-de-Bretagne, attacking early and hard on the climb to succeed where he fell short in 2015. That time, he was second to Alexis Vuillermoz of AG2R. This time he holds off Pierre Latour, also of AG2R. The drama doesn't stop there. Chris Froome looks laboured on the climb and loses a few seconds, as does Rigoberto Uran.

We'd been waiting for the big favourites to trade blows on this Tour, but hadn't meant for it to be as literal as it turns out to be. Romain Bardet and Tom Dumoulin collide and Dumoulin comes off worse, sustaining broken spokes in his front wheel, which forces him to swap wheels with his teammate Simon Geschke.

The twisty roads and ensuing confusion caused by the fractured peloton leaves Dumoulin isolated and he has to chase alone. He loses 53 seconds and is penalised a further 20 by the race jury for drafting behind a car. He tumbles from seventh to 19th overall. It feels like the first really significant moment of the Tour.

We head to our hotel, an impressive and recently restored building in a quiet little Breton village and record the podcast on the terrace before heading indoors for dinner. Unfortunately, the hotel's Wi-Fi is very slow and as we're in a remote village there's no 4G or 3G reception on our phones. My laptop says it will take two hours to upload a 15-minute audio file to Dropbox, from where our producers can download it and start editing.

Not once in five years have we failed to get an episode online at the Tour de France, but the lack of signal is causing a concern. In the end we decide to get in the car. The plan is that I will drive while Richard holds his phone up in the air, hoping to catch a strong signal.

It turns out there's a tiny patch of 4G in the hotel car park. I reverse backwards a few metres and Richard says 'No, hold on, go back. That's it, don't move, I think we're in business,' as if we're adjusting the aerial on an ancient transistor radio trying to tune into the football commentary.

Friday, 13 July

Stage 7: Fougères–Chartres, 231 km
Stage winner: Dylan Groenewegen
Yellow jersey: Greg Van Avermaet

Today was like going back in time 15 or 20 years in Tour de France history. You could be forgiven for thinking that this was the peak of the Jean-Marie Leblanc era. It's a long, boring stage across the breadbasket of northern France, with only the stunning views of the cathedral in Chartres to boost the spirits. And even then we come into town from the wrong direction, and don't really see it in all its glory.

Very early on a sizeable break is snuffed out by Dylan Groenewegen's LottoNL–Jumbo team and what follows is a day-long stalemate.

Yoann Offredo of the Wanty–Groupe Gobert team breaks away with 195 kilometres left. He builds a lead of more than seven minutes and is out on his own for almost 100 kilometres. At one point he jokingly motions to the TV motorbike to take a turn at the front. Last year Offredo told

François of his irritation that so few riders seemed interested in going in the breaks.

The threat of crosswinds sparks the peloton into life and Offredo is put out of his misery. Then Laurent Pichon of Fortuneo–Samsic tries something, but by now the sprinters' teams are keen to take control. Despite the fast finish, the race finishes well down on schedule. It's gone six o'clock by the time Groenewegen has won the stage – a fine reward for his teammates who worked so hard to shut down that early break, even if it did neutralise the race somewhat.

I wait near the Wanty–Groupe Gobert bus and watch as Offredo arrives back. He's met by his wife and young children. His body language confirms his frustration. Then one of the team cars pulls up and sports director Hilaire Van der Schueren gets out in a hurry.

Van der Schueren is 70 years of age – the oldest manager in the convoy of team cars. And despite never having raced a bike at any sort of level, not even as an amateur, he's part of the fabric of Flemish cycling. His first Tour de France was in 1980, meaning he's been at this on and off for nearly 40 years.

I try to catch his eye as he gets out of the car but he darts across the grass and heads for the nearest tree to answer what appears to be a fairly pressing call of nature. I'm sure that I can see his shoulders relax as I watch him from a distance.

When he eventually returns, I say, 'How long have you needed the toilet?'

He puffs out his cheeks. 'Three times I stopped the team car and went on the roadside,' he says. 'A long day.'

It *has* been a long day. And it turns out to be a long night too. Our hotel is a shoebox with shutters on a light industrial estate on the outskirts of town.

There are two of the same chain hotels more or less across the road from one another. We park up at one and find that – naturally – our rooms are in the other one, so we wheel our cases across the road because we can see from a distance that the car park is already full of vehicles from the publicity caravan.

It looks like something from the opening credits of *Wacky Races*. There's a giant red, white and blue chicken parked across three spaces in the corner of the car park among the novelty vehicles that drive ahead of the race advertising stuff to the public.

After checking in, we call a taxi to take us into town for dinner. Now the car park is full of the young people who smile and wave from the publicity caravan's fibre-glass vehicles all day. They have beers and boxes of wine, packets of crisps and a large set of speakers playing music. It's their Friday-night party in the car park, although I suspect they may do this every night.

It's late by the time we return from a very fine meal at the restaurant Saint-Hilaire, which is well worth a visit if you're ever in Chartres.

I'm relieved to see that the party in the car park is dying down when we arrive back. Unfortunately, it seems that half a dozen or so of the noisiest ones have continued things in the room adjacent to mine, and I'm woken frequently by laughing, screeching and music that manages to be both tinny and bassy at the same time.

'Irritating young people,' I think to myself. 'Why can't they just go to bed at midnight? Don't they know that the Tour de France continues tomorrow?'

Saturday, 14 July

Stage 8: Dreux–Amiens, 181 km
Stage winner: Dylan Groenewegen
Yellow jersey: Greg Van Avermaet

Bastille Day. Groundhog Day, more like. My word, what were they thinking when they plotted the two-day journey to take the Tour from the edge of Brittany to Amiens in the Somme department?

To be fair, criticising the Tour route on the basis of the landscape is an exercise in futility. We all know that the Tour goes where the money is. And if the local authorities of Fougères, Chartres, Dreux and Amiens have the money, that's where the Tour shall go. Complaining that there are no mountains in northern France is a waste of energy.

Fortunately, as it's Bastille Day we're due to enjoy the closest thing to a day off that it's possible to have on the Tour.

We have an appointment with Richard's in-laws and extended family in Croissy-sur-Celles to watch the Tour as the French do on their national day of celebration – from the roadside with a barbecue and a glass of wine on the go. We're not even going to go to the finish. It feels like bunking off school, but as the call is made by head prefect Moore, François and I are not going to complain.

The race is due to pass the house where Richard's aunt and uncle live, and when we arrive the courtyard is busy with people and barbecue smoke and a convivial atmosphere. It takes literally seconds to relax. Richard sees his wife and young son for the first time in a week and I'm hit with a pang of homesickness again.

I fill the void in my stomach with sausages from the barbecue and salad. François tucks into the *andouillette*, a truly awful offal sausage and declares it to be delicious. I think he's winding me up. I say this whenever the occasion demands, but it's become something of a public service now to warn unsuspecting holidaymakers of the perils of *andouillette*. It is tripe sausage and it is disgusting. It has the texture of elastic bands crammed into a verruca sock. It smells of drain water, or sewage. If you're not careful, it can linger for days.

I stick to the pork and herb and Toulouse varieties – much more civilised.

When the race approaches, everyone heads to the roadside and we watch the breakaway riders whiz past and then the bunch follows a minute and a half later. The leaders are Fabien Grellier of Direct Énergie and Marco Minnaard of Wanty–Groupe Gobert, but they are destined to be caught by the bunch well before the finish.

The convoy of team cars flies through and only then do I appreciate just how quickly the riders are going. The cars are smashing the speed limit and it feels like they're on the edge of keeping it on the road.

We watch the final 20 kilometres on the television with a cup of coffee and a piece of cake. Dylan Groenewegen wins for the second day in a row. 'Oh well,' says François, 'at least we didn't miss much at the finish.'

Back at Richard's in-laws' house a bit later, as we wait to be well fed for the second time in a matter of hours, François and I sit in the garden and record something for an episode of *Kilometre 0* about breaking the story that almost broke the Tour.

It turns out to be a riveting half-hour or so listening to François talk about the mechanics and ethics of journalism – how stories broke in the not quite pre-Internet age, but certainly in the pre-social media age, and how a simple phone call led to the Tour de France almost grinding to a permanent halt in 1998.

François is so modest that it has taken some time to draw from him the fact that he was instrumental in breaking the story of one of the biggest scandals in cycling's history – the Festina affair.

It's 20 years since all that EPO and other banned drugs were found in the back of a car boot of a Festina team car heading across the border between Belgium and France on its way to the Tour, which was about to get underway in Dublin.

François was working in the office of the Reuters news agency when he received a call from a trusted stringer – a freelance journalist with impeccable contacts in the police and judiciary in north-eastern France. The team car had been stopped on the border, the drugs had been found and Festina's *soigneur* Willy Voet was in custody.

The thing that fascinated me most was how François trusted his stringer enough to break the story, even though it was against the Reuters policy of requiring further corroboration from a second source and identifying the source.

News broke more slowly in those days and Reuters enjoyed their scoop for hours before other news outlets caught up with the story. It may only be 20 years ago, but listening to François talk it feels like a different world.

Sunday, 15 July

Stage 9: Arras–Roubaix, 156 km
Stage winner: John Degenkolb
Yellow jersey: Greg Van Avermaet

It's the day everyone has been eagerly awaiting. The cobbles are back at the Tour de France. It's become something of a tradition that I go out onto the course with Simon Gill in his camper van and try to capture some of the atmosphere. We first went *pavé* hunting at the Tour in 2014 when the rain fell and churned up the mud between the stones.

Lars Boom won that day, but what I remember was that when the team cars came past they sent a wave of muddy water over my new Adidas Gazelle trainers. The following year it was dry and dusty and so my trainers survived intact, and the weather is fine again today.

This time I've decided to make an episode of *Kilometre 0* on the *pavé*. The inclusion of so many sections, and particularly some difficult sections, has divided the peloton – especially because the stage comes relatively late in the race.

Over the past few days we've canvassed opinion among the riders and team managers, and views have ranged from one extreme to the other. Some say the cobbles are too much for the little climbers who have little experience of racing on them.

Others say that any road in France is fair game for inclusion. Alain Gallopin – the boss of Trek–Segafredo – has no sympathy at all, saying that the climbers have the opportunity to win every stage race on the calendar, so they shouldn't complain about being asked to race on the cobbles one day in the year.

We *rendezvous* at Simon's camper van in Arras and head out onto the course. I have the roadbook on my knee and Google Maps on my phone, and we set off for a dizzying cross-country journey to see the race on several stretches of cobbles, starting with the first one – sector number 15. I hear that Richie Porte has crashed and is out of the race before they've even reached the *pavé*.

Once the peloton has thundered past us on section 15 we run back to the camper van and head to our next point. This time we see some exuberant Belgian fans who've clearly enjoyed a few beers, a man with a homemade sign that reads 'Froome, go home', and then when the race arrives I barely recognise it from before. Everything has changed, as if the riders have been sucked up by some invisible force and placed back on the road in a random order.

There are groups all over the place. Rigoberto Urán and his EF Education First teammates are off the back. The road is so clogged by team cars and spectators their passage is blocked and one of the riders has to slam his hand on the side of the car to make room for them to pass. It really is a battle for survival out there.

We see the race again towards the end, knowing that we won't make it to the finish, and it seems that a semblance of order has been restored. By the finish I'm stunned to scan through the results to see that almost all of the overall favourites finished together. That seemed an impossible outcome at one point. Landa and Bardet lose just seven seconds, having looked in real trouble earlier on. Urán's Tour chances are probably over, and Porte is out of the race, but the cobbles have been relatively merciful.

We record the podcast sitting in the grandstand of the famous Vélodrome André-Pétrieux, which hosts the finish of Paris–Roubaix every April. Every so often there's a cheer that tells us France have scored another goal and I feel slightly guilty that François is missing the World Cup final. But we can't hang around while he watches the game because we've got to get on the road to head south.

After a weeklong discussion about our rest-day transfer strategy, I've got my way. My preference was to drive a couple of hours tonight and do the rest of the drive to Annecy on Monday morning – overruling the suggestion that we just get on with it and drive into the small hours. It at least means we can have a meal and an early night.

As our hotel is next to the motorway junction near Reims, we order a bottle of champagne to toast the French World Cup victory, Simon's arrival and the close of the first phase of the Tour.

by Richard Moore

Monday, 16 July

Rest day: Annecy

Riders in the *gruppetto* have to make quite complicated calculations on the move. These can be high-stakes decisions about making, or not making, the time cut, and we are not immune from having to wrestle with important dilemmas ourselves. After Stage 9 finished in Roubaix on Sunday, for example, we had to get ourselves to Annecy for Stage 10 on Tuesday: a seven-hour drive.

The question was, should we try to do the bulk of the journey on Sunday night, giving ourselves a late night but a relaxing rest day? Or should we drive a couple of hours and stop in order to be able to have dinner, even though that left us with a longish drive on Monday?

In the late 1960s, an experiment was carried out on some children – it was known as the Stanford marshmallow experiment. What happened was that a child was given a choice between one immediate reward (a marshmallow, biscuit or sweetie) or, if they waited 15 minutes, two rewards. In follow-up studies some years later, it appeared that the children who exercised patience, and waited for the bigger reward, had 'better life outcomes'.

Here, in a modern re-enactment of the Stanford marshmallow experiment, our choice was dinner now or a beautifully relaxing day 12 hours later. Dinner won.

Luckily, François – a little more relaxed about these things than Lionel – was sanguine about the World Cup final, in which France were playing Croatia while we were driving south. But he was happy, in his nonchalant way, when they won.

Near Reims, we stopped at a hotel by the motorway, had a mediocre meal (it would have been good for my analogy if marshmallows had been on the menu; they weren't), and this morning, with all day to complete our five-hour drive, we meander off with no real sense of urgency.

'What are all these red lines on Google Maps?' I ask Lionel as we leave the car park. I don't really need to ask: I know very well what they are. Traffic. To cut a very, very, very, very, very long and tedious story short, we endure the very worst of rest-day transfers. The Stanford marshmallow experiment was right: taking the immediate reward of dinner has not resulted in a good life outcome for us.

Abandoning any hope of picking up Orla from Geneva airport, we crawl towards Annecy, getting increasingly anxious because we have an event in the evening. Having left at 9am (OK, 9.42am), we get there just before 6 pm, to find Orla poolside, sipping a cool drink (her cab having dropped her here about an hour earlier).

We jump in the swimming pool to cool off, then shower, dress and head down to a small cinema for an event, hosted by Base Camp, before about 100 people. There is a surprise for the audience – and for us – when Jonathan Vaughters and Doug Ellis, head honchos at EF Education First, turn up and then join us on stage to take part in the discussion. Ellis on the business of cycling and Vaughters on aerodynamics – and the art of time-trialling – are absolutely enthralling.

You had to be there. (You literally did have to be there, because it wasn't recorded.)

Tuesday, 17 July

Stage 10: Annecy to Le Grand–Bornand, 158.5 km
Winner: Julian Alaphilippe
Yellow jersey: Greg Van Avermaet

An early start because as well as Stage 10 of the Tour, today is the day of La Course, the women's race. As Orla and I drive to the start we begin recording our thoughts about the race for the podcast. You won't hear that conversation, because it is so unrelentingly negative that we decide to bin it. But to summarise: we think this year's race, a short mountain stage starting early on a Tuesday morning, barely 48 hours after the end of the Giro Rosa, is a piss-poor effort by ASO.

You also don't hear it because the race itself is an absolute belter. Well played, ASO! It is attacking and aggressive from the start, with one team, Cervélo–Bigla, taking it on and putting the strongest riders under pressure. There is a nail-biting finish when Annemiek van Vleuten pips Anna van der Breggen in the last few metres. And there is a gushing interview with Cecilie Uttrup Ludwig, the young Danish rider, that endears her to anybody who witnesses it or happens to be watching TV on a Tuesday morning.

One of my favourite things about La Course is seeing television's Daniel Friebe so out of sorts, frantically searching Google Images for the riders he's about to interview. Daniel doesn't follow women's cycling as closely as he follows men's – which, before anyone gets angry, is fine. There are only so many hours in the day and I don't think people *have* to watch it. If they want to follow only men's cycling, that's fine. If they want to follow only women's cycling, that's fine, too. I enjoy watching it, but don't think the way to make it more popular is to shame people for not watching it. But there's a lot of this sort of thing on social media. And of course there's a lot of virtue-signalling, and some of my colleagues are not immune. Quite a few harrumph at how little coverage La Course gets in the next day's papers – a legitimate grievance if they had actually bothered to go to the race themselves.

Postscript: Julian Alaphilippe wins Stage 10 of the men's race a few hours later.

Wednesday, 18 July

Stage 11: Albertville–La Rosière, 108.5 km
Winner: Geraint Thomas
Yellow jersey: Geraint Thomas

Lionel and I think we'll be smart at the finish and drive from the press tent to the team buses, just down the hill. Our heavily branded Skoda is parked just outside. Starting the engine, I notice something on the bonnet, glistening in the scorching sun: a dog turd.

I am pretty sure it is plastic, but not confident enough to not go in search of a stick with which to remove it. Eventually I find one, give the vile object a poke and… it *is* plastic.

We never do find out who put it there. We scan colleagues in the press-room for shifty looks and furtive glances, and our suspicions centre on Rob Hayles, though he denies it under intense questioning. I'd say he remains the number one suspect.

It is a dog turd sort of a day. In the morning we stop for petrol. I fill the car up, and then at the start in Albertville realise my wallet is missing. Once the stage is underway, we drive 45 minutes back to the petrol station. No sign of the wallet. The 45-minute drive back, retracing our steps on a twisting mountain road, passes in an uncomfortable silence.

Few things put a dampener on a day like a lost wallet: the emergency €150 that was in it, the tedious phoning of banks and cancelling of cards, the knowledge that for the rest of the Tour I will be relying on Lionel to pay for everything. Oh well, every cloud…

A lot happens in the stage, but one experience that will stay with me is over an hour after Geraint Thomas wins the stage at La Rosière. Lionel, Orla and I are making our way back to the pressroom after doing some interviews when, just beyond the line, we bump into Rod Ellingworth, the Team Sky coach. 'I just thought I'd come down to see Mark,' he says – meaning Mark Cavendish, his former protégé.

Cavendish has been way off the back all day but, despite being certain to finish outside the time limit, he has carried on. In doing so, he is holding up the entire entourage of the Tour – all the team cars have to wait until the last rider is through before they can head down the mountain – but it seems more important to Cavendish to finish. It says a lot about Ellingworth that, despite winning the stage and having riders placed first and second overall, he makes the effort to come and support Cavendish in his hour of need.

We stay in an enormous and beautiful house that a listener, Simon Lund, offered us – he emailed us over the winter. The enormous interior isn't quite finished, but it doesn't matter – the house is situated at the foot of the climb to La Rosière and it is spectacular. As is the food Simon has arranged for us: a large chicken, huge dishes of lasagne and moussaka, all the snacks we can eat and enough beer and wine to last us a week (or a night, as it turns out). We want for nothing. But it is strange cooking in a house rather than eating in a restaurant, which we do every night at the Tour. There is a different atmosphere. It is rowdier.

Perhaps that is also because there are more of us than usual: as well as François, Lionel and me, there are Orla, Simon the photographer and his friend, also Simon. We call the friend Simon 2, and decide to call the original Simon, the photographer, Simon 7. Don't ask. Then we are joined, close to midnight, by Rob Arnold, an Australian journalist who's phoned in distress – on driving over an hour to his hotel, he discovered that his hotel no longer exists. Perhaps it never existed.

As the wine flows, the conversation echoes around the bare walls and gets louder and louder, and more and more animated. It is a lot of fun, though the podcast we recorded before dinner perhaps lacked fun. Although it had been an exciting stage, we'd had a difficult day.

There was the fruitless hour-and-a-half detour for the wallet, the loss of it and associated hassle, a faff at the finish when our 'smart' drive to the team buses also ended fruitlessly, then, finally, a wrong turn on the way back down the mountain, which meant a 20-minute drive ended up being closer to an hour. To cap all that, Orla seems not quite herself. Travel sick, perhaps (she spent the day in the Cofidis bus with Cédric Vasseur). She is a little quieter than usual – more like someone with normal levels of energy.

Unfortunately this all contributed to the podcast being a little flat, though I think this also owes to a sense – conveyed strongly by François, who is generally right about these things – that the race is over. Sky have been too strong, again, and the only question for François is who will win, Thomas or Froome.

Well, I know what I think, and say it with feeling on the podcast. 'I think it's completely fanciful to think that Geraint Thomas is a potential Tour de France winner,' I say. 'I just don't see it happening.'

Thursday, 19 July

Stage 12: Bourg-Saint-Maurice–Alpe d'Huez, 175.5 km
Winner: Geraint Thomas
Yellow jersey: Geraint Thomas

A touching scene at the start in Bourg-Saint-Maurice. Edvald Boasson Hagen, the former Team Sky rider now at Dimension Data, swings by his old team, looking for Servais Knaven. The previous day, Boasson Hagen's bike gave up on him at the foot of the final climb. With his team car nowhere to be seen, he was stuck until Knaven, in Sky's second team car, offered him one of the Sky Pinarellos. It got Boasson Hagen to the finish but taking another team's bike is against the rules and earned him a penalty. Knaven was also fined €150 for the transgression.

When he finds Knaven, Boasson Hagen reaches into the pocket of his jersey and pulls out a bundle of euros – €150. He wants to reimburse Knaven. I manage to get a picture of this exchange, posting it to Twitter and inadvertently starting a conspiracy theory concerning my missing wallet, which of course had €150 in it. 'Did Boasson Hagen find it?' some wonder, while the more cynical conclude that he must have actually stolen it, perhaps pickpocketing me at the start. I don't imagine many of the riders as potential pickpockets, but Boasson Hagen would be close to the bottom of any such list I might compile.

It's only François and me in the car today, with Lionel travelling ahead with Simon 2 and Simon 7 to camp out for the day on Dutch Corner for an episode of *Kilometre 0*. Orla, meanwhile, is spending the day with Rod Ellingworth and Xabier Artetxe of Team Sky. She has had to be persistent to get a seat in their car on the Alpe d'Huez stage because of some sensitivity in the team about what she might witness – and then report on. The hostility directed by some on the roadside at Team Sky has presented them with a dilemma, namely whether to make a fuss or not, when making a fuss could make it worse.

Orla has managed to get a seat in the car and, although she sees nothing of the race, she does get some great insights from Ellingworth and Artetxe on the stage as it unfolds and ends with another win by Thomas, who is another of Ellingworth's *protégés* from the British Cycling Academy.

It has been said that the Tour is won on Alpe d'Huez. Not this year. As I said last night, there is simply no way that Geraint Thomas can win the Tour de France. Not. Going. To. Happen.

Friday, 20 July

Stage 13: Le Bourg-d'Oisans–Valence, 169.5 km
Stage winner: Peter Sagan
Yellow jersey: Geraint Thomas

A phone call from Chris at Chalet La Giettaz, where we stayed on Tuesday night. A local *gendarme* has called him to say that he has discovered a wallet with €150, some bank cards and a bundle of receipts. It was by going through these that he has managed to work out the last hotel we stayed at, and then phoned it. Nice work, *Monsieur le Détective*.

The *gendarme* in question, Eric Piau from the Brigade de Gendarmerie de Ugine, then emails me and offers to post it back to my UK address. When it arrives, a week or so later, I tweet my thanks, which gets a great response – in my experience, and contrary to what you might think, good news stories tend to get more of a reaction than bad news stories on Twitter. I am then contacted by a journalist on a local newspaper, *Le Dauphiné Libéré*, who wants to write a story about it. There was a time when I might have fancied appearing in *Le Dauphiné Libéré* for my exploits in the race they gave their name to rather than for losing my wallet. But never mind.

Unfortunately, their story contained an appalling mistake, the headline reading: 'Un journaliste anglais remercie un gendarme uginois qui a retrouvé son portefeuille.' I demanded that it be changed for the online edition to 'un journaliste *ecossais*'.

It would be harsh to say that the news of my wallet is the most exciting thing that happens today, which is so hot that I can barely function, but nor would it be entirely inaccurate. Peter Sagan wins a bunch sprint missing most of the top sprinters: Mark Cavendish, Marcel Kittel, Fernando Gaviria,

André Greipel, Dylan Groenewegen have all been casualties of the Alps, most of them climbing into the broom wagon on the stage to Alpe d'Huez.

Meanwhile, another mystery is solved. Orla had not seemed herself – only about 50% as bubbly and enthusiastic as she usually is, which still meant she was 50% more bubbly and enthusiastic than the rest of us. After Alpe d'Huez she had to leave early the next morning for a mysterious but important hospital appointment. She messages to reveal what it was: the three-month scan of her unborn baby.

Saturday, 21 July

Stage 14, Saint-Paul-Trois-Châteaux–Mende, 188 km
Stage winner: Omar Fraile
Yellow jersey: Geraint Thomas

Some mysteries remain, and we love them all the more for that. At dinner last night we bumped into Ciro Scognamiglio. We were staying in a cheap hotel in Valence and ate in the restaurant next door. At some point Ciro appeared and sat down – there was a spare seat at our four-person table, after all. After a few minutes he got up again.

'Where are you going, Ciro?'

'I'm sitting over there,' he said, pointing to another table.

'You can join us.'

'Oh no, I always eat on my own,' he said, batting us away, and he was already off, sitting down and opening his newspaper while tucking into his dinner. But this is why we love Ciro. He is wonderfully, gloriously, eccentrically, courageously himself.

I spend the day with Andy Schleck, the 2010 Tour winner. He opens up about how difficult he has found retirement, in a way that I find unusual and even quite moving. Over the course of the day I can't help but notice how good he is with the guests he's there to entertain in his role as a VIP ambassador for Skoda. Basically, every day he and other ex-riders welcome some guests of the Tour, who are there on a corporate jolly which involves travelling the early part of the stage by car then jumping in a helicopter, seeing some of it from the air, then landing and getting back in the cars. With around 50 kilometres to go there's also a lavish picnic by the roadside – and I mean lavish.

On top of that, the days start with a bike ride, though Schleck says that he doesn't take part in that every day. All in all, it's a gruelling routine – not as hard as riding the Tour, but hardly easy. Meeting new people every day, having to make conversation and give them a memorable experience, must be quite draining, I imagine. Schleck does it all with great humour and charm. I like him.

Speaking of lavish meals, we have a real treat tonight. We are staying with friends of François, Peter and Virginie. They live deep, and I mean deep, in rural France. Deep as in at the end of miles and miles of disintegrating single-track road. Deep as in no phone signal. The Petit Château de Roquetaillade in the Aveyron department, in the south of the Massif Central, is our home for the night, and it is wonderful – so peaceful that it could not feel any further away from the noise and bustle of the Tour de France. My nostrils twitch on the way in at the scent of something familiar but so unexpected that I don't twig what it is.

Later, in one of the very last places I would have expected it, we are served – cooked by Peter's fair hand – a delicious chicken curry.

Sunday, 22 July

Stage 15: Millau–Carcassonne, 181.5 km
Stage winner: Magnus Cort Nielsen
Yellow jersey: Geraint Thomas

Just before I hand over to François Thomazeau, I will note that yesterday morning he told Seb Piquet, the voice of Radio Tour, that he should interview Omar Fraile. Fraile duly won the stage. This morning he interviews another Astana rider, Michael Valgren, who will end up in the break, where he helps set up his teammate, Magnus Cort Nielsen, to win the stage. He knows his stuff does François.

Ian Boswell should have spoken to him. I meet Boswell, who's keeping an audio diary for friends of the podcast, as he's rolling down to the start, past the other team buses. He looks confused. 'Why is everyone warming up?' he asks. 'I've been told to try and get in the break today. Now I'm worried.'

Ian doesn't make it into the break.

At the risk of alerting the cliché police, today's is a transition stage. Nothing much happens. Or so we think. But an hour or two after the finish word reaches us of an edgy-looking Dave Brailsford and Nicolas Portal loitering by the offices in the Permanence, the organisation's HQ. In the first 800 metres of the stage, it transpires, Gianni Moscon threw a fist at Élie Gesbert of the small French team Fortuneo–Samsic.

I remember Gesbert as the rider who (accidentally) set fire to his hotel room on the second rest day of last year's Tour.

Moscon is kicked off the race in disgrace, adding to a lengthy list of transgressions and confirming him as cycling's bad boy. He is clearly a huge talent, but his talent isn't much use to Team Sky now that he is at home. On the podcast, I wonder whether he will now be sacked. Lionel thinks not. Indeed, a week later he will be welcomed to Paris and to the Team Sky celebration party.

In Carcassonne on the eve of the second rest day, I don't necessarily foresee a Team Sky celebration party in Paris, because I believe that, with Chris Froome showing signs of fatigue, Tom Dumoulin is the Tour champion in waiting. One thing I remain quite convinced of is that Geraint Thomas will crack. Geraint Thomas win the Tour? LOL. Not going to happen.

I guess the lesson is that I should listen to François more. I think it's best that he guides you through the final week.

by François Thomazeau

Monday, 23 July

Rest day: Carcassonne

Another Monday, another rest day. It has been said repeatedly, but I shall say it again. Rest is nowhere to be found on the Tour. *The Cycling Podcast* has rented a flat atop a medical centre on the outskirts of the medieval city of Carcassonne and the heat, combined with a looming hangover, is to make my night rather uncomfortable.

I have a brilliant dinner in possibly the best restaurant in town, La Barbacane, with my old Reuters colleague Julien Pretot, who, fortunately at first – quite embarrassingly later in the evening – is best friends with the wine waiter. As a result, we are not offered a special glass of wine with each dish, but two, not to mention the *aperitif* and the *digestif,* both served in double portions as well.

It is quite a bizarre evening as the restaurant terrace is just opposite the main open-air theatre in Carcassonne, which is hosting a concert by my fellow-Marseillais rappers – some of them friends – IAM. The volume is deafening and the not-so-young couple sitting at the next table in their best gear obviously expected a little more intimacy. Imagine recording a podcast episode in the middle of a Sleaford Mods gig and you get the picture. The décor is also slightly surprising as we are sitting just under one of the main keeps, which is splattered with yellow stripes that only make sense from a distance when they all join together to form a target.

Lionel, Richard and I – or should I say Lionel, myself and Richard in that order – stay in bed quite late and Richard and I finally decide to head for the Cité de Carcassonne, the medieval part of town. It is a bit of a tourist trap, and it is certainly a cyclist trap on that very morning, as we discover when we stroll around the winding little streets to find the whole of Team Sunweb, led by Tom Dumoulin, lost in the middle of the crowd. Their GPS does not seem to help them too much. Who said electronic devices on bikes should be banned?

As we make our way back to the house, I spot a couple of Cofidis riders appearing at the end of a lane on the hill just above us. I take a quick picture of Christophe Laporte, which turns out so well when I tweet it that the team ask me if they can use it for their official website. Sorry Simon (7), there are now two professional photographers in the *Cycling Podcast* team!

In the afternoon, after a quick lunch in the lively central square, we sit at the dinner table in our flat to answer a few questions for our *Press Conference* series. I have given up for now on my probably flawed theory that Geraint Thomas cannot win the Tour because he is not enough of a bad guy.

My point of the day – probably as questionable as the previous one – is to describe the typical profile of a Tour de France winner as a time trial specialist turned climber. And I strongly reject the idea that Bradley Wiggins, Chris Froome or Geraint Thomas belong to a new breed of Tour winners, none of them being a natural climber. It is the old guy's prerogative to give some historical perspective, however approximate, to our discussions.

The day ends on a great meal with most of the British cycling press at a decidedly unvegan place called Au Lard et au Cochon ('The Bacon and Pork'). While I cannot face a *cassoulet* in this heat, a couple of bottles of Minervois finally settle my hangover. I even manage to walk over a long bridge on our way back to the house, overcoming one of my worst phobias. It is called *gephyrophobia*. Now you have learnt something!

Tuesday, 24 July

Stage 16: Carcassonne–Bagnères de Luchon, 219 km
Stage winner: Julian Alaphilippe
Yellow jersey: Geraint Thomas

Back in the nest at the back of the *Cycling Podcast* car and not unhappy to be. Like a sailor on a ship, the Tour *suiveur* (follower) knows that he is only passing through and that the call of the road is stronger. It will only cease when we reach Paris and even then, touching base will leave us dizzy and unsettled for a while.

I have a breakfast of bad tea and a croissant in a bar close to the start with our beloved agent David Luxton – he truly is beloved, honest... – and make a speedy return to the car, which is parked under the dreaded bridge. To be honest I can't face walking over the bridge again and take a long shortcut to avoid it.

The third week of the Tour is a strange animal. In most of the editions I have covered, the race is already decided at this stage however hard the organisers try to make the last seven days tricky and unpredictable. It is fairly common to assess that the first week of the Tour is the most boring but it's probably wrong. The third week is actually more often than not an anticlimax. This will be no exception.

Our debates on whether Geraint Thomas can retain the yellow jersey have become half-hearted. Of course we know that he's always faltered in Week 3, that Chris Froome has needed time to recover from the Giro and might move up a gear thanks to his better experience of Grand Tours and blah blah blah...

We note that Tom Dumoulin is still within reach of victory and I even dream, without daring to express it bluntly on the podcast, of a Dutch coalition with the LottoNL–Jumbo guys, all becoming more impressive as the race unfolds. But let's face it: we no longer sincerely believe that Team Sky can be beaten and we are now convinced that Geraint Thomas is the strongest rider, especially as he does not have to face the open hostility of the French crowd towards Chris Froome.

While the outcome is beyond serious doubt, the Tour keeps enough resources to provide interest and controversy. Early in the stage to Luchon, demonstrators try to stop the race. They are dispersed by *gendarmes* using tear gas. So French! Unfortunately, traces of the gas remain in the air while the riders try to start again and a few of them are back in the saddle with headaches and tears in their eyes.

Bagnères-de-Luchon is the town where I joined the Tour for the first time as a journalist in 1986. I've often told the tale of how, on my very first day on the race, I ran away from the press tent towards the finish line to find myself unwittingly face to face with a man on a bike with a yellow jersey on his back. Bernard Hinault! The Badger shoved me away ruthlessly as I tried to ask a question and this inconsiderate gesture marked the start of a long jinx for French cycling as Hinault lost the yellow jersey that day and no Frenchman will ever win the Tour again until I retire.

With the yellow jersey permanently out of sight, the French have now set their sights on more modest goals and especially the king of the mountains jersey. After all, it's even easier to spot than the yellow jersey and it embodies virtues of courage, boldness and excitement. It appeals to the national pride as a valid consolation prize, quite similar to the famous French flair in rugby, a British invention, to pretend that we play an exciting, running game, scoring brilliant tries while being thrashed by the oh-so-boringly disciplined *rosbifs*.

Hinault actually won the polka-dot in 1986, followed by Thierry Claveyrolat in 1990, then Richard Virenque continued the trend by winning seven of them between 1994 and 2004. Laurent Jalabert took over in 2001 and 2002, taking advantage of the early climbs to score points at the expense of pure climbers. Teammates Anthony Charteau and Thomas Voeckler relented to the same tactics in 2010 and 2012. In 2017, Warren Barguil conquered it in turn, claiming he had given up on the idea of becoming a Grand Tour contender to focus on the mountain classification and stage wins.

The same applies this year to Julian Alaphilippe, who like Barguil a year ago wins two stages and claims the garment ahead of its last two holders, Barguil and Poland's Rafał Majka. It is nice to see Alaphilippe doing so well in a year when he finally delivered, winning the Flèche Wallonne, the Clásica San Sebastián and the Tour of Britain, all well-deserved rewards for one of the most exciting riders in the peloton. French flair, I said.

Luchon is a Tour de France classic and we end up eating trout in a fine restaurant on the Allée d'Etigny where the whole of the Tour caravan seem to have booked a table. As the AirBnB flat we hired can hardly accommodate the three of us, I end up in a suite in the hotel of the Tour management. On my first Tour, 32 years ago, having failed to make hotel reservations as I was sent unexpectedly to cover the race for Reuters, I had spent the night in a disco a few numbers down on the same road.

Call it gentrification.

Wednesday, 25 July

Stage 17: Bagnères-de-Luchon–Col de Portet, 65 km
Stage winner: Nairo Quintana
Yellow jersey: Geraint Thomas

In the age of fake news, the most talked about subjects are not always the most relevant. And this morning at the start line on Allée d'Etigny, the talk of the bunch is all about the grid start introduced by Tour designer Thierry Gouvenou as a launch pad to the short stage up to the Col de Portet. To be honest, we do not have time to watch the start as we have to set off for Lionel and Richard to take the lift up to the day's finish line. Me? Take the lift? Do you seriously believe that a man suffering from gephyrophobia would set foot in a lift hanging by a thread over cliffs and ravines? No way!

We definitely need to spread our forces and keep one of us in the press tent set up on a tarmac car park at the bottom of the climb. It is actually a good idea for me to stay behind as the team buses are parked on the said car park and are duly besieged by the press mob after Nairo Quintana has clinched only his second stage win in the Tour. We have reached that moment in the race when hapless team directors and also-rans keep hanging around the buses nodding at us, desperate for questions that do not come.

By contrast, there are lots of questions being asked around the Team Sky bus as Chris Froome has lost more time on Geraint Thomas and has dropped to third behind Tom Dumoulin. Froome is on the way down on his bike and little do we know as we scrum around the bus that at this very moment he is being pushed off his bike on the descent by an overzealous French *gendarme* who has mistaken him for an amateur rider. Froome's romance with France continues.

For lack of Froome and Thomas, who is still at the top on podium duties, we talk to the amicable Egan Bernal, the up-and-coming Colombian who has been impressive since the start and is foreseen by Team Sky *aficionados* as the future winner of a dozen Grand Tours at least. I spurred a controversy of sorts by claiming that it might be a bit too early for a 21-year-old to ride a three-week race at the front at the risk of using up most of his youthful energy.

My suggestion is deemed ludicrous by several colleagues and notably Daniel, even though other aging specialists like Trek–Segafredo manager Alain Gallopin, who looked after riders of the calibre of Jan Ullrich, Andy

Schleck or Alberto Contador, tend to agree with me. My opinion is backed by the impression that Team Sky have had a tendency to wear out and waste first-class *domestiques* like Richie Porte, Mikel Landa, Leopold König or Michał Kwiatkowski in the past.

It has always been an unwritten rule of the peloton that a young rider should take it lightly in his first Grand Tours so as to discover the race and build up his engine gradually. That's the way Greg LeMond or Miguel Indurain prepared for their Tour de France conquests. Notable exceptions were Fausto Coppi or Gino Bartali, who both won the Giro at 21, while Eddy Merckx and Bernard Hinault, although they both won the first Tour de France they entered, were both in their fourth professional season when they did.

In the stage to the Col de Portet, a young French rider also aged 21, David Gaudu, finishes 14th, while Bernal is 7th. Gaudu, who won the Tour de l'Avenir in 2016, a year before Bernal, was not supposed to ride the Tour this season and only entered after an exhausted Thibaut Pinot pulled out. Gaudu has been asked by the Française des Jeux staff to take it easy, open his eyes and learn. He finally finishes 34th overall and 4th in the young-rider classification by racing from behind and saving his energy.

Will Gaudu perform better or worse than Bernal in the future? Which was the right approach? Are they both valid when applied to different riders? Only time will tell. My money is on Gaudu, just for the sake of agreeing with myself for once.

Thursday, 26 July

Stage 18: Trie-sur-Baise–Pau, 171 km
Stage winner: Arnaud Démare
Yellow jersey: Geraint Thomas

Ah, press chiefs! Some are good, some are useless, some helpful, some incompetent; some are here to help you talk to riders, others to make sure you never come close to any of them. Some are pros, some are former riders in search of a career; the worst are probably former journalists eager to avenge the frustrations of their previous career on their old colleagues. The friendliest of all is probably Direct Énergie's Blaise Chauviere, the perfect companion for long flights, airport transfers or hotel lobby last beers.

When it comes to talking to Sylvain Chavanel, it is a different ball game. Today is the veteran Frenchman's 365th day on the Tour de

France, a full year in the saddle on the cobbles and the climbs, in the heat and the rain, through the echelons, sporting the colours of teams Bouygues–La Boulangère, Cofidis, Quick-Step, IAM Cycling and Direct Énergie. Along the way, Mimosa, as he is called, has won three stages and held the yellow jersey for two days in 2010.

'Aaah… He won't be able to talk to you because there's a little ceremony at the podium for him and then there's the TV.'

Of course! The daily routine of the cycling writer or podcaster. TV comes first. Our television colleagues often break into your head-to-head interviews with riders because they are in a rush. Of course, you have all the time in the world because nobody reads you or listens to you, do they? One day when I raised an objection to this unfriendly behaviour, I was told, 'We *pay* to be here, you don't!' I even at one time considered walking around the buses and mixed zones with a fake camera to receive a little more consideration.

Never mind. I head for the podium and the first rider coming down is Sylvain Chavanel. He greets me with a broad smile – we've been around, both of us – and is duly impressed by the hairy kitten on my *Cycling Podcast* microphone, which looks more like a dead hedgehog to be honest. He answers my questions for nearly 15 minutes, leaving a queue of TV colleagues stomping nervously around me. I also talk at length with Direct Énergie manager Jean-René Bernaudeau for an episode of *Kilometre 0* on the man who is now the longest ever serving Tour rider, with 18 editions entered and 16 completed.

We head towards the familiar direction of Pau, overtaking a rather fit-looking man on a bike along the way – Sir Dave Brailsford keeping in shape. The pressroom is as usual set in the Palais Beaumont, the place where Richard Moore interviewed me about the 1986 Tour de France for his book *Slaying the Badger* back in 2010. This was really the chance to get to know each other better and, as you can see, the encounter led to even greater things. With the day's ride as flat as can be, the stage is set for a bunch sprint.

There was some controversy at the start over a tweet posted the night before by André Greipel, accusing Arnaud Démare of cheating to make the time cut in the previous day's stage to Saint-Lary. The Frenchman has quite a reputation in this respect and if you listen to Italian riders jealous of his 2016 victory in Milan–San Remo, you would swear he only got out of the FDJ team car in the final stretch that year. Démare has had to produce his Strava data on Twitter to settle the row with Greipel and the German duly apologised before the start, apologies the Frenchman bluntly rejected.

Greipel, who quit on Stage 12, is one of many sprinters to have given up since the beginning of the Tour and Démare easily fends off the challenge of fellow Frenchman Christophe Laporte and Norway's Alexander Kristoff to snatch his second stage win after the one clinched in Vittel in 2017. At the FDJ bus, manager Marc Madiot is in a state like usual, but the whole of the staff, usually pretty laid back, is in a vengeful mood, obviously incensed by Greipel's allegations and by what they see as an unfair reputation given to their rider. Démare himself sounds more bitter about the doubters than happy with the win, relieved as well to deliver at last after the odd experience of the last Tour, when his teammates were disqualified *en masse* for failing to take him to the finish line inside the time cut.

And now is the time to head to Le Viscos.

Friday, 27 July

Stage 19: Lourdes–Laruns, 200.5 km
Stage winner: Primož Roglič
Yellow Jersey: Geraint Thomas

Le Viscos in Saint-Savin, a small medieval village with an old abbey overlooking Argelès-Gazost, is like a second home to me. When I open the window to my room, Hautacam is straight ahead and at the right end of the valley, the Tourmalet appears, its summit peppered with small clouds. The smell of fried bacon and eggs is an open invitation to breakfast.

Last night was one of our traditional dinners at Le Viscos with chef Alexis Saint-Martin and his father Jean-Pierre, the sixth and seventh generations of Saint-Martins to run the place, treating us like family. Both are cycling fans, while Alexis's brother Aurelien, who is the *maître d'hôtel*, is a keen cyclist himself. Alexis tells me that the annual visit of Tour de France journalists and fans is like a holiday in the middle of a busy summer. Alexis cooked *presse de porc*, a tender part of a pig's leg, which is best eaten rare. The food is delicious as usual, the portions enormous, the whole menu the equivalent of a Pyrenees stage.

Saint-Savin used to be a halt on the road to Santiago de Compostela in the Middle Ages and Le Viscos is now a pilgrimage in itself for many Tour followers. French colleagues from *Le Monde* and *Le Dauphiné* are staying here as well as legendary Italian writer Gianni Mura, who still used a typewriter to report on the race only two years ago. Gianni's Tour de France bible is not the roadbook but the *Michelin Guide*.

A freak incident took place as we were sipping down a glass of armagnac because the fire alarm started shrieking and would not stop for nearly an hour. Some of us took it as an excuse not to go to bed and muffled chitchat and the clatter of glasses could still be overheard at nearly five in the morning.

The day's start is in Lourdes, at the foot of the basilica built near the small grotto in which Bernadette Soubirous purportedly encountered the Virgin Mary in the 19th century. The mixture of cycling gear, team buses, pilgrims, priests and nuns is a colourful one. Everybody admits it would take a miracle for Geraint Thomas to lose the Tour now.

Lourdes is a dreadful place, which always makes me nervous not because of the presence of God but because of his very absence and the long gloomy processions of gentle souls desperately hoping for him to give them a sign, however small. It is like a huge spiritual lottery thriving on the desperate hope of a divine jackpot at the end of the day. In the meantime, the much more down-to-earth bonanza goes to the keepers of the countless souvenir shops and aptly named hotels the Pilgrim, the St. John, the St. Saviour, St. Catherine, St. Therese, Solitude, Joan of Arc and so on. Think Blackpool with cassocks and leather sandals instead of bikinis and flip-flops.

The stage goes to Laruns, a small town at the bottom of the Aubisque, renowned for its cheese. Several attempts have taken place, involving Mikel Landa, Romain Bardet or Rafał Majka, but all the favourites made it back on the last climb, leaving Primož Roglič to surge on the descent and go for his second stage win after Serre-Chevalier a year ago. The Slovenian former ski jumper is now briefly on the Tour podium. Should he aim for more in the future?

While LottoNL–Jumbo have been impressive for the whole Tour, they may have lacked focus with three potential leaders, Roglič, Steven Kruijswijk and Robert Gesink, and Dylan Groenewegen going for bunch sprints. Movistar are in a similar situation with Alejandro Valverde, Mikel Landa and Nairo Quintana all vying for Tour leadership. As for Tom Dumoulin, with Michael Matthews in the team and rather weak support from the rest of the Sunweb riders, did he really stand a chance? Team Sky's domination might also be explained by the flaws of their rivals.

Saturday, 28 July

Stage 20: Saint-Pée-sur-Nivelle–Espelette time trial, 31 km
Stage winner: Tom Dumoulin
Yellow jersey: Geraint Thomas

The final time trial of the Tour de France has not crowned the overall winner since 2011 and the victory of Cadel Evans. Nobody seriously thinks Geraint Thomas can lose the Tour today over 31 kilometres between Saint-Pée-sur-Nivelle and Espelette. The forecast is for a battle between Tom Dumoulin and Chris Froome for the stage laurels and podium places. And that's exactly what happens as Dumoulin takes the stage after a short moment of uncertainty when Froome, who is one second down, is initially announced as the winner.

Nobody really cares as Geraint Thomas crosses the line with the third fastest time, thirty seconds slower than the Dutchman, contradicting my prediction that he would win the penultimate stage to top it off. The Welshman walks towards the podium to find his wife Sarah waiting for him unexpectedly behind a roundabout where we're all standing as race stewards fend off photographers and cameramen. The emotion is overwhelming and even for an old insensitive hack like me, it is quite moving to see a few tears on the face of a man widely respected as one of the nicest guys in the peloton.

Who would have thought? Well me actually! I'm suddenly remembering the many times I asked Dave Brailsford what he believed Thomas could do and only got embarrassed replies. Looking into my files, I even discover two stories I wrote about Thomas in 2011 and 2016 (available on request!), hinting that he might be the third step in Team Sky's domination of the Tour. While G (sorry guys) is swallowed by his sudden fame, his podium and media obligations, the finish area is turning into a confessional. The general atmosphere is one of relief. It's done. Tour over. Home soon.

It seems like every rider completing the course wants to stop by and talk to you. Pierre Rolland hangs around and is still chatting to journalists half an hour after his race is over. Yoann Offredo tells us how he broke his brakes and had to scream to the public to get out of the way in the descents. Dan Martin learns from us that he has been named the most aggressive rider of the whole Tour. It is a reward he does not take lightly. 'Wow, of course I race to win but I try my best every day. And it really means a lot,' he says.

On the way back to the car, I bump into Movistar team director José Luis Arrieta, who is also in relief mode. He insists that they had a great

Tour with a stage win for Quintana and the best team classification. I bet he does not really believe what he says.

We head for Biarritz, where we are spending the night and where Richard has planned a few days holiday with his family. I had in mind the image of an old-fashioned Victorian seaside resort for elderly pensioners, a bit like Scarborough or Whitby, but it turns out to be very lively, pretty and full of partying young people.

We booked a table on a rooftop terrace at a place called Les Baigneuses, which means 'The Bathers', to find on arrival that it is the trendiest place in town. On spotting *The Cycling Podcast*'s microphones and equipment spread over the table, the charming landlady, Sabine, comes to us and tells us her best friend used to be a pro rider!

'Oh! And what's his name?' I ask.

'David Millar,' she says, adding that he was there the night before with Ned Boulting and the whole of the ITV crew. A selfie of the *Cycling Podcast* team is quickly taken and sent to Millar.

I think of his book *Racing Through the Dark* and his fond memories of Biarritz, the town where he lived and was eventually arrested by the police in June 2004 as he was dining with Team GB coach Dave Brailsford. No Briton had ever won the Tour de France at the time. I remember a discussion I had with Cyrille Guimard, the former manager of Bernard Hinault and Laurent Fignon at roughly the same period, in which he insisted that Millar, in his view, had the potential to be a Grand Tour contender. We'll never know.

We end the meal with patxaran, a bittersweet local spirit which stays with me all night.

2018 VUELTA A ESPAÑA

by Lionel Birnie

Saturday, 25 August

Stage 1: Málaga time trial, 8 km
Stage winner: Rohan Dennis
Red jersey: Rohan Dennis

Last year Richard accused me, not entirely unfairly, of treating the Vuelta like the holiday Grand Tour. As I board my EasyJet flight to Málaga I realise I'm just about the only person who is not jetting off for a week or two sitting by the pool, sipping sangria. Fine by me, I don't really like sangria.

The Vuelta is a bit more relaxed than the Tour but flying out the day of the time trial leaves me no room for error. A 90-minute delay to my flight and then an hour's wait at the car-hire desk means I'm cutting it fine. But after collecting my accreditation I'm reunited with the sunny disposition of Fran Reyes and we reach the centre of Málaga just in time to see the first riders roll down the start ramp.

Because the time trial is due to finish late – the last rider will cross the line at 8.30pm – Fran and I record as the race unfolds. The early story of the day is Richie Porte's poor performance. Having crashed out of the Tour de France in the cobbled stage, he had been tipped as a pre-race favourite for the Vuelta. All the signs point in the opposite direction, though.

Porte has been ill before the race and he's just announced his long-rumoured transfer to Trek–Segafredo on social media with a piece to camera that had all the ease of a hostage video.

Porte finishes well down but his BMC Racing teammate Rohan Dennis is on top of the pile, making amends for his near-miss in the opening time trial at the Giro d'Italia in Jerusalem. It means he ends the Vuelta's opening day in red for the second year running, because last year BMC won the team time trial in Nîmes.

Fran shows me the old town, which has all the charm that the more modern bits lack. We wrap up the podcast at about 9.30pm and make plans for dinner. Fran has booked the table for 11pm so my plan is to check into my hotel a few kilometres away on the outskirts of Málaga and then head back to the old town to meet up with Fran and a group of other journalists.

Unfortunately, the hotel's car parking is haphazard. I'm allocated a space in an impossibly tight underground car park and just about manage to open the car door enough to wriggle out. (No sniggering at the back.)

When I return to the car 15 minutes later to head back into Málaga, someone has parked right in front of me, blocking me in.

I go to reception but the owner of the car cannot be traced so I'm stuck. I head to a nearby tapas restaurant for an extremely average plate of assorted things with chips and later learn that Fran and co had a lovely meal in town. ¡Viva la Vuelta!

Sunday, 26 August

Stage 2: Marbella–Caminito del Rey, 163 km
Stage winner: Alejandro Valverde
Red jersey: Michał Kwiatkowski

The hire car is an absolute wreck and it smells like an ashtray, despite multiple 'No smoking' signs on the dashboard. The suspension feels shot to bits, the aircon blows smoky air at me, and the electric window on my side doesn't work.

This book is too short to detail the full cock-up at the car-hire place, but suffice to say I never cease to be amazed by the industry's ability to overcharge you for something you didn't book. I long for the day when I pay the quoted price for the car I've ordered. How can the price escalate several hundred euros between booking online and collecting the keys? What are all the charges that get added on? How do they get away with it?

Anyway, as I pull out of the car park it strikes me I'm going to be driving this thing solo a couple of thousand kilometres to Madrid over the next week. Fortunately, the first three days are all based around Málaga, which I had thought would give me a fairly gentle start.

Daniel is moonlighting for ITV and travelling with his cameraman Scott. I had tried to check in to the same hotels as them but their place in Málaga was full so I found somewhere down the road. However, Daniel neglected to tell me that they'd checked out of their place and headed for the hills because the on-street parking was not secure enough to enable Scott to leave any of his camera equipment in the car.

With Fran staying on the other side of town, it means I'm left somewhat isolated without teammates. I resolve to make the best of it by going for a run along the beachfront before breakfast. I opt to take the coast road from Málaga to the start in Marbella, or Marbs as it's known by British holiday-makers. On the way I pass the meccas of Torremolinos and Fuengirola.

I must admit this stretch of Spanish coastline is not really my cup of tea. I'm too pink-skinned to enjoy baking in the Costa del Sol's rays for too long, and the way the tower blocks and golf courses crowd out anything of charm that remains after decades of development leaves my heart feeling slightly heavy.

Caminito del Rey on the other hand is delightful, a series of beautiful reservoirs and unspoilt countryside that will give us a wonderful calming view as we record the podcast after the stage.

On the climb, Laurens De Plus of Quick-Step tried to pull a fast one but he was quickly overhauled by Michał Kwiatkowski, who takes the red jersey, and Alejandro Valverde who wins the stage.

Valverde calls on years of experience to time it just right. Valverde's popularity in Spain is not in question, especially since Alberto Contador retired, but there is a reluctance in Spain to discuss his suspension for doping and his role in the Operación Puerto case, and that does make it harder to hail him as one of the greats of his era.

I head back to my hotel, decide against visiting the dodgy tapas bar for a second night running and end up in an all-you-can-eat Asian buffet restaurant instead. The food is OK, but the failure of the other diners to put the serving spoons back where they belong means that everything has a slight taste of everything else.

Fran is aghast when he finds out where I had dinner. I can't help feeling that I'm getting the Vuelta all wrong. It's just that you need a little bit of local knowledge to get away from the places designed to trap the tourists, and my guide is staying miles away.

Monday, 27 August

Stage 3: Mijas Playa–Alhaurín de la Torre, 178 km
Stage winner: Elia Viviani
Red jersey: Michał Kwiatkowski

I make a rookie error and head to Mijas, a town just inland from the coast, not realising that the stage is actually starting in Mijas Playa just down the road. Whoops! It's easily done because the roadbook lists Mijas as the start town, but when I arrive there I find the place eerily deserted. When I see a banner for an intermediate sprint, I know I'm in the wrong place.

Luckily, I'm early enough to get down to the coast in time to speak to a few riders, including Ian Boswell. He kept an audio diary at the Tour de France, where his Katusha team finished with only four riders, although their leader Ilnur Zakarin managed to climb into ninth place in the final week with all the determination of a man hauling himself in through an upstairs window after locking himself out of the house.

I wanted to know whether or not Katusha counted the Tour as a success or a failure, and the way Boswell puffs his cheeks out doesn't really tell me one way or the other. Where I do slightly empathise with him is recognising the mental strength it must take for the *domestiques* to raise themselves for the Vuelta just four weeks after arriving in Paris for the end of the Tour.

Simultaneously, it feels like a lifetime ago and yet just the other day.

It's a nice, short drive from Mijas to Alhaurín de la Torre and so I park up outside the pressroom and walk down into town to find a place for lunch. I order another selection of things, including some *croquetas de patatas*.

Inadvertently, Daniel and I spark the first major controversy of the Vuelta by describing *croquetas* as being made of potato. Fran is aghast (again) the next morning when he points out that they are in fact made out of a rich, stiff bechamel sauce. In my defence, the *croquetas* I had were definitely described as potato on the menu. A few people point out to me on Twitter that in touristy places slightly lazy restaurants sometimes use them rather than the fresh ones because they freeze better.

Elia Viviani wins the stage, his fifth Grand Tour victory of the season after four at the Giro in May. But my job for the afternoon is to wait at the Caja Rural team bus for a young Australian rider by the name of Nick Schultz.

This is one of Richard's ideas for an episode of *Kilometre 0* and it turns out to be a good one because Schultz has a great story about his circuitous route towards a World Tour contract and he's able to tell it very well. We stand and talk for about 10 or 12 minutes, but as large blobs of rain begin to fall I feel we should perhaps wrap it up.

Schultz is too polite to cut the interview short so I do it for him. Getting an episode of *Kilometre 0* in the bag is not worth making a rider stand in chilly rain and putting them at risk of getting a cold. After all, I wouldn't want Schultz to be cursing *The Cycling Podcast* if he got sick in the second week.

Tuesday, 28 August

Stage 4: Vélez-Málaga–Alfacar, 161 km
Stage winner: Ben King
Red jersey: Michał Kwiatkowski

Before breakfast I record the links to an episode of *Kilometre 0* called *King Kelly's Vuelta and the Missing Trophy*. It's about Sean Kelly's Vuelta victory in 1988 and his near-miss the previous year when a painful saddle sore forced him to pull out when he was just a few days from clinching a first Grand Tour win.

I'd spoken to Kelly back in April when he was over in London to commentate on the Classics for Eurosport but hadn't been quite sure what to do with the interview.

The missing trophy angle appealed to me and I thought about trying to track it down for him. It turned out that the whereabouts of his Vuelta trophy has been a mystery for more than 20 years, although he reckons he's narrowed the search down to a pizzeria in Vitoria in the Basque Country.

It may only be a 26-minute episode but it's taken a lot of back and forth between me and our producer Tom Whalley to get it into shape. I enjoy this process a lot, especially now I've learned a bit about what works and what doesn't. Snipping up the quotes and scripting the links to join the whole story together is a bit like writing features for magazines.

Tom does an amazing job with the final edit and when we put it together with some original artwork by Annette Kelly of Grand Tour Art, I'm really happy with the finished result. I'm even happier when the episode is shortlisted for an international sports media award in Lausanne.

The fact it's in the can before the nick of time is a bonus too, because it means I can get on with the next episode of *Kilometre 0* by seeing Nick Schultz at the Caja Rural bus again to pick up where we left off yesterday.

Today I have some company for the drive to Alfacar, a natural park above Granada, because Fran's regular companion is away from the race today and it means Fran can drop in with me.

We chat about the Vuelta and Spanish cycling on the way. Fran calls Granada home these days and he's ridden the final climb many times. He's even taken people on dates up there, he says, which is perhaps more than I need to know. It's a peaceful, tranquil place where the trees and rock complement one another. There's also absolutely no mobile-phone signal and no facilities for the press either. So we are, relatively speaking, cut off for the afternoon.

I opt for a restorative siesta in the warm shade before watching the last 60 kilometres of the race on TV. Then I dash down towards the finish line and speak to a few riders, including Pierre Rolland, who came up just short at the finish after missing the crucial split before mounting a strong but doomed chase. I also speak to Steven Kruijswijk, whose LottoNL-Jumbo team did a pretty good impersonation of Team Sky on the final climb.

The stage winner, though, is Ben King, who gives Dimension Data their first World Tour victory of the year, leaving just EF Education First on *nul points* as the clock ticks down towards the end of the season.

After the stage we head down to Granada, record the podcast over a cool local beer outside a bar, and the cooling effect is multiplied by a fine mist being sprayed over the customers from some pipes in the wall. We then have dinner at just gone 10pm – early by Spanish standards.

Wednesday, 29 August

Stage 5: Granada–Roquetas de Mar, 188 km
Stage winner: Simon Clarke
Red jersey: Rudy Molard

Before heading to the start, I drive up to the Alhambra, the stunning palace for which Granada is famous and decide that the views of it from the middle distance make it look more impressive than it does up close.

The traffic crossing town is heavy and I'm in danger of missing the start, so I ditch the car in a little car park and walk to where the team buses are parked. I want to speak to Ben King about ending Dimension Data's World Tour drought so brilliantly on the climb yesterday and I'm struck by his sense of relief as well as joy at the achievement.

It's quite hard to win a World Tour bike race, especially if you're not a sprinter. For a rider like King to put himself in the position to win and then execute it so clinically should not be underestimated.

As François says, professional cycling is a team sport practised by individuals and I wonder about the cumulative negative effect of going month after month without a top-level win. OK, so Dimension Data have picked up victories in smaller races, but the World Tour is what really counts and as the season has ticked towards its conclusion they knew the chances were running out.

As the race rolls out of town, I check the season's race results on my phone and confirm that King's victory leaves EF Education First as the only World Tour team still waiting for a World Tour win this season. I wonder what their riders were thinking as they cruise through the neutralised zone?

The whole coastline down Roquetas de Mar is dominated by greenhouses growing tomatoes and other fruit and vegetables. All you can see for miles around are plastic greenhouses. It's startling later to look on Google Maps, turn on the satellite view and see that the whole landscape for miles shows up as white.

It's a lumpy old day for the riders on their way to the greenhouses and when the finish boils down to a fight between Alessandro De Marchi of BMC Racing, Bauke Mollema of Trek–Segafredo and Simon Clarke of, yes, EF Education First, I can't help but quietly hope Clarke can do it – simply because it will be the best story of the day.

Sure enough, Clarke pulls it off. No mean feat considering his team's season was all but hinging on it. I wait at the EF Education First bus and the team's Spanish sports director Juan Manuel Garate is trying to keep his obvious delight from boiling over.

In the press conference later, Clarke is brilliant. He talks at some length about the team's season, his own difficulties, his previous positive experiences at the Vuelta, and the planning that went into today's stage and how he executed it at the finish.

He talks for so long and so eloquently that some of the journalists give him a spontaneous round of applause afterwards. It's rare to glean quite so much insight from the artificial question-and-answer format of the press conference, where the riders must sometimes feel they are tiptoeing through a room of invisible tripwires and dull questions.

Daniel and his cameraman are staying miles away, closer to tomorrow's start than today's finish. As they head off, I begin to regret booking a hotel down here near the coast because it means another night with only my own brain for company.

My hotel is big, but old-fashioned and impersonal – the sort of place that feels like its heyday was decades ago. I stroll down to the beach for a pre-dinner beer and hear a shout from across the road. To my delight it's Dutch journalist Dan Hakkenberg coming back from, I think, a dip in the sea. We have a beer and end up going for dinner where we share a seafood platter of variable quality – with items that range from very, very good to seemingly fished out of a drainpipe.

Dan used to be a crime reporter before switching to cycling and he has arrived at a time when the Dutch are enjoying their best spell of Grand Tour results since the 1980s. He's got Dumoulin, Kelderman, Kruijswijk, Poels and the sprinter Groenewegen to follow, not to mention the likes of Oomen and Tolhoek coming up behind.

We swap notes about British and Dutch cycling and the peculiarities of life on the road, and he asks me about Brexit with a puzzled expression on his face. I'm afraid I'm not able to enlighten him much.

After dinner we head back to the hotel where a live singer is entertaining a small audience who are sitting around the swimming pool. When the singer starts *Highway to Hell* by AC/DC, I decide it's time for bed.

Thursday, 30 August

Stage 6: Huércal-Orvera–San Javier, 155 km
Stage winner: Nacer Bouhanni
Red jersey: Rudy Molard

A quiet day ends in chaos. A traffic island 25 kilometres from the finish that was neither signalled nor softened by hay bales or padding causes a crash and the peloton splits. Those splits are made worse by the wind and with Bora–Hansgrohe and Quick-Step driving the pace the peloton is hacked into bits.

Nacer Bouhanni wins the sprint, but as is so often the case with the Cofidis sprinter, controversy swirls around him like a tornado. Yesterday he was accused of slapping his team car in frustration, which he and his team denied. But this was also coming just days after he was penalised for taking a length sticky bottle after a crash.

Thibaut Pinot is the worst affected by the crash when it comes to the GC riders, he loses a minute and three quarters – as does Wilco Kelderman who was lying sixth overall this morning, although the cause of his problem was a puncture that happened around the same time as the crash.

The chaos continues just after the finish line when the downdraft from a low flying helicopter operated by either the race organisers or the host broadcaster – it's not clear which – blows a chain of plastic barriers across the road and into the riders. Only in the Vuelta.

The other notable thing about the day's stage is the sight of Richie Porte in the break, with escape specialist Luis Ángel Maté and Jorge Cubero. When I speak to Porte after the stage he says he enjoyed the experience. It's been a long time since he's been off the front on a flat stage, and it gave him a renewed sense of respect for the riders like Maté who attack day after day and toil away in the lead knowing they are unlikely to fight it out for the stage win.

I meet up with Daniel and Scott for dinner at our hotel – some sort of quasi-religious retreat in the hills. We order a T-bone steak, which arrives so rare it could probably keep up with the *gruppetto* if it had to. It's also disconcertingly cold in the middle so we send it back and a few minutes later it returns steaming hot but with one piece missing. It's the last piece of T-bone we're told – so it's either that or choose again from the menu.

Friday, 31 August

Stage 7: Puerto Lumbreras–Pozo Alcón, 185 km
Stage winner: Tony Gallopin
Red jersey: Rudy Molard

I manage to accidentally park in the wrong place and lose my press accreditation this morning. I search everywhere in the car for it and start to wonder whether I can cover the remaining three days of my Vuelta stint as a rogue, unofficial outsider, rather than bother the staff and the press office for another pass.

Fortunately, it's a very low-key start with a tiny crowd of people and no barriers keeping the people away from the team buses, so I'm able to do what I'd normally do, although I feel somewhat underdressed without my official Vuelta pass and lanyard.

I tick off a few people on my hit list for an episode of *Kilometre 0* we're making on cycling's transfer market. It's always struck me how dysfunctional the market is. Depending on the circumstances, some riders hold the upper hand, but most often it's the teams who call the shots.

Every August when riders and teams are allowed to begin announcing their plans for the following year, it feels a little like a game of musical chairs. As we've seen with the Richie Porte transfer from BMC Racing to Trek–Segafredo, sometimes a team's future hinges on the destiny of one particular rider. Often riders are competing in the last of the season's Grand Tours – the Vuelta – knowing they're riding out their notice period with their current teams too.

When Daniel and I discuss the way the transfer market works for the podcast, I indulge another of my flights of fancy – suggesting that there could be a week of the season when the transfers are announced one after the other at a special event, with all the drama and razzmatazz of the NFL or NBA draft.

Football manages to make a soap opera out of the transfer window with the rumours and deals being discussed endlessly, but cycling's negotiations are all still endearingly cloak and dagger.

As for the Vuelta, Tony Gallopin wins the stage, making it another fine day for the French, because the Frenchman Rudy Molard is still in the red jersey. It turns out Molard was a junior world champion at winter triathlon, which involves running and mountain biking on snow, and cross-country skiing. Daniel asks me what my ideal triathlon would be, and I wonder if darts, cycling and competitive *cassouleting* could become a thing.

The evening's episode is bolstered with an exclusive interview Richard has done with Aqua Blue Sport's team owner, Rick Delaney. A few weeks ago, I asked their rider Conor Dunne if he'd keep an audio diary for us at the Tour of Britain, but the team had subsequently gone pop – leaving the riders and staff out of a job.

As always with these things, sympathies lie with the riders, not unreasonably, but there is always more than one side to a story like this, and it feels like it will be weeks before a fuller picture emerges.

It seems strange to think that a year ago Aqua Blue were here at the Vuelta, just about keeping their noses above water until that brilliant stage win by Stefan Denifl at Los Machucos.

Saturday, 1 September

Stage 8: Linares–Almadén, 195 km
Stage winner: Alejandro Valverde
Red jersey: Rudy Molard

I find my accreditation pass in the passenger seat footwell of the tin can and feel legitimate again. After the opening few days where everything was quite straightforward logistically, it feels like Spain is opening up before me. There's a lot of driving to do on tricky roads. Some of the scenery is spectacular, but it's remote and I know there is a lot of ground to cover today.

In the morning I meet LottoNL–Jumbo's Sepp Kuss, a young American who impressed recently by winning the Tour of Utah and looked very good on the climb to Alfacar a few days ago. His enthusiasm is infectious and just what I need to brighten the podcast because for the next two days I'm without Fran, who has left the race to attend a friend's wedding.

Kuss is enlightening on what it's like to ride a Grand Tour for the first time and not knowing quite what to expect other than that it's going to be hard and might get harder.

In Almadén, we walk the final few hundred metres from a tricky dead turn and Daniel and I debate whether it's a Valverde finish or a Sagan finish. In the end, we have to agree it is ideal for both because Valverde wins the stage, although it's arguable that Sagan, who finishes second, is quite a few notches below his Tour de France peak here.

The presence of sprinters like Danny van Poppel and Giacomo Nizzolo just ahead of the climbers like Simon Yates, Steven Kruijswijk and Rigoberto Urán means the results make for interesting reading. I love finishes like this where riders with such different skillsets are able to go toe-to-toe.

After the stage there's a long, boring drive in search of the remote guesthouse Daniel has booked. Twice I drive a dozen kilometres up the same stretch of road looking for the tiny turn-off. Twice I stop to look at the directions on the guesthouse website. Eventually, I decide to interpret the instructions in exactly the opposite way to the way I'm understanding them. I end up two or three kilometres off the road on a gravelly rocky track which eventually peters out into a field.

I'm starting to panic a bit. I can't get hold of Daniel on the phone, I don't know where the guest house is, and it's getting dark.

Up ahead I see a plume of dust and the red brake lights of a car. I watch as it does an 11-point turn and comes back towards me. It's Daniel and Scott, much to my relief. Eventually, after another few wrong turns and a couple of phone calls to the place, we find it. Even by Daniel's standards it's remote. But we're rewarded with a good dinner, and beautiful views of the sunset.

Sunday, 2 September

Stage 9: Talavera de la Reina–La Covatilla, 195 km
Stage winner: Ben King
Red jersey: Simon Yates

It's another long drive to the start at Talavera de la Reina and a couple of wrong turns and a lack of phone signal means Google Maps doesn't know whether I'm coming or going.

The satnav takes me along a very small, very rough track – a detour of 15 or 20 kilometres – and then pops me out no more than two kilometres further along the main road I'd already been on. The detour costs me at least half an hour and it means I've lost confidence in the satnav's ability to take me the quickest way.

I have no co-pilot to navigate and I know that one more mistake could cause me to miss the start and then force me to spend the rest of the day fretting about getting up to La Covatilla in time. So, I decide to take the sensible decision to skip the start and in a heartbeat I go from running horribly late to being blissfully up on schedule.

I now have hours to get to La Covatilla and have time to stop *en route* for lunch. The Spanish motorway service station is strangely old-fashioned, but I have a good *café con leche* and a *bocadillo*, morale rises and I watch on TV as the Vuelta peloton rolls out.

It possibly sounds like I'm complaining too much about the logistical difficulties, but this week at the Vuelta has reminded me just how much covering the Grand Tour is a collaborative effort, not just on the mike but off it.

It's so easy to take for granted having someone else to help with the directions and the driving. I don't mind admitting that after nine days I'm ready to climb off and hand over to the Buffalo. I also have the perfect excuse because, just like Dan Martin, who will also call it a day after this opening nine-day phase, my partner is heavily pregnant, and the plan was always to abandon the race on the first rest day.

Before I go, I see Ben King win a second stage in even more impressive fashion than the first, and I see Simon Yates regain the leader's red jersey. In the press conference afterwards, Yates seems relaxed but incredibly focused. He swats away questions about his dramatic collapse at the Giro d'Italia. When he's asked whether he and his team have discovered what went wrong in Italy and what he's learned from the experience, he more or less dismisses the question.

I find it hard to believe Mitchelton–Scott haven't at least analysed the data from the Giro, but it strikes me as entirely credible that Yates would park that disappointment and push on. There's a steely determination not to be defined by that fateful Friday at the Giro, and I drive the 250 kilometres to Madrid after the stage thinking to myself that Yates is in with an excellent shot of completing a British clean sweep of the Grand Tours this year. Not that I go in for such speculation, of course.

by Richard Moore

Monday, 3 September

Rest day: Salamanca

A new shift takes over at the Vuelta. I am jetting in to replace Napalm and Madrid Airport is swarming with people wearing team-issue clothing.

After *rendezvous*ing with Fran at the airport we drive two hours to the pretty university city of Salamanca, meeting Daniel and his cameraman Scott in the Plaza Mayor, reckoned by the *Lonely Planet* (who says I don't research this stuff?) to be Spain's most beautiful central square: 'a remarkably harmonious and controlled baroque display'.

Busts of famous figures adorn the plaza and until just over a year ago they included one of the former fascist dictator, Franco.

It doesn't feel like Spain's most beautiful plaza, and harmonious it certainly ain't, because a team of workers are hammering and clanking away assembling the infrastructure required for tomorrow's stage start, which is taking place right here. And it's raining.

My shift hasn't properly started yet but I feel tired and a bit under the weather and then I feel my mood plummet when Fran offers to put the *Prensa* ('Press') sticker on the windscreen. He goes at it with too much gusto – I should have known – and makes a dog's dinner of it, meaning that for two weeks I'll have, at the top of my field of vision, as I drive the long, straight and empty roads that are a feature of so much of Spain, a crinkled, wrinkly, squinty *Prensa* sticker. A bit like having an eyelash stuck in your eye, for two weeks.

Tuesday, 4 September

Stage 10: Salamanca–Fermoselle, 172.5 km
Stage winner: Elia Viviani
Red jersey: Simon Yates

A long sleep has sorted me out (I think yesterday I was just tired) and I'm raring to go. Dan Martin isn't. Like Lionel, he has abandoned the Vuelta, and for similar reasons to Lionel: Martin's wife is expecting twins and he wants to be present for the birth. (Update: the Martin twins didn't actually arrive until September 19th, three days after the Vuelta finished. Baby Napalm arrived two days before that. So both Martin and Birnie could have finished the Vuelta after all. Noted.)

Today sees a rare thing on the Vuelta, a bunch sprint, won by Elia Viviani. The drama comes towards the end when there's a spate of punctures – at least 15, including an incredible number of favourites. It looks almost suspicious but at the finish the culprit is revealed as tiny thorns from the thistles that cover the plains in this part of Spain, close to the border with Portugal. The thistles have been washed onto the road by the rain. And the rain isn't done. Out for dinner in Zamora we have to move inside when it starts absolutely hammering down.

Thistles, rain – it's enough to make this Scotsman feel right at home.

Wednesday, 5 September

Stage 11: Mombuey–Ribeira Sacra, 208.8 km
Stage winner: Alessandro De Marchi
Red jersey: Simon Yates

The sense of discombobulation continues. When I think of Spain, I don't think of places like Lugo. Driving into the Galician town in the evening – it's raining, natch, and with every swish the windscreen wipers catch the corner of my lopsided, crinkled *Prensa* sticker – is as jarring as being in the middle of Clackmannanshire and driving into Florence.

Nothing against Lugo – it just doesn't feel very Spanish. It's dark and the wet streets are streaked with yellow, the reflections of the streetlights. It is more reminiscent of a November night in Glasgow.

But as Fran told me, the image of Spain that we are sold is not very accurate. When the country opened up to tourism a strategic decision was taken to sell the country solely and exclusively as a destination for sun, sea, sand and sangria– the story of how Benidorm the party town was effectively created by the local mayor is fascinating, but I'll save it for another day. Most of Spain is not like that – thank God! – and this has been underlined today and will be repeatedly over the next few days as we travel through the north-west corner of the country and explore rugged Galicia, a region with a spectacular landscape and coastline but whose towns and villages can feel a little threadbare.

Standing at the finish of the stage, at the top of a short climb, we huddle together for warmth in the press tent, the TVs hanging from the frame, swinging in the wind like saloon doors. I am standing with the Katusha contingent who are watching their man, Jhonatan Restrepo of Colombia, try to stay with Alessandro De Marchi, the BMC rider whose face always appears fixed in a permanent frown. I remember Restrepo from the Vuelta in 2016, when he was only 21, and looked like a great prospect. When I mention this to the Katusha press officer, he shakes his head. 'He's not getting a new contract. Nice guy, but lazy. Eats too much.' It seems harsh on a rider still so young, and I find myself rooting for Restrepo. But my silent cries of support are in vain: he's dropped as the road climbs up and De Marchi wins the stage, crossing the line and flashing a beautiful scowl.

Thursday, 6 September

Stage 12: Mondoñedo–Punta de Estaca de Bares, 177.5 km
Stage winner: Alexandre Geniez
Red jersey: Jesús Herrada

Today's finish is a perfect example of a story for the social-media age, in that it is very easy to form an instant opinion about what appears to happen – and who the culprit is – without knowing any of the facts, the people involved or the actual circumstances.

On a day that some thought might finish with a bunch sprint, a group of three arrive together. And thank goodness for that. Any more and there would be carnage, because the finish is the narrowest I have ever seen. With the photographers packed on one side of the road just beyond the line, there is barely any room for Alexandre Geniez, the winner, and Dylan van Baarle, the runner-up, but to make matters more complicated, there is a race official scurrying back from the line just as they cross it. The official gets between the photographers and the barriers at precisely the wrong moment; Geniez hits him square on, then Van Baarle goes barrelling into both of them and is hurled over the handlebars. It is a sickening crash. And it looked to be entirely the official's fault.

When Daniel and I convene to record the podcast outside the press centre an hour or so later, Daniel is initially distracted by the sight of Fernando Escartín, twice second at the Vuelta, in 1997 and 1998, walking past eating a banana. 'You know what I'm like around late 1990s climbers,' coos Daniel. He looks thoughtful, before adding, 'That's quite a green banana – I like them like that too.'

Then someone else appears, an older gentleman with an almost comically large bandage on his head. It is Chema Rodríguez, head of media operations, and the man, of course, at the centre of the finish-line controversy. It is a relief to see that he is OK, and also eating a banana.

It is easy to lambast the hapless functionary, or 'Bungling Vuelta official,' as British newspaper *The Sun* will declare in its headline the following morning – perhaps the only coverage of the Vuelta in *The Sun*. But as the evening wears on I learn a bit more about Rodríguez, not least from Fran, who tells me about the regard in which he is held in Spanish cycling circles, first as a respected journalist, more recently in his role at the Vuelta. The picture he paints is very much not one of a bungling official.

By the following morning, Rodríguez has resigned and the Vuelta organisers appear to happily accept his resignation, thereby, it seems to me, making him the scapegoat for a fiasco that I thought was largely their fault.

The finish was far too narrow, that was clear. Rodríguez's job, to make it safe, seemed impossible. As if that weren't bad enough, we later learn that just minutes before the riders appeared, he had to deal with a local politician refusing to take the official deviation – the turn-off from the finishing straight, a couple of hundred metres before the line – and driving instead through the finish. This was why Rodriguez was not where he should have been, behind the photographers. He was dealing with an obstacle on the finish line just before the riders were due to arrive: he was trying to make the finish safe.

According to Iban Vega, a Spanish cycling journalist, Rodríguez is known universally as 'a serious, rigorous, demanding guy'. Yet after working on the last 40 Vueltas, he has left the 2018 race in disgrace. It seems to me like an injustice – but one that, conveniently enough, leaves the organisers off the hook.

By curious coincidence, this incident happened barely 24 hours after David Millar announced his intention to stand for president of the CPA, the riders' union. Equally curiously, within an hour of the incident happening, a press release lands in my inbox from Gianni Bugno, the incumbent president. The email, headlined 'Gianni is angry!', is critical of the Vuelta for the accident beyond the finish line. It is the first email I have ever had from Bugno and the CPA. If Millar achieves nothing else, he has at least forced Bugno to send an email.

Millar's campaign had been a topic of conversation at the start of today's stage. In the tiny, one-horse town of Mondoñedo, I was talking to Ian Boswell about it when Richie Porte stopped alongside us. He seemed very relaxed as he began to chat, initially also about Millar's bid. Millar had phoned him that morning and Porte said he could count on his support in any campaign to oust Bugno.

I wondered why Porte was still riding the Vuelta when he appeared so far from his best, especially when he didn't appear to enjoy a great relationship with his soon-to-be-former team, BMC. I couldn't really understand why Porte didn't use the illness he had at the start of the Vuelta as an excuse to go home.

The conversation continued and Porte began talking about his three-month-old baby, back home in Monaco, a development to which he was still adjusting. ('Aha,' I thought, perhaps uncharitably, but with some recent experience of my own of having a newborn, 'so that's why he's still riding the Vuelta.')

Friday, 7 September

Stage 13: Candás–La Camperona, 175.5 km
Stage winner: Óscar Rodríguez
Red jersey: Jesús Herrada

This morning I seek out a couple of riders who've been critical of the previous day's finish, Marcus Burghardt and Michael Morkov, the latter a member of Quick-Step's lead-out train.

Morkov has been around for years – we covered his travails at the Tour a couple of years ago when he was struggling with crash injuries and he was *lanterne rouge* for a bit. But this year he has been prominent in helping Elia Viviani to several of his victories. This is something we see all the time in cycling – a rider who is familiar, but whose talents we don't fully appreciate and whose role isn't too clear, though invariably these two things are linked.

It is especially the case with the riders in a lead-out train, who only get any credit if their sprinter wins. If they don't, they are all but invisible. This is the point the 33-year-old Morkov makes to me in his gentle, Danish way. He's not doing anything differently this year, he tells me, and he's not any better. He just happens to be working for Viviani rather than Alexander Kristoff – no disrespect to Kristoff.

Today is not a stage for Morkov or Viviani, though Morkov tells me that yesterday's, with that dodgy finish, was one they thought might end in a bunch sprint. He's relieved it didn't.

As for finding himself at the tender age of 33 performing at a new level, he admits that 'sometimes I have to pinch myself to believe that I ended up here and found my second youth as a rider.'

He explains, 'My career started with Saxo and Bjarne Riis and that team was never going for sprints. Being in that team I always tried to help and develop myself as a climber and be part of the Grand Tours. When I went to Katusha and became part of Kristoff's lead-out I realised that was the job I was supposed to do. I did more or less the same job last year at Katusha, though obviously we didn't succeed as many times with Kristoff as we do with Elia. At this team we always start with a clear plan of how to win each race.'

Today there's a big surprise when Óscar Rodríguez, a rider I confess I know nothing about, appears from nowhere to win the stage. Le Camperona is a steep little climb, and when Rafał Majka goes clear near the bottom and Dylan Teuns joins him, it looks like they'll fight it out. Rodríguez just seems to judge it better, ignoring the early attacks but riding it at his own pace, bridging up to the leading two, then going straight past them. On the podcast I tie myself in knots trying to explain the difference between the Euskadi Foundation team, now run by Mikel Landa, the Euskadi–Murias team, which Rodríguez rides for, and the old Euskaltel–Euskadi team, which Landa used to ride for.

Fran is delighted for Rodríguez, who rode for the development team that he helps run, but he spends much of the day looking traumatised. It was here, on the Vuelta's last visit to Le Camperona in 2016, that he and his colleague Víctor ran over a dog. The ghost of the dog haunts him, and clearly affects his performance – after interviewing Rodríguez about his triumph atop Le Camperona he realises that he forgot to press *Record* on his recorder.

He perks up over a splendid dinner, in a magnificent old monastery where Daniel is staying, close to the foot of the climb.

Saturday, 8 September

Stage 14: Cistierna–Les Praeres de Nava, 167 km
Stage winner: Simon Yates
Red jersey: Simon Yates

A typical Vuelta finish with the pressroom in one place, the finish in another and the team buses somewhere else. There are three choices: stay in the pressroom to watch the finish, go up the climb to the finish or go to the buses and get the riders as they arrive back there, hoping there's enough 3G to watch the stage on my phone. I opt for the buses. Wrong choice.

The buses are spread over about 2 kilometres on a narrow, winding road. It's a case of picking one and waiting. Michał Kwiatkowski is one of the men of the day, featuring in a strong break that survived until late in the stage. Did he come to the Vuelta wanting to find out what he could do on GC, or is he using it to prepare for the world championships? I decide to wait by the Team Sky bus to try and find out – and because Kwiatkowski is an interesting guy, with lots going on, including his cycling school back home in Toruń.

It's a long wait. After doing the stage the riders are met by a *soigneur* at the top of the climb, given some warm clothing (I haven't mentioned the weather for a few days, because I'm used to it now, but it's still cold!), then they have to ride around 10 kilometres back down the hill to the buses – almost a daily, and I imagine pretty tedious, ritual at the Vuelta. Eventually Kwiatkowski appears, looking glum.

'Hi Michał, any chance of a qui…'

'After shower,' he says as he throws his bike against the bus and stomps aboard. The fact that he didn't so much as glance in my direction tells me that he won't be reappearing after his shower.

'There goes your interview,' says Chris Slark, the bus driver.

It is pretty annoying. I understand that Kwiatkowski has had a difficult day and is pissed off – as the team's press officer will confirm later. But I'm pissed off too, because I have driven 20 minutes to the buses and waited there for almost an hour to speak to one rider – Kwiatkowski. Not that he knows this. But it's not as if at the Vuelta there are hordes of journalists trying to speak to him every day. If he didn't want to speak he could have said that he'd had a difficult day and wasn't in the mood, and maybe we could do an interview another day. That would have been mildly irritating but I would have understood. I end up stomping away myself, thinking that it isn't media training some riders need, it's just basic manners.

To make myself feel better, I send an angry, curt text message to the team's press officer, who, later, will probably reflect on the fact that some journalists just lack basic manners.

Hey, we all have difficult days!

The stage itself has been a cracker. Daniel thinks the 'novelty finishes' might have gone a little too far – on this one, in a national park where the road was controversially surfaced for this first visit by the Vuelta, it's so incredibly steep that the riders look like they're taking part in a slow bike race. Spectators who start to run alongside them have to slow down to keep pace until they are jogging, then walking, then walking very slowly. The final kilometre takes about 45 minutes. Simon Yates wins with a late, brilliantly judged effort, suggesting that this time, maybe, just maybe... but it's too early to talk about that. I'm sticking with my podium of Quintana, López and Kelderman. Fran, meanwhile, is sticking with Fabio Aru for the win.

Sunday, 9 September

Stage 15: Ribera de Arriba–Lagos de Covadonga, 185.5 km
Stage winner: Thibaut Pinot
Red jersey: Simon Yates

At the start I am taken aback to be gently admonished by Friend of the Podcast Tao Geoghegan Hart. He calls me over to tell me that he disagrees with something I tweeted a couple of nights ago about Chema Rodríguez, the race official at the centre of the crash at the end of Stage 12, which brought down Alexandre Geniez and Tao's teammate, Dylan van Baarle.

It was a tweet that basically said what I said a couple of diary entries ago: that Rodríguez had been made a scapegoat. But this opinion appears to be counter to that of the peloton, who, like any group of colleagues, often take a collective view of things, and seem to have decided that the official was to blame. I tell Tao that I thought Rodríguez's job was impossible in the circumstances, and also that he had to deal with a local politician being where he shouldn't be just minutes before the riders arrived.

One point that strikes me, as I'm speaking, is that the riders don't really know what Rodríguez's job was. Tao asks why there were so many photographers there, but there were no more than any other day – it was just that the road was narrower (which was not Rodríguez's fault: he had to try to make the best of a bad situation).

I don't mean this as an insult, but the riders have a very narrow view – they have no idea what all the people working on the race do, a point that Adam Hansen made when Lionel interviewed him at the Tour. Hansen had just finished his run of 20 consecutive Grand Tours but was blown away by the infrastructure and the sheer number of people working on the Tour. 'I had no idea it was so big,' he said.

'You should never turn your back to the riders,' argues Tao. This is a fair point, but on the larger point we agree to disagree. Throughout this robust but civil exchange Tao is warming up on his turbo trainer outside the Sky bus, alongside my new *bête noire*, Michał Kwiatkowski, who throws me the occasional frosty glance, which I return with extra frost. (I don't, of course.)

A big performance from Astana today. One of the fascinating things about this Vuelta as we head into the final week is that there's still no one in charge. It's still all to play for, and we see teams make grand statements of intent, hoping they become a self-fulfilling prophecy. Act like you're the boss and others will believe it. But it's Thibaut Pinot who wins the stage at the summit of the spectacular, mystical Lagos de Covadonga, while Nairo Quintana – who won when we came here two years ago – crosses the line seventh and immediately congratulates Superman López on the victory. López was second. Admittedly it is foggy up there, but for me this is the first sign that Quintana may not live up to the favourite's billing that I have assigned him.

Monday, 10 September

Rest day: Santillana del Mar

Rest days usually promise so much and deliver so little. This one is the opposite. I awake in Santillana del Mar (having driven here last night), a town I didn't know but which, I will discover, is absolutely gorgeous.

At breakfast there are a couple of quite large men sitting in very animated conversation a couple of tables away, speaking loudly and passionately but in a language I cannot make out. It takes about 10 minutes for me to realise that the language they're speaking is English but with very strong Irish accents. I hope the people who will soon decide on my Irish passport application are not reading this.

After breakfast, as I'm walking towards the car, I hear a voice yelling, in a broad Irish accent, 'Is that the Buffalo? I thought that was you at breakfast, so I did.' Turns out the two gents are from Cork; they got the boat to Santander, just along the coast, and are here for a few days to see the Vuelta. We have a pleasant chat. I hope that *they* are the people who will decide on my imminent Irish passport application.

The first challenge on a rest day is finding a laundrette. Here, there's one just across the square, beside a café. While my pants, T-shirts and socks tumble in the soapy suds, I have a coffee and open my laptop to do some work – by which I mean checking Twitter, Facebook, Instagram and email, before going back to Twitter to begin another dreary lap of the Internet.

Midway through my third lap of the Internet the next table begins to fill with people who, when I look up from my important work, I see are wearing Team Sky uniform. It's some of the riders and staff out recceing tomorrow's time trial, which starts here. Among them is Michał Kwiatkowski, who can't get away from me now. He has to walk past my table to get into the café. 'Hello Michał,' I say, with, hopefully, a slightly menacing edge to my voice.

'Oh, hello,' he says.

'The coffee here is good,' I say.

'OK,' he says.

'That looked a nasty crash yesterday,' I say.

'Ah, it's OK,' he says. 'I'm fine.'

'Enjoy your coffee,' I say.

'Thanks,' he says, and moves on – though in truth he didn't really stop moving.

Sometimes getting a Kwiatkowski exclusive is just about being in the right place at the right time. I saved that interview for this diary – hope you enjoyed it.

From there, I wander into the old town to meet Daniel for lunch. It's a beautiful place: winding cobbled streets, old buildings, lots of very smart restaurants to choose from. After lunch I drive 5 kilometres to the BMC hotel to do a couple of interviews, with Brent Bookwalter and Jackson Stewart, two stalwarts of a team that will soon morph into CCC.

Then I get back to Santillana del Mar in time to do some pilates on the yoga mat that I brought with me – it was about time I christened it – before lying on my bed to read my book/have a snooze. Then I meet Fran to record one of our *Press Conference* podcasts, then I meet Daniel to finish it off and go for another fantastic meal. Truly, the first rest day worthy of its name.

Tuesday, 11 September

Stage 16: Santillana del Mar–Torrelavega, 32.7 km
Stage winner: Rohan Dennis
Red jersey: Simon Yates

A time trial means a late start, which means more time in Santillana del Mar. Frankly, I could stay here for ever.

I need cash, so I join a small queue at a cash machine in the centre. While waiting, Fabio Sabatini, the Quick-Step rider, joins the queue behind me. The couple in front seem to be having trouble working the machine, but eventually there's a whirring sound and the banknotes appear. They take them and walk away, but when I get to the machine their card is still in the slot. I pull it out, and turn to call them. Getting their attention and returning their card takes about five seconds. This is all it takes for Sabatini to insert himself into the gap and his card into the machine.

I guess that's the Wolfpack for you. Totally ruthless.

Rohan Dennis is also ruthless today on two fronts, in winning the time trial and in casually announcing in his press conference that that's it for him, he's off – outta here. He says he's leaving the Vuelta to prepare for the World Championships. Perhaps we should admire his honesty. But the etiquette is to make up some excuse for leaving a Grand Tour early – a made-up illness, a family emergency, the imminent birth of a child (but not that imminent, eh, Dan Martin and Lionel Birnie?).

It seems a bit disrespectful to the race to leave in such circumstances. (Looking at you, Lionel Birnie.)

Wednesday, 12 September

Stage 17: Getxo–Oiz, 166.4 km
Stage winner: Michael Woods
Red jersey: Simon Yates

Michael Woods is a rider it's easy to warm to. In my diary from last year's Vuelta I quoted something he said to me off the record the night before the race started, when he lambasted 'the so-called golden generation of Spanish cycling – Contador, Valverde and Sánchez,' adding that he couldn't wait to see the back of them. It was the kind of thing that some riders say in private but are reluctant – quite understandably, I think – to see in print. But I was keen to use it in my Vuelta diary for last year's book so I emailed Woods to ask if he would mind, and he replied immediately: 'Of course, man, go for it.'

Lionel put it best about Woods when he described him as a human being. Not to say the other riders aren't – most if not all of them are human beings. But Woods is very human indeed. He has a great backstory as a runner, which we've covered extensively, but as he adds to his cycling palmarès, his human qualities come even more to the fore. And he has never been more human than today, as he toils up yet another uber-steep Vuelta finish, the fog-enshrouded Balcón de Bizkaia in the Basque Country, with Dylan Teuns chasing and never allowing Woods to relax – not that you could on such a climb.

Woods is out of the saddle the whole way – standing up, which suits him best as a former runner – his face contorted, as though crying with the effort, which he might well be. He hasn't taken out his earpiece. He has his DS, Juanma Garate, in his ear, urging him to do it for his family. This is not mere motivational talk but a message that could not have more meaning for Woods. At the finish, after winning his first stage in his third Grand Tour, he speaks about his son, who was stillborn at 37 weeks just two months earlier.

'We lost a little guy – his name was Hunter,' says Woods. 'The whole time I was coming up the climb, I was just thinking of him.'

He is speaking spontaneously, as he always seems to do – just telling people what is on his mind and in his heart, and what has given him the strength to go so deep, as he has had to do. It is such a human moment. Woods begins crying before he can finish the interview. He is not alone.

Thursday, 13 September

Stage 18: Ejea de los Caballeros–Lleida, 180.5 km
Stage winner: Jelle Wallays
Red jersey: Simon Yates

On paper today promised nothing. But what a stage!

At the Vuelta last year, I spent a couple of days stalking Jelle Wallays, the Lotto–Soudal rider whose continued participation in the race seemed like a miracle. He had horrendous crash injuries, and kept falling off to add more. Then there was an incident at the summit of the Calar Alto Observatory, beyond the finish line, when a car stopped beside him and the door opened violently, smashing into Wallays's torso. Fran witnessed it. Wallays screamed and doubled over, crying with pain. He would find out on finishing the Vuelta – because he did finish – that he had ridden most of the race with broken ribs.

What struck me when I interviewed him during that Vuelta was how positive he was. Let's be clear: he wasn't transformed into Orla Chennaoui. He was phlegmatic, in that Belgian way, but there was no self-pity: he shrugged and said, with a smile, that he'd just have to get on with it.

When I later ask Thomas De Gendt for his highlight of this Vuelta, he selects today's stage and Wallays's stage win, even though De Gendt himself wins the king of the mountains. The win today is testament to Wallays's strength, cunning and determination, because there is no way he and his breakaway companion, Sven Erik Byström, should have stayed away. Normally the bunch plays with the breakaway; today it's the other way around. They save their big effort for the final 20 kilometres, and after crossing the line Wallays heads immediately to the Quick-Step bus to rub their faces in it – he celebrates loudly and ostentatiously, apparently having been annoyed by Rik Van Slycke, one of the Quick-Step DSs, who laughed at him earlier in the stage.

In Lleida I have an odd experience, entering my Ibis Hotel only to find that it is in fact two Ibis Hotels sharing one reception. After checking in you turn left for standard class, right for budget. I turn right, and find that in the same corridor as my small, moulded plastic 'pod' are riders from the Burgos BH team.

In the relative luxury of standard, meanwhile, are Sunweb, LottoNL–Jumbo, Cofidis – Cofidis?! – and Daniel Friebe. It gives me a brief, tantalising glimpse of how the other half lives.

Friday, 14 September

Stage 19: Lleida–Naturalandia (Andorra), 157 km
Stage winner: Thibaut Pinot
Red jersey: Simon Yates

Andorra is the real reason Lionel went home early. In a curious twist, the other father-in-waiting, Dan Martin, lives here, and will even turn up at the stage start tomorrow.

Today's is a cracking stage, that more or less confirms Simon Yates as champion. He has ridden a very impressive race, apart from a strange lapse today, when he drops back to the team car on the approach to the climb to Naturalandia. Doesn't he have people to do that for him? While he's there, a crosswind picks up and Movistar drill it at the front, forcing splits. It leads to about 10 minutes of excitement before it all comes back together. Movistar are at least trying. As they begin the climb Quintana attacks, going up the road, as Daniel says later, 'like a burst football'.

Valverde, who still looked like he might win the Vuelta this morning, also resembles a punctured football. He looks every one of his 38 years as he battles up the climb, finally falling out of contention.

Tonight we are staying in Escaldes-Engordany. Recording with Fran in one of the main squares is an odd experience. Feral children run wild, then gather round us more or less as soon as I press *Record*, as though we are celebrities or something. I think they are trying to put me off. Or perhaps I have spent too much time with Lionel, and have so internalised the anti-Andorra prejudice that I am now paranoid.

Saturday, 15 September

Stage 20: Escaldes-Engordany–Coll de la Gallina, 105.8 km
Stage winner: Enric Mas
Red jersey: Simon Yates

Sorry to keep going on about Andorra, but it's such a strange place. And yet the riders who live here seem to love it, and not just for tax reasons they assure us even while managing, in one or two cases, to keep a straight face.

I can only think that there's another side to it that I haven't seen. The main town, where today's stage starts, I find garish, tacky and claustrophobic.

On my way to the start I run into Dave Brailsford, who has been for a bike ride and is now trying to find the Team Sky bus. It isn't here yet, I tell him. He's too early. I leave him standing in the centre in his Team Sky kit, waiting for the bus and feeling – I imagine – distinctly uncomfortable.

I am heading to Leigh Howard's café. Howard is the Australian rider who was with Aqua Blue Sport last year but now focuses just on the track. He also runs a cycling-themed café a few minutes' walk from the centre – he is working the coffee machine as I walk in. It's packed, mainly with cyclists. Simon Clarke, the Education First rider, is here with his family.

Howard's coffee is good, but the highlight of my day comes later at the summit of the Vuelta's last climb, the Coll de la Gallina. Fran and I are standing with 200 metres to go, watching the race unfold on the big screen, when a ripple of applause and cheering travels slowly up the mountain towards us. It's not clear what is happening until, finally, a man appears with a young boy in tow. I had seen the boy at the start – a six-year old in full kit, on a racing bike adapted for his diminutive size, with saddle attached by zip-tag – and now here he is, having ridden all the way up. He gets as big a cheer as the riders an hour or so later. It's a lovely moment.

Not quite as young – but not that much older – are the two surprises of the day, Miguel Ángel López and Enric Mas, who leapfrog Alejandro Valverde and Steven Kruijswijk to occupy the steps of the podium beneath the champion, Yates.

Yates has just one bit of unfinished business, and I don't mean the final stage in Madrid, which – on account of it being a seven-hour drive away – I am boycotting. After being presented with his red jersey, as he makes his way to the team car waiting to take him down the mountain, Yates makes a slight detour to have a word with a journalist – me.

'You guys have got to come up with a better nickname than the Flying Black Pudding,' he says. I mumble that I'll have a word with Lionel, thereby making it clear that I am not to blame.

In the same square as last night, with the same children running wild, Fran and I have a farewell beer and toast the end of the Vuelta. He will go to Madrid; I will go home, via Girona, where I'm staying for a couple of nights to do some interviews. It's been fun, and it was a good race, but it's been a little different to the other Grand Tours. The three of us – Daniel, Fran and I – have travelled separately. When we travel together, we talk about the race in the car on a fairly constant basis, and the podcasts are really a continuation of that conversation. Without that, it's been as if an ingredient has been missing – though on the plus side, while driving through Spain on my own I've listened to lots of great podcasts.

But next year, we have resolved, we'll do the Vuelta a little differently.

See you on 24 August on the Costa Blanca. Stage 2 starts in everybody's favourite party town, so I'll be able to tell my Benidorm story.

Daniel, Richard, Lionel and Orla in action during one of The Cycling Podcast's live shows at the Round Chapel in Hackney, March 2018

Tom Dumoulin, La Rosière, 2018 Tour de France

Off the back, alone and outside the time limit: Mark Cavendish at La Rosière, 2018 Tour de France

On his way to winning the stage, Geraint
Thomas at La Rosière, 2018 Tour de France

Adam Yates, La Rosière, 2018 Tour de France

Shadowing the yellow
jersey, Chris Froome
and Geraint Thomas,
Alpe d'Huez, 2018
Tour de France

On his way to 14th in the opening time trial at the 2019 Giro d'Italia,
few were talking of Ecuador's Richard Carapaz as a likely winner

The tallest man in professional cycling, and talented audio diarist for The Cycling Podcast,
Conor Dunne tackles the Colle della Guardia on stage 1 of the 2019 Giro d'Italia

Scorching up the Colle della Guardia on stage 1 of the 2019 Giro d'Italia,
Primož Roglič sets the best time to win the stage

Primož Roglič in the first pink jersey of the 2019 Giro d'Italia a day after
winning the time trial in Bologna

Orbetello, 2019 Giro d'Italia

Pascal Ackermann wins his second stage of the 2019 Giro d'Italia in a wet Terracina

A gloomy Tom Dumoulin contemplates another day in the rain 24 hours after his crash at the 2019 Giro d'Italia. He abandoned just a few kilometres into stage 5.

Riding to nowhere: Egan Bernal begins his descent of the Col de l'Iseran during the 2019 Tour de France. It was the move that won him the Tour, though the entire race was stopped a little bit further on as the storm closed in.

Into the storm: dark clouds await the riders as they reach the summit of the Col de l'Iseran, stage 19, 2019 Tour de France

Matt White, the Mitchelton-Scott sports director, in the thick of things as the riders stop and prepare to be evacuated from the summit of the Col de l'Iseran

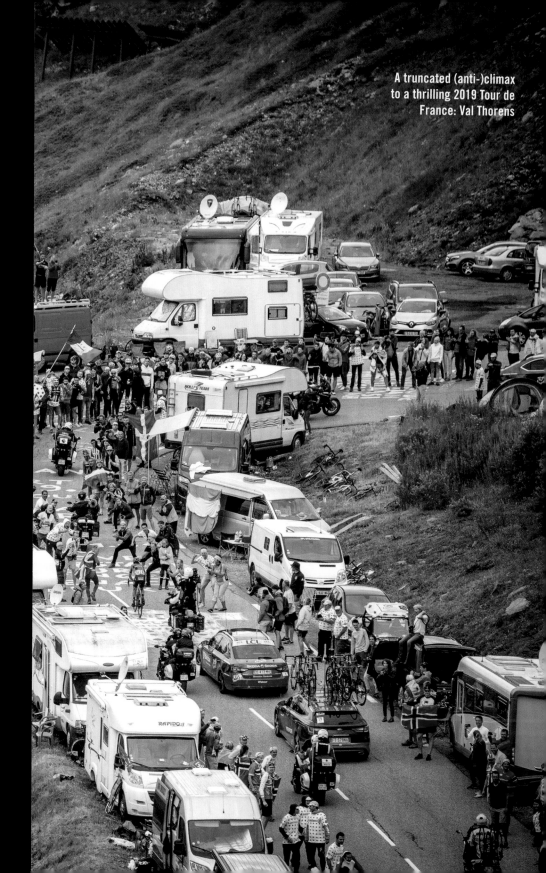

A truncated (anti-)climax to a thrilling 2019 Tour de France: Val Thorens

Richard, Lionel and François recording the
podcast in Gap at the 2019 Tour de France

2019 GIRO D'ITALIA

by Lionel Birnie

Friday, 10 May

The 2019 Giro d'Italia gets off to a cracking start when Richard spills hot EasyJet tea all over his tan-coloured Rapha chinos midway through the flight. In response to Richard's call for dry napkins to mop up the mess, I look the other way and pretend my earpiece radio isn't working, like the world's worst *domestique*.

We land in Bologna, home of Europe's oldest university, a city that considers itself the tastebuds and stomach of Italy, and the place that welcomed the finish of the very first stage of the Giro d'Italia in 1909. That first Giro set off from Milan, only about 220 kilometres away as the crow flies, although the route took them via Lake Garda to make the stage almost 400 kilometres long. The race was won by Dario Beni, while the eventual Giro champion Luigi Ganna had a level crossing to thank because he'd fallen behind the leaders and only caught up when they had to stop and wait for a train to pass. You should have seen the hoo-ha on Twitter about it!

Bologna has several nicknames. *La Dotta* (the learned one, on account of the university), *La Rossa* (because of its historically communist politics and red brick buildings) and *La Grassa*, or the fat one, because of its reputation as the capital of Italy's food culture. Over the course of a couple of days in Bologna I am impressed at Daniel's restraint from nicknaming me *La Grassa*. It must be killing him.

The Giro's pressroom is at Eataly World, which is apparently a huge warehouse-type place next to the motorway, opened with great fanfare a few years ago to showcase not just Bolognese cuisine but to gather together the best Italy has to offer under one roof covering 100,000 square metres. I'd seen it described as being like Ikea for food and so I'm far from unhappy when Daniel announces that he has already collected our accreditation passes and so there's no need to visit. The pun is leaving a sour taste all by itself, although I can't decide which is worse: Eataly World or the Giro's slogan, The Fight For Pink?

We head to our delightful bed and breakfast in the hills, which offers a glorious view of Bologna below us. The place is clearly owned by someone who has a flair for interior design. We step into a room dominated by two large coffee tables made from what look like reclaimed railway sleepers, upon which sit a pair of ornate bronze buffalos.

'It's as if they knew you were coming, Richard,' I say.

As we drive into town to sample the best Bologna has to offer, I spot a branch of Domino's Pizza.

'I can see where the city gets its reputation,' I say. Daniel is sitting in the front seat with his back to me but I'm pretty certain he rolls his eyes.

We head to a restaurant called La Drogheria della Rosa, a charming little place in an old apothecary. The interior is all dark wood panels and shelves stacked with bottles and jars. We're joined by Daniel's parents, who are holidaying in Italy, and we accept the recommendation made by the restaurant owner to try a couple of pasta dishes followed by the steak.

One of the pasta dishes is a neat little swirl of tagliatelle topped with a traditional Bolognese ragù. I'd once left Daniel askance when I said that at home I sometimes like to serve my sauce on top of the pasta and stir it in as I eat. He said this was something the Italians would never do, and so I make a big show of photographing my plate of pasta with the ragù stacked on top.

To irritate Daniel further I declare it my mission for the weekend to discover the perfect spag bol recipe and I have to say this seems pretty good.

'There's no mushrooms, carrots or Worcestershire sauce in this one, I don't think,' I say. Daniel rolls his eyes.

The steak that follows is beautifully cooked and accompanied by a rich balsamic vinegar sauce that has developed the consistency of Marmite.

The owner of the bar joins us at the table, gently swilling a fish bowl-sized glass of red wine by its slender stem as he tells us about Bologna and its traditions.

He offers us a glass of limoncello to round off the meal. Daniel declines.

'You don't like it do you, lovey?' Daniel's mum says.

'Of course he doesn't,' I say. 'Daniel probably prefers an obscure liqueur made from kumquats.'

Saturday, 11 May

Stage 1: Bologna–Madonna di San Luca time trial, 8 km
Stage winner: Primož Roglič
Pink jersey: Primož Roglič

It turns out to be a funny sort of day. The time trial course offers everything you could wish for – a fast opening half, a dead U-turn at the bottom of the hill and a spectacular, steep climb alongside the famous portico up to the basilica at San Luca. With Tom Dumoulin, Simon Yates, Primož Roglič, Vincenzo Nibali and co in the field it should have made for an intriguing afternoon.

And yet there's a sense of anti-climax because the weather forecast has predicted rain for the early evening and so all of the overall favourites – bar Mitchelton–Scott's Simon Yates – are scheduled to set off in the first 20 minutes of the stage, making it an upside-down sort of opening time trial.

We drive to the bottom of the hill and park near the Stadio Renato Dall'Ara, home to Bologna's football team and the scene of England's second round win over Belgium in the 1990 World Cup, immortalised in the lyrics of Baddiel and Skinner's song, *Three Lions*. John Motson's line, 'England have done it. In the last minute of extra-time,' greeted David Platt's volley. I mention this to Richard and remind him that Scotland lost to Costa Rica in the group stage at that World Cup. He curls his lip and walks off. Usually I can't resist a look round a football stadium whenever our travels take us to one but the ground is all locked up.

There are much better views of the stadium from further up the hill. We set off to walk up under the portico, which, at 3,700 metres, is one of the longest in the world. There are more than 600 arches and it takes us all the way up to the church with its elegant domed roof. Thousands of spectators are already on the hill as we walk up and the enclosed archways promise to amplify the cheers, making for an electrifying atmosphere.

Usually, the suspense builds during a time trial like this but with 2017 Giro champion Dumoulin first to set off I speculate that there's the distinct possibility he could set the best time and spend the rest of the evening in the hot seat.

Over the next quarter of an hour there's a flurry of excitement as Miguel Ángel López beats the Dutchman's time by a fraction of a second and then Nibali goes five seconds quicker. All of them are swept away by Roglič, who goes 23 seconds faster than Nibali. And that's more or less it for three hours because no one else can get within half a minute of Roglič's time until Simon Yates crosses the line, 19 seconds down, by which time it's nearly eight o'clock.

We're already back down near the football stadium by this time, as are many of the fans who had hiked up the hill to see the stars before drifting down again over the course of the evening. Those who set off in the second half of the field have the surreal experience of riding up the hill as fans walk down on the road either side of them.

As it turns out, the forecast rain never arrives and even the latest starters are able to ride in the dry.

I see tweets from fans turning on their televisions to watch the last hour of the time trial only to find the result is more or less done and all the favourites have already finished. I make the case that in circumstances such as this the organisers should be allowed to set the starting order themselves so the stars set off at the end but it's not an argument I'm fully committed to. The teams should be able to take into account changing weather conditions even if it does rob the stage of its drama.

We record the episode in a bar and are somewhat distracted by a developing situation at the fruit machine. One man had been feeding coins into the fruity for a good half-hour before leaving it to order a drink. In the meantime, another man nips in and within minutes we hear the clack-clack-clack of coins being dispensed. When the first man returns there's a heated discussion over who is the rightful winner of the jackpot. In many ways, it's a bit like cycling. You can put in all the coins you like, but if someone else presses the button that causes it to pay out there's very little you can say.

Dinner is at a terrific restaurant in the centre of the city, but I make a series of errors when it comes to ordering and end up looking enviously at everyone else's meals. The starter of Bologna ham and cheese sounds promising enough, but the ham is like luncheon meat, arranged into cones that look like wizards' hats. The main course of meatballs with peas is just that – four small meatballs and peas in a sauce. Not even any pasta to pile it onto.

Sunday, 12 May

Stage 2: Bologna–Fucecchio, 205 km
Stage winner: Pascal Ackermann
Pink jersey: Primož Roglič

At the start, I speak to the Irish champion, Conor Dunne, for an episode of *Kilometre 0* about parenthood and the peloton. Dunne's partner Stacey gave birth to their son Jesse on May 1, meaning he had just eight days with his new family before heading to Italy for the start of the Giro.

'I really want to do him proud here,' says Dunne outside the Israel Cycling Academy team bus. 'I've got to keep him in nappies and porridge. That's the reality of life now. I've got to support my family.'

I must confess, parenthood is not something I'd thought much about before the arrival of my daughter last year, but I reflect on the fact that professional cyclists are away from home a lot, often for weeks at a time. With all the training camps and stage races many World Tour riders can be away for a third of the year or more, and when they are at home they need to train, rest and sleep as well as possible. None of those things, it strikes me, are terribly compatible with having a baby at home.

Dunne admits he's looking forward to sleeping through the night and getting up relatively late. 'I never thought I'd come to a Grand Tour and treat it like a holiday,' he jokes.

I speak to some former riders and sports directors, who give the impression that being away from home was harder in the old days, before FaceTime and WhatsApp made it easier to call home and see family members face to face.

Once the race has rolled out, Richard and Daniel head to the finish and I get into the car with Simon the photographer and David Luxton, super agent to the cycling literary world and the man who has the job of keeping morale high among *The Cycling Podcast*'s team, and we drive down to the famous San Baronto climb. Richard describes it as Tuscany's Box Hill. It's a climb that generations of professionals have trained on and the 2013 World Championship road race tackled it early on too.

I must admit I find it slightly underwhelming when we get there, not least because there's nowhere to stop for a coffee. It's also chilly, with a howling tailwind behind the riders as they crest the top, although the morning's rain has at least receded to a light drizzle.

We watch the finish on my phone in the warmth of the car and just about manage to see Pascal Ackermann of Bora–Hansgrohe win his first Grand

Tour stage ahead of Elia Viviani, Caleb Ewan and Fernando Gaviria. There's a good field of sprinters in this Giro and for Ackermann to get off the mark at the first opportunity presumably eases the pressure on him. The young German was selected instead of Ireland's Sam Bennett, who won three stages in last year's Giro only to be told he would ride neither of the season's first two Grand Tours this time round.

The other talking point arises from Richard's assertion yesterday that Primož Roglič has the Giro's pink jersey sewn up already. In case you don't know, the Slovenian is a former ski jumper. His form so far this season has been impressive. He's raced relatively lightly but has won all three stage races he's started – the UAE Tour, Tirreno-Adriatico and the Tour de Romandie.

Not everyone sees it the same way as Richard. At the start, Mitchelton–Scott's sports director Matt White tells him that no one has won the Tour de Romandie and the Giro d'Italia in the same season in the modern era, suggesting that being in great form 10 days before the Giro even began might not help Roglič when the race reaches its final week.

Once the podcast is aired, someone points out that Stephen Roche won the Tour de Romandie and Giro d'Italia back-to-back in 1987, which sparks a debate about what counts as the modern era. I argue that if colour television footage exists it counts as the modern era. Richard laughs because when White was regaling him with his inaccurate fact this morning, the man standing right next to him was none other than 1987 Tour de Romandie and Giro d'Italia champion Stephen Roche.

Dinner is sensational. The speciality of the Agriturismo Casetta near Vinci is steak Florentine. The owner makes an elaborate ceremony of showing us the raw steaks before they are chargrilled. While they cook, we enjoy a delicious risotto served in little edible bowls made from parmesan crisps.

Monday, 13 May

Stage 3: Vinci–Orbetello, 220 km
Stage winner: Fernando Gaviria
Pink jersey: Primož Roglič

Vinci is apparently a beautiful little walled town. It's the birthplace of Leonardo da Vinci, of course, and from the little I see, the townsfolk have celebrated him beautifully. There are floral displays all over and I spot a wood carving of his Vitruvian Man.

But I don't get any closer than a glimpse through the car window because we head straight to the team buses, which are parked three kilometres away in the car park of what looks to be an olive oil bottling factory. Round the back are pallets stacked with bottles of olive oil, which is what leads old Columbo here to that particular conclusion.

It's windy and the talk among the sports directors is the danger of crosswinds when the peloton hits the coast. What follows is an extremely cautious day of non-racing. Sho Hatsuyama of the Nippo-Vini Fantini team is the lone attacker and he spends half the stage out in front. There are no significant attacks after that because the sprinters' teams keep the pace high. Days like this are especially stressful for the riders – they're constantly on the lookout for danger, wary of splits caused by crashes or the wind – but as a spectacle it's got little going for it.

My sense is that the finish in Orbetello should be stunning. Google Maps gives me the impression of a pretty little seaside town close to a beautiful nature reserve. However, we're stuck at the ugly end of town. The grey skies take the blue shine off the sea and the whole place feels a little sorry for itself.

Daniel and I head down to the deserted car park where the team buses are parked in rows. We spot a smart looking camper van and peer through the window at a man who looks like an older version of Elia Viviani.

'That's Viviani's dad,' says Daniel.

Viviani's dad is following the Giro in style. His camper van has a satellite dish on the roof so he can watch the stage on TV. The leatherette seats swivel so he can watch in comfort. We peer in through the window as the race enters the final few kilometres. I feel a bit awkward watching his TV like this, but feel a little less so when he tilts the screen so we can see it more clearly.

The sprint unfolds, Viviani looks the fastest. Viviani is the fastest. Viviani Senior leans forward in his seat, rocking a little as if trying to help push the pedals for his son. Viviani hits the line first by which time Viviani Senior is out of his seat. He lets out a big whoop of delight, smiles and opens his little side window. Daniel is already recording. We capture a little moment of joy, and it's a reminder that every race, victory and defeat puts the riders' family and friends through the spectrum of emotions.

But wait. The joy is short-lived. As we arrive back in the pressroom the televisions are showing a defiant-looking Viviani striding along the finishing straight, ducking past the cameramen and photographers. It doesn't take a body language expert to work out he's not happy.

A slow-motion replay of the finish explains more. We watch as Viviani comes off Ackermann's wheel and moves to his left, forcing Trek-Segafredo's young sprinter Matteo Moschetti to stall. It's a clear deviation from his line and so the decision to disqualify Viviani is probably the right one, but even Fernando Gaviria, who inherits the stage victory, lacks the enthusiasm to celebrate.

Not to worry, we say, Viviani's day will come. Little do we know...

'Relegation is too good for him,' I joke. 'He should be made to ride stage four in just his bib shorts.' Viviani deserves a sanction for his unique – shall we say – take on the Italian national champion's jersey. Instead of the classic tricolour with thick bands of green, white and red, Viviani and his Deceuninck–Quick-Step team have gone for vertical stripes. They say it's to honour his appearance in his home Grand Tour but to me it looks like a Carlisle United away shirt from the late 1990s.

Every day in the podcast, we try to make sense of the Grand Tours even though the Grand Tours rarely make sense, especially at the beginning. Millions of things happen during each stage that may, or may not, gain greater significance later in the race. We focus on the favourites but sometimes we miss something that turns out to be critical. Today is one of those days.

With nine kilometres to go, Movistar's Ecuadorian rider, Richard Carapaz, has a mechanical problem and has to change bikes. He has teammates to help him chase back but they don't make it and Carapaz, a stage winner and fourth overall last year, loses 46 seconds. This evening it feels like a footnote to the stage. Little do we know...

Tuesday, 14 May

Stage 4: Orbetello–Frascati, 235 km
Stage winner: Richard Carapaz
Pink jersey: Primož Roglič

Never let me complain about Italian breakfasts again. The buffet at our remote *agriturismo* – the Podere de Priorato – is sumptuous. There's a huge ham and cheese tart, baked eggs in a rich tomato sauce, a tortilla swollen by chunks of potato and topped with slices of courgette. And that's before we even get to the sweet things.

The race heads to Frascati today so Daniel announces he has a wine lesson for me. Naturally, it doesn't concern Frascati at all. Far too mainstream. Instead we stop as we leave Orbetello to buy a bottle of Est! Est!! Est!!! It's from the Montefiascone region, which, like Frascati, is near to Rome.

Daniel explains the story of the wine's peculiar name. In the 12th century a German bishop travelled to the Vatican to meet the Pope. He sent a minion ahead of him with the sole job of seeking out the best wines along the route. If the wine was reasonable, the minion was to write Est! on the door of the establishment. If it was a cut above passable, he'd scrawl Est! Est!! And if the wine was really exceptional he'd write Est! Est!! Est!!! That way the Bishop and his pals would know where to stop for a really good session of spiritual wine drinking. It's a great story, but possibly an apocryphal one.

As we peruse the shelves in the supermarket one obvious question occurs to me.

'Daniel, if this Est! Est!! Est!!! is such good stuff, why is it €2.99 a bottle?'

In the supermaket's entrance there's a display of bikes, jerseys and photographs that a small cycling museum would be proud of. On closer inspection, most of the jerseys are replicas but there's an old *ciclamino* jersey – awarded to the points competition leader – that appears to be a genuine one from the late 1970s. There's also a Decathlon-branded Time bike and Cofidis jersey that once belonged to Massimiliano Lelli, a fairly notorious ex-teammate of David Millar's, who is from a town not too far inland.

When we arrive in Frascati, Daniel announces another culinary assignment. We're off to find the three-breasted honey bread woman, *La Pupazza di Frascati*. Legend has it that the region's infants are nursed on wine as well as milk and that the three-breasted woman dispenses milk from two of the breasts – so far, so normal – and wine from the other.

Again I have questions that Daniel can't answer. For example, is the wine dispensed from the middle breast? That would seem most logical. And does it dispense fizzy wine?

We purchase a three-breasted woman in a cafe and commence a taste test. I'm terribly disappointed. I'd been anticipating a sweet, soft dough, perhaps not quite with the tang of a good gingerbread man (or woman) but certainly sweet enough to suggest it's a treat. The dough is hard – stale almost – and bland. I'm unimpressed by the delicacies the Lazio region has to offer so far.

The stage itself is stale and tasteless too, at least until the end. It's too long, especially coming after two other stages that bust the 200 kilometre mark. The cold rain makes it even more miserable. Very little happens until everything happens at once, when the drama comes in its most unwelcome form. There's a big crash inside the final 10 kilometres and then, a little further on, Dumoulin and Yates fall as they tackle a roundabout made slick by the rain. It means the finish is contested by fewer than 25 riders, and on the climb to the line Richard Carapaz takes a flier to surprise the remaining sprinters. Caleb Ewan of Lotto–Soudal gets closest, and is undoubtedly travelling faster than the Ecuadorian ahead of him as they approach the line, but it's too little too late.

I head to the Lotto–Soudal bus and endure the most embarrassing moment of this, or any other, Grand Tour. I call Caleb Ewan 'Cadel' by accident. For a few minutes I think I've got away with it. Perhaps he didn't hear me. For some unknown reason I decide to make certain at the end by apologising for calling him 'Cadel'. 'Oh… er… yeah, that's okay,' he says, sounding suddenly crestfallen. I put it down to being drunk on Est! Est!! Est!!! and the contents of the honey bread woman's middle breast.

Next I head to the Sunweb bus thinking that perhaps I can kick Tom Dumoulin on his injured knee to complete my day.

I get there just as the 2017 Giro champion hobbles across to a waiting ambulance. He has wounds on both knees and what looks like the imprint of a chainring on his calf. To my untrained eye, it looks like his Giro is over.

At dinner, Daniel stitches me up by photographing me in a way that makes it look as if the sprawling banquet for four is all mine.

Wednesday, 15 May

Stage 5: Frascati–Terracina, 140 km
Stage winner: Pascal Ackermann
Pink jersey: Primož Roglič

Frascati could be amazing. It has everything a tourist destination requires. Quaint cobbled streets, quirky nooks and crannies, grand old churches. Popes lived here, back in the day. It's also twinned with Maidenhead, Theresa May's constituency, so, I mean… print that in the brochures Frascati Tourist Board.

But it's so run down and lacking fizz. The buildings need a good scrub, the streets are cracked, the park I run round before breakfast is strewn with litter and dog mess. What it lacks in tidiness it more than makes up for in character, though. I pop my head into a fishmonger's shop, no more than a hole in the wall, really, and see a startling array of fresh fish beautifully presented on ice. Glassy eyes peer at me, the scales are crisp and clear and there's that fresh scent of well-kept fish that doesn't smell at all fishy. The greengrocer a few doors down is more like a garden allotment overflowing with greenery and vibrant fruit and veg. In London these guys would be working towards their second Porsche and holiday home in Padstow by now but here there's a sense that it's all rather under-appreciated, which is a shame.

I also learn that the Gregorian calendar, the one we observe today, was adopted at the grand Villa Mondragone up on the hill overlooking the town. That was down to Pope Gregory XIII, who commissioned a calendar that meant people wouldn't have to keep adding or subtracting days from the year to make the clocks keep pace with the spinning of the Earth and avoid night falling in the middle of the afternoon every so often. Of course, the ordinary folk thought they were being diddled out of a day's wages or something so the move was terribly unpopular but old Gregory had science on his side and common sense won the day. Clearly people hadn't had enough of experts back then. It meant that the 10 days between 4 October and 15 October 1582 didn't happen. I'm sure we've all had days when it's felt like we've woken up 11 days after we went to bed but back then it really did happen.

One man who probably wishes he could have had 11 days' recuperation in a single night is Tom Dumoulin. At the start, he reverses down the steps of the Sunweb bus like a nervous non-swimmer lowering himself into the pool for his first session without armbands. The fact he's even starting the race raises questions about cycling's relationship with the pain barrier. Dumoulin is one of the most valuable assets in the sport, a man who could win the Tour de France this summer, and yet he feels he needs to start this stage to prove something to himself, or perhaps to others. I wonder whether it's all worth it. Dumoulin isn't going to reach Terracina, let alone Verona. And the rain in Frascati is ludicrous again this morning. It's bouncing up off the road to ankle height.

Dumoulin makes it through the neutralised zone, then another kilometre-and-a-half and then he calls it a day, quite sensibly.

After the riders have rolled out, we shelter in a cafe in the hope the rain might ease off. It's 10 past 12 but I order a nice warm cappuccino despite Daniel's objections. We buy a coffee for Flavia Cappellini, who makes films for the television show, *InCycle*. She explains that when the weather is cold and miserable, a late cappuccino may be permitted. She also points out that she's young and that young people are less conservative or stuck in their ways about these things. I enjoy the fact that Daniel's adherence to the 11am cappuccino cut-off puts him in the fuddy-duddy camp.

The rain falls all day and intensifies again as we arrive in Terracina. This most un-Giro-like weather is starting to take its toll. It also makes the two-kilometre walk from the pressroom to the team buses feel unappealing, so I ask Ciro Scognamiglio if he can give me a lift in *La Gazzetta Dello Sport*'s car. Ciro has a driver who drops him off exactly where he needs to be and waits while he works before taking him back to the pressroom.

Pascal Ackermann wins his second stage ahead of Gaviria, Démare and Ewan. The big absentee from the top 10 is Viviani, whose legs and rear derailleur lock up in the final few hundred metres. Ciro's intensity in finding out what went wrong for Viviani explains why the riders might be tempted to come up with multiple excuses when things don't go to plan.

In the press conference, Ackermann cuts a confident dash for a Grand Tour first-timer but falters slightly when he's asked about the damage the doping undertaken by previous generations has done to cycling's reputation in Germany. It's a question Marcel Kittel and others have faced with aplomb but Ackermann seems unprepared for it and gives the sort of non-answer you'd have heard a decade ago. In a way, I can understand why someone who was 12 years old when Jan Ullrich was snared in the Operación Puerto doping net might think events from half a lifetime ago bear little relevance to him. But cycling's relationship with doping is complex and I also think it is the responsibility of the teams and their staff to ensure younger riders have a decent grasp of the sport's recent history.

Thursday, 16 May

Stage 6: Cassino–San Giovanni Rotondo, 238 km
Stage winner: Fausto Masnada
Pink jersey: Valerio Conti

San Giovanni Rotondo is our destination and it turns out to be quite a long drive. If you think of the country as a high-heeled cowboy boot, as I do, San Giovanni Rotondo is right over in the east, where the spur should be attached.

On the way, Daniel explains to me that the town was home to the venerated priest Padre Pio of Pietrelcina, until his death in 1968, and so it's a popular place for Roman Catholic pilgrimages. I have in mind an Italian version of Lourdes – my least favourite town in France – but I am pleasantly surprised because it is quiet and understated and no one seems to be selling holy water in the sort bottles that windscreen washer fluid usually comes in.

We park up and walk towards the modern church, which towers over everything. As we reach the entrance we pass a gift shop which has a small forecourt at the front upon which sit dozens of statues of Padre Pio, from a life-size golden one sitting on some sort of throne, to an army of smaller garden gnome-sized ones. With their grey hair and beard and long brown robes, they seem very familiar.

'They look like Obi-Wan Kenobi,' I say, referring to the character played by Alec Guinness in the original *Star Wars* films.

Daniel is non-plussed.

'These are not the priests you are looking for,' I say with a chuckle.

Daniel walks off, another 20th-century Anglo-American cultural reference completely passing him by.

I read up on Padre Pio and learn he was a priest who had visions, was said to have the gift of reading souls, and also suffered stigmata – bodily marks and pain in the locations corresponding to Jesus Christ's crucifixion wounds.

Meanwhile, in the Giro, there's a breakaway. Thirteen riders get clear early on and build a big lead, which the peloton shows little enthusiasm for reducing, especially after a crash leaves Primož Roglič with a big tear in the arse of his shorts. With about 30 kilometres remaining, two Italians, Valerio Conti and Fausto Masnada, break away from the rest and commit fully to the effort. Conti knows the pink jersey will be his and so Masnada can be confident of being allowed to win the stage. With this agreement apparent to all, the pair trade turns all the way to the line.

Masnada rides for Gianni Savio's Androni Giocattoli–Sidermec team and so a stage victory is more than enough to justify their wild card place in the race for another couple of years. Savio, the silver fox of Italian cycling, is one of the Giro's most charming characters. He's in his early seventies but could easily pass for 60. He usually pairs a smart suit with an open-neck shirt and box-fresh trainers and, having seen him out running, I reckon he could beat me over five kilometres.

Savio has been running cycling teams for more than 25 years. He's old school, in the sense that he recognises that having a high profile himself brings in the sponsors, and so he never turns down the opportunity when there's a television camera or microphone around. After every stage, he strolls round the pressroom, chatting to journalists.

Daniel considers him to be an avuncular uncle and will often tease him about his team tactics. 'What's your formation today, Gianni?' he'll typically ask, and Savio will play along, comparing a cycling team's line-up to that of a football team. Today, he gave Masnada a free-role and it paid off handsomely. Tomorrow, he might go for a more conventional 3-3-2 formation. Who knows with Padre Gianni?

The team's primary sponsor, Androni Giocattoli, is a chain of Italian toyshops, which seems appropriate because there's something slightly Father Christmas-y about Savio. But behind the smile and the twinkle in his eye, there's a shrewd operator too. It's easy to mock the dozens of company logos on the team bus but he's developed a savvy business model. He spots young talent, most notably in South America, persuades the riders to sign long contracts, and then sells them on. In recent years he has struck gold with Egan Bernal and Ivan Sosa, who are both now at Team Ineos. Rumours are already circulating that Masnada will go to CCC next season.

The break has shunted the top 10 riders in the general classification down a bit and, with a lead of 1:41, Valerio Conti can look forward to spending at least the weekend in pink. Roglič is still the leader in the clubhouse, as Daniel puts it, as his advantage over everyone who really counts is unchanged.

Once we've recorded the podcast, Simon the photographer and I are in a hurry to get on the road. I'm leaving Daniel to his own devices for the weekend because I'm making a whistle-stop return home to see my team, Watford, take on Manchester City in the FA Cup final.

As I bid farewell to Daniel he nods towards the church. 'Have you said a little prayer?' he asks, presumably referring to the Androni Giocattoli–Sidermec versus Team Ineos-style clash at Wembley.

'Oh don't worry,' I quip, 'I'm sure the podcast is in very safe hands.'

Friday, 17 May

Stage 7: Vasto–L'Aquila, 185 km
Stage winner: Pello Bilbao
Pink jersey: Valerio Conti

Saturday, 18 May

Stage 8: Tortoreto Lido–Pesaro, 239 km
Stage winner: Caleb Ewan
Pink jersey: Valerio Conti

It's Saturday afternoon – FA Cup final day – and the Giro d'Italia is due to arrive in Pesaro.

Watford has five twin towns. Mainz in Germany, Nanterre in France,

Novgorod in Russia, Wilmington in Delaware, US of A. And – wait for it – Pesaro in Italy.

I mean, if that isn't an omen, what is?

On the day Watford play in the FA Cup final for only the second time, the Giro d'Italia will reach one of its twin towns.

It's meant to be, surely?

Final score: Watford 0, Manchester City 6.

Oh well, back to the cycling.

Sunday, 19 May

Stage 9: Riccione–San Marino time trial, 34.8 km
Stage winner: Primož Roglič
Pink jersey: Valerio Conti

My alarm goes off at 4.30am, a taxi arrives half an hour later to take me to the airport and I arrive back in Bologna later that morning with a bump, nine days after I first landed here. It's pretty surreal that the Giro has been going on for more than a week and it's back (almost) where it started.

I take a taxi to the railway station and then buy a ticket for the train to Rimini. There's only a €4 difference between a second- and first-class ticket so I decide to treat myself, only to discover, once on board, that there's absolutely no difference between the second- and first-class carriages.

Daniel picks me up at the station and I resist the urge to make a comment about the state of the back seat of the car, which is covered with his running kit and scrunched up newspapers. We drive through heavy rain into San Marino, then get drenched walking a few hundred metres from the car to the pressroom.

Only the early starters in the time trial avoid the heavy rain and for a long while it looks like the World Hour Record holder and European time trial champion Victor Campenaerts will win the stage. And he might well have done but for a mishap in the final 1,500 metres on the climb towards the line. During a gear change, the Belgian's chain falls off. Because the road is uphill to the finish, Campenaerts's mechanic gives him his road bike instead of the back-up time trial machine. Unfortunately, the chain on the road bike is set in the big ring, making it difficult for Campenaerts to get going again. To make matters worse, his mechanic has turned away to pick up the time trial bike, leaving it to a spectator to give Campenaerts a push off. It's difficult to know for sure how much time this costs him, but it's likely to have been more than the 11 seconds Primož Roglič ends up beating him by.

Speaking after the finish, Roglič sympathises with Campenaerts but points out that the Belgian rode in better conditions whereas he was rained on from start to finish. That makes Roglič's victory all the more impressive and does nothing to change my opinion that the Giro is his to lose. Although Valerio Conti has defended the pink jersey and still leads Roglič by a minute and 50 seconds, the Slovenian has hammered everyone. Nibali is a minute slower, Carapaz is almost two minutes down, Landa and Yates over three.

Having got soaked standing at the finish line waiting for the riders, Daniel and I decide to get out of San Marino and try to find a warm bar in which to record the podcast. This is the first in a series of mistakes which end up costing us dearly. In fact, we have a bit of a Campenaerts ourselves.

Failing to spot a suitable recording venue on our journey, we drive the best part of an hour towards Riccione and end up in a hotel bar. I'm conscious that time is ticking on and so I hurriedly set up the recording equipment and we start to review the stage. It's a lively episode, fuelled partly by the fact I've been up since the early hours after the hectic return trip home.

I upload the audio files and Daniel and I begin to contemplate our dinner plans when our producer Tom sends a message to say that there's something wrong with the files we've sent. Tentatively, I listen. It sounds like Daniel and I have recorded the episode using a couple of yoghurt pots and a length of string. I check the settings on the recorder and a sinking feeling sweeps over me as I realise I'd been recording using the wrong mic ports.

The look on my face says it all.

'What's wrong?' asks Daniel.

'Er… The podcast hasn't recorded properly.'

To be fair to Daniel, he takes it very well. We record again, sharper and more urgently this time, and he winds up by explaining that the restaurant he had planned to visit has closed, before running through a list of the delights and delicacies we now won't be enjoying.

Instead, we end up in a pretty ordinary pizzeria where we see Mitchelton–Scott's sports director Matt White, who admits that after losing another three minutes the race for the pink jersey is over for Simon Yates. Perhaps that's why White is nursing a large glass of red.

It's gone midnight when we get in the car for the 10-minute drive to our hotel in Gradara. It's not until we've been driving 20 minutes that I realise we're heading in the wrong direction. Unbelievably, according to our sat-nav at least, there are two towns called Gradara a little way from each other. I swing the car round and we drive in silence to our hotel where the owner, who has been waiting up for us, checks us in with barely a word.

Fortunately, it's a rest day tomorrow.

Monday, 20 May

Rest day

Our plan is to drive to Cesenatico, Marco Pantani's home town, and head straight to the museum that houses a shrine to his life and career but, after dropping in to the Mitchelton–Scott team's hotel for Simon Yates's informal meeting with the media, we're rushing to make it before the museum closes for a three-hour lunch break.

If you want to visit it, the museum is more or less next to the railway station. It features two main rooms named after the great mountains of the Giro d'Italia and Tour de France that Pantani conquered: the Mortirolo and Alpe d'Huez.

Each room is an Aladdin's cave of trophies, bikes, jerseys and memories. There's Pantani's first racing bike, a steel Vicini dated 1982, and large woollen jerseys from his junior and amateur career that must've swamped him like a child wearing a duffel coat. The memorabilia from his professional career also look dated now. The sky blue and yellow Bianchi bike and *maillot jaune* from the 1998 Tour de France are 21 years old now, of course. In one of the rooms, a huge TV shows race highlights and news reports. The walls are plastered with photographs and newspaper cuttings and there's a surreal painting of Pantani being thrown backwards while riding a fierce looking Roman bull that has bicycle wheels attached to its legs. It's striking but it's not exactly a Caravaggio.

Pantani's legacy troubles me. I started working in cycling journalism in August 1998, in the immediate aftermath of the Festina Affair which exposed the extent of organised doping in the peloton. Even then, eyebrows were raised at the idea that the swashbuckling Italian was the saviour of the Tour. The following year, he was kicked out of the Giro at Madonna di Campiglio after trouncing everyone in the mountains and having been just a couple days from clinching overall victory. The way he climbed was undoubtedly exciting. He gripped the drops of the handlebars and rode out of the saddle for so long it was almost like watching an escapologist holding his breath during a death-defying underwater stunt. But it was only a mat-ter of time before it was revealed to be fuelled by doping.

I am struck by how old Pantani looked as a boy in the photos. He was already balding in his teens and clung onto the dark back and sides for too long. His big ears meant he was given the unflattering nickname Elefantino, the little elephant, before he reinvented himself as il Pirata – the Pirate – by shaving his head and wearing a brightly coloured bandana and hooped earrings. When I study the photographs I sense the same vulnerability in all of them, although that could be because I know how Pantani's story ended. The performance-enhancing drugs, the depression, the cocaine, the hurt, and the lonely death at the age of 34 in a hotel room in Rimini.

Our next stop is the Piadineria Pantani, the family-owned sandwich shop right at the other end of Cesenatico, where Daniel hopes to talk to Marco's sister, who runs the place. I am already nervous about the intrusion because I imagine that the Pantani family have been visited by enough journalists and camera crews since he died on Valentine's Day in 2004.

Pantani's sister is friendly but reserved and says she'd prefer not to talk about her brother or cycling, which I am secretly quite glad about, so we sit down and order a *piadina*, which is a grilled flatbread sandwich. Mine is filled with sausage and caramelised onion.

As we eat, a man at the next table – who looks so similar to Pantani I am convinced it could be his older brother or a cousin – eyes me suspiciously. I am worried that the presence of two journalists from the Giro has caused a stir in the cafe. I nudge Daniel and whisper that I'm getting eyeballed.

Daniel sparks up a conversation and it turns out the man is not related to the Pantani family at all, which stuns me because it seems almost impossi-ble. The reason he's been staring over at us is because he thinks I'm Bjarne Riis, the 1996 Tour de France winner.

For a moment I'm almost flattered...

After lunch we head on to Ravenna, where we are staying. I go for an early evening run round the town and discover why it is so popular with tourists. This feels like the real Giro at last. Later, Daniel and I stroll back into town to record our rest day press conference episode, answering ques-tions from the listeners, and at dinner I order what I hope will be a delicate dish of pork loin for the main course. It follows a sharing selection of really excellent pasta dishes and so by the time it arrives I am already quite full. The dish turns out to be a huge chunk of pork leg clinging for dear life to the bone. It's the sort of thing you might throw to a particularly large and fierce dog and I neither relish nor finish it.

Tuesday, 21 May

Stage 10: Ravenna–Modena, 145 km
Stage winner: Arnaud Démare
Pink jersey: Valerio Conti

It's a short, flat stage, which means a late start and plenty of time to enjoy a leisurely morning in Ravenna. I go for another run, enjoy a relaxed breakfast and then a coffee in the centre of town before strolling off to find the team buses. This is more like it, I think.

This stretch of the Giro may feel more typical but there's definitely a sense of compromise about it too. This year's edition was supposed to start in Matera, right down south in Puglia, but there was some kind of fall-out over who was putting up the money and Bologna stepped in at relatively short notice. It means we have consecutive flat days across the plains of Emilia-Romagna to get within touching distance of the mountains. It also means there is barely a pimple on the course for two days, so we know we are in for a couple of sprint finishes.

At the start, I head to the Trek–Segafredo bus to see if I can have a word with their Dutch rider Bauke Mollema, who is up to 12th place overall after an excellent third place in the time trial. Considering Mollema's previous Grand Tour results include fourth place at the 2011 Vuelta a España (soon to be upgraded to third following winner Juan José Cobo's disqualification for doping), sixth place in the 2013 Tour and seventh at the 2015 Tour and 2017 Giro, I wonder whether he considers himself a serious contender for the podium. (Note: Mollema eventually finished the Giro in fifth place).

I ask the team's young press officer if it might be possible to have a word with Mollema.

'Has he won *Pédaleur de Charme*?' he asks hopefully.

'Er… no… not this time,' I say.

The press officer pops onto the bus and returns moments later.

'Bauke doesn't want to do any interviews this morning,' he says.

I had assumed, because today's stage promises to be relatively stress-free for a rider like Mollema, that he might be happy to talk but it turns out that on days like this he prefers to keep things as low-key as he possibly can. It seems counter-intuitive but, I'm told, Mollema would be more likely to speak to the media before a big mountain stage when he knows he has to be switched on for the race. I can see the logic in that.

On the way to Modena we stop at the motorway services and, seeing the big sign for the Fatti Furbo Maxi meal deal offer, I notice Daniel hang back and take his phone out of his pocket in the hope he can get a picture of me in front of it.

The joke's on Daniel because I actually don't enjoy what Fatti Furbo has to offer. The pizza bases are thick and doughy and the toppings too sparse. The bolognese-filled *arancini* are claggy and under-seasoned, but I order one anyway.

The stage is leisurely. At times the riders in the peloton are almost squeezing the brakes to avoid catching the escapees. Things hot up at the finish, though, and a bad crash rules out Pascal Ackermann. Frenchman Arnaud Démare wins the sprint and by luck, rather than design, Daniel and I speak to nearly all of his Groupama–FDJ teammates about the lead-out, which our producer edits together into a neat montage that tells the story of the sprint.

There's another heavy rain shower but as we leave Modena the skies brighten to reveal a stunning rainbow that I choose to interpret as a tribute to Niki Lauda, who died yesterday. We're deep in Ferrari country here – the team's base is 20 kilometres down the road in Maranello – and Lauda won two of his Formula One world titles in their famous red livery, breaking an 11-year drought for them in 1975. Throughout the afternoon, I've noticed dozens of people wearing Ferrari baseball caps, jackets or T-shirts.

Wednesday, 22 May

Stage 11: Carpi–Novi Ligure, 221 km
Stage winner: Caleb Ewan
Pink jersey: Valerio Conti

I'm always suspicious when I check into a hotel and the heating is on in the room, as it was last night. This morning, I wake up with a ticklish cough and the scent of damp in my nostrils. The hotel is in a sturdy-looking building but it's obvious the flat lands of Emilia-Romagna are prone to flooding. After all, they grow rice in these parts. I suspect keeping the moisture out of the thick, old stone walls is an impossible job.

Last night we were welcomed with a large gin and tonic and recorded the podcast as half a dozen or so cats lapped round our feet and jumped on the table. The owner told us that only two of the cats belonged to him.

Three of them started visiting after an earthquake in the region a few years ago and one of them comes every May for three weeks' holiday but does not so much as pop in at any other time. Disconcertingly, one cat is missing its tail and another has a nasty-looking sore behind its ear.

This morning I wake up to see two cats curled up at the end of my bed. You've guessed it, my two lodgers are the tail-less one and the wounded one. Suddenly I feel a bit itchy. I have no idea how they got into my room because to the best of my knowledge they weren't there when I got back from dinner last night and none of the windows were left open.

Yesterday morning, in Ravenna, we had our pre-race coffee in a little independent cafe that just happened to be called Costa Cafe. Today in Carpi, I notice we are in Caffè Nero. What next, I ask Daniel, a trip to Starbucks? He rolls his eyes for the first time in a few days.

The stage is again uneventful but the finish line is a couple of hundred metres from the large Villa Coppi, once home to the legendary Fausto, now lived in by his son, Faustino. The villa is a grand building but the trees have enveloped it giving it a dark, almost haunted quality, and the brickwork and grounds could do with a tidy up. We record the opening section of the podcast outside the villa and then head to Novi Ligure and a museum dedicated to Fausto's life and career to do the rest.

The museum is actually a celebration of Italian cycling in general and my eye is drawn to the bike Francesco Moser used to attempt the hour record in 1988. With its huge rear disc wheel, steeply sloped top tube and upturned 'cow horn'-style handlebars, it looks almost impossible to ride but Moser managed to exceed 50 kilometres, even though he fell short of his existing record set four years earlier.

Once we've wrapped up the episode, we head to what turns out to be the finest hotel and meal the 2019 Giro d'Italia has to offer. It's on the hillside in Barbaresco, surrounded by vineyards. The wine, made with Nebbiolo grapes, is lighter, softer than its more famous near-neighbour Barolo. It goes equally well with my first course of ravioli with butter and nutty, woody black truffle and my main course of rolled, stuffed rabbit, also with black truffle. What is staggering, though, is the price. I'm speculating here, but a meal like this would cost three or four times more in the UK but we pay not much more than you'd expect to part with in one of the more upmarket chain restaurants in Britain and yet it is a meal that hits the heights.

Thursday, 23 May

Stage 12: Cuneo–Pinerolo, 158 km
Stage winner: Cesare Benedetti
Pink jersey: Jan Polanc

We're past the halfway mark and yet there's a sense that no one is really holding the reins in this Giro. The Jumbo–Visma team does not appear to be all that strong. They lost the talented climbing *domestique* Laurens De Plus through illness at the end of the first week. Richard, who returned to the race today, teases me that De Plus's illness was my fault because I kept him chatting in the cold as the sun dipped behind the basilica after the opening time trial.

Truth be told, Jumbo–Visma have no obligation to keep an iron-grip on things because Roglič is not wearing the pink jersey, although they are secure in the knowledge that his major opponents are minutes behind. However, there's the looming sense that all the most difficult stages are to come.

Today's stage is eventful but afterwards it's tricky to analyse what it all means. Twenty-five riders break away early on and open a big gap. UAE Team Emirates appear unconcerned about chasing to protect Valerio Conti's overall lead because they have Jan Polanc in the break and know he stands to inherit the pink jersey at the end of the day.

The gap between the break and the bunch stretches to more than 12 minutes at one stage so all eyes are on the race for the stage victory. Things burst into life on the Montoso, the first category one climb of the Giro, as five riders break clear. They split up as they hit the final cobbled hill and it appears to be a head-to-head scrap between two Italians – Gianluca Brambilla of Trek–Segafredo and Eros Capecchi of Deceuninck–Quick-Step. Ireland's Eddie Dunbar reaches them on the descent and for a short while the trio look to be in the clear. But they do not reckon on Damiano Caruso of Bahrain–Merida and Cesare Benedetti of Bora–Hansgrohe getting across to them in the final kilometre.

I am standing under the gazebo just past the finish line, watching on the television with other journalists and the team *soigneurs*. I don't mind admitting that as soon as Benedetti bridges the gap, I am rooting for him to win the stage. Yesterday, we released an episode of *Kilometre 0* called *Hail Cesare!* which looked at the role of one of the most respected but unheralded support riders in the peloton. The subject, 32-year-old Cesare Benedetti. In 20 minutes or so listening to him, his teammates and sports director talk about his role as the Bora–Hansgrohe road captain I feel I've got to know him a little bit. In

10 years as a professional, he has never won a race (apart from a couple of team time trials). His job is to work for others, look out for his teammates on the road, provide the link between the leaders and the sports directors when tactics have to be decided. And here he is, 500 metres away from winning a stage of his home Grand Tour. Make than 400 metres... 300...

Benedetti goes early, as if he knows this chance may never come his way again, surging to the front and sprinting in what looks like a huge gear. I never cheer for riders but I don't mind admitting that I did a discreet little fist pump when Benedetti crossed the line first. As I walk back to the press-room, I check Twitter and I'm taken aback by how many of our listeners were also cheering on Benedetti after hearing him on the podcast.

The other story that has re-emerged is the Operation Aderlass (which means Bloodletting) doping scandal, focusing on a German doctor and several Slovenian riders. With two Slovenians occupying first and second place overall it's an important story and after the stage Daniel interviews the only Slovenian reporter working on the race to find out more. There's no suggestion that either Polanc or Roglič are anything to do with it but Kristijan Koren, a Slovenian riding for Bahrain–Merida, was pulled out of the Giro early on after being linked to the doctor in question. Borut Božič, a sports director at Bahrain–Merida, and a coach called Milan Eržen, who has an unofficial role at the team, are also said to be involved. Croatian Kristijan Đurasek of UAE Team Emirates is provisionally suspended and we already knew that Stefan Denifl, a stage winner at the 2017 Vuelta, and Georg Preidler, a teammate of Tom Dumoulin's when he won the Giro, were implicated. I'm all over the details, of course, incorrectly calling it Operation Anderlass throughout the podcast.

Friday, 24 May

Stage 13: Pinerolo–Ceresole Reale, 196 km
Stage winner: Ilnur Zakarin
Pink jersey: Jan Polanc

We're right in the north-west corner of the Italian Alps. As the crow flies, we're only about 15 kilometres away from Tignes, where stage 19 of the Tour de France is due to finish later this summer. At last, almost two weeks in, the Giro has reached the proper mountains.

The mayor has laid on polenta for lunch for the journalists and staff working on the race in a little dining room close to the pressroom at the bottom of the Colle del Nivolet so we're well-fed before we take the shuttle bus up to the finish.

We stand under the impressive dam wall and Daniel tells me the incredible story of a Northumberland Fusilier called Alfred Southern, who was one of 39 who escaped from a prisoner of war camp in November 1944 hoping to make it to Val d'Isère. The group split up and many of the men slipped to their death, others perished in the cold and only Alfred survived. I'm on fire at the moment because I end our recording calling him Albert. I'll put it down to the altitude, because we're at well over 2,000 metres.

I forget to mention that Ceresole Reale, where the stage finishes, was also the location for the cliffhanger ending of the 1969 film *The Italian Job*, in which Michael Caine and his gang of thieves are left teetering on the brink in a bus.

Today is the day the Giro comes alive, or at least opens its eyes. Ilnur Zakarin wins the stage for the beleaguered Katusha–Alpecin team – it's only their third World Tour victory in 20 months – and soars to third place overall, now only 31 seconds behind Roglič. I see Katusha's sports director, Dimitri Konyshev, who is delighted by the stage win but doubtful about Zakarin's chances of challenging overall. I wonder if it's a double-bluff because Zakarin has podium pedigree in the Grand Tours and, at the very least, is a dangerous man to let back into the picture.

Polanc has lost time but keeps hold of the pink jersey, although it's surely only a matter of time before it passes back to Roglič. Of more than minor concern to him would have been the time gained by the Movistar duo Mikel Landa and Richard Carapaz, who are both closing in a bit, although only at the pace of a pair playing a game of Grandmother's Footsteps at this point.

We record the podcast in a bar at the bottom of the mountain and by the time we've finished it's getting late. Daniel reveals that throughout the afternoon he's been receiving increasingly agitated messages from our host, who seems very anxious to know what time we'll be arriving for dinner.

'How far is it?' Daniel asks, as we set off.

'About an hour and 20 minutes,' I say.

'I'll tell him it's an hour.'

A few minutes later Daniel says, 'He says he'll wait for us before eating.'

This conjures an image in my mind of our host and his other guests sitting at the table waiting for the arrival of a shambolic trio who've been at the Giro d'Italia. I am already rehearsing my apologies for delaying their dinner.

The reality is much more disconcerting. We're the only guests. Our host is a short, bald, muscle-bound man in, I'd guess, his late 40s. There's an edgy atmosphere. Even Daniel, usually so at ease when we arrive at a guest-house or hotel late, seems uncomfortable.

'He says dinner will be served upstairs as soon as we're ready,' Daniel tells Richard and me, as we dump our bags.

I head up the staircase and poke my head round the door to what I assume is his private kitchen and living space.

'Oh, mi dispiace,' I say, thinking that I've intruded on his personal space.

But he waves his hand in the direction of the table and ushers me to sit down.

I wait for what feels like an uncomfortably long time before Richard and then Daniel arrive.

For once, I am glad I don't speak Italian because it leaves Daniel to do the heavy lifting. I can already tell conversation is going to be a struggle.

Nervously, I take in my surroundings. All the plates and cutlery on the table are plastic, which I think is a little odd. A giant television behind us shows some sort of terrible game show. It cuts from women in swimsuits and high heels singing karaoke to women in swimsuits and high heels trying to crawl the wrong way up a slide covered in gunge.

'He says this is the best programme in Italy,' says Daniel.

As he serves the food, our host has that insistent manner that makes me nervous that unless I express unbelievable delight at every mouthful he will take great offence, so I mmmm and aaah at every mouthful. To be fair, the meal he's laid on is perfectly nice, except for the lump of quivering tongue he demands I try.

Richard and I try to continue quiet conversation rather than sit in silence but that leaves Daniel to keep things going with the Italian Bruce Willis look-a-like. I can tell things keep hitting the occasional bump and later learn of our host's displeasure whenever Daniel suggested that immigration and not being white weren't terrible things. Even I picked up on the statement that there was such a thing as 'good Europe' and 'bad Europe'.

At the end of dinner, and after a *digestif* it felt unwise to decline, he shows us his gun. A replica, apparently, although I didn't fancy hanging around long enough to find out.

Once we've been excused, we scurry downstairs and along the corridor.

'Make sure you lock your door, Napalm,' says Daniel.

Saturday, 25 May

Stage 14: Saint-Vincent–Courmayeur, 131 km
Stage winner: Richard Carapaz
Pink jersey: Richard Carapaz

After sleeping with my eyes open and my suitcase pushed up against the door, I rise early and go for a run. In daylight I notice that this beautiful property – a lovingly restored old mill with the milling stones still in place – is surrounded by an unnecessarily tall metal fence with sharp edges on the top. It's also guarded by CCTV cameras. Something tells me our host has a thing about his security.

At breakfast, I notice there are wooden bowls in the centre of every table. The edge of the bowl on our table has broken off. It was like that when we arrived.

After serving coffee, our host notices the broken bowl.

'Who did this?' he asks Daniel in Italian.

Instinctively I know what he's asked and say, 'Tell him it was like that when we arrived.'

He sweeps the bowl and its broken lip away with a passive-aggressive huff.

I visualise him holding me responsible for the breakage, squeezing my neck and saying, 'If only people would respect other people's things we wouldn't have all this nasty business, would we?'

There's a TV in the corner of the room showing a film about the history of the mill but I'm no longer in the mood to make appreciative noises, I just want to get out of there.

Today is a day to concentrate on the race anyway. It feels like the ground-work for an overall battle was laid yesterday and although today's course is not as hard, I have a feeling the hangover from yesterday's efforts may catch out a few. We learn pretty early on that Konyshev was not bluffing about Zakarin. The Russian clearly went deep yesterday because he loses more than seven minutes.

The star of the show is the Ecuadorian, Richard Carapaz, who sails to the stage win. We watch and count down the seconds as he takes the pink jersey from Primož Roglič by a fine margin. Carapaz's overall advantage is only seven seconds but when I see Roglič's face after he crosses the line the Tour de Romandie and the Giro's opening time trial that he dominated so completely suddenly feel a very long time ago. The Movistar rider's quiet threat can be ignored no longer.

Remembering the 2016 Giro, I still feel Vincenzo Nibali can make up a minute and 47 seconds in the final week, and Mikel Landa might not be out of it, but for now the Giro looks to be about two men whose form is heading in two very different directions.

I head to the team buses to speak to sports director Max Sciandri, who left BMC for the mañana world of Movistar at the start of the year and seems to be loving it.

Earlier in the day, we saw the times for yesterday's final climb, which told us that Carapaz was the quickest. I ask Max about this. 'Yeah, yeah, I talked to him about this. I said to him at the time trial in Bologna that he was the fastest on the climb. We knew if we could get him out there he could climb. We've got some hard stages in the mountains to come but altitude is no problem for him, he was born at 2,800 metres or something.

'He hasn't done much recon of the course so every morning I make sure he's on the iPad looking at the information we've prepared. He's a super quiet guy. On one of the stages, which one was it…? It was raining, but that doesn't narrow it down. I hear this voice on the radio,' Sciandri adopts a small, meek voice, '"Por favor, tengo frio [I'm cold]." He wants his jacket, you know?'

'When was the last time a rider said please when they asked for a jacket?' I say.

'Never,' jokes Sciandri. 'Where I've come from it would be: "Bring me the jacket. Now." Now he's in pink let's see what's going to happen.'

Finally I ask Sciandri about Movistar's reputation for chaotic, contradictory race tactics, where they seem to work against each other, or at least collaborate in unconventional ways. 'What's different here? Is it the riders? Is it the personnel?' I ask.

'I don't want to say it's me,' says Sciandri, saying it's him, 'but the other day I came to the dinner table and the guys said, "Cheers to the new director". I don't want to say it's me but I really work on balancing out the team. If you work in a happy environment how much more can you give, you know?'

Our guesthouse could not be more different to last night's – a charming place run by a man who works in the merchant navy based in Genoa and who spends a lot of time in Plymouth. He points us in the direction of a pizzeria for dinner and insists we sample a little from each of the bottles of grappa in his drawing room when we return.

Sunday, 26 May

Stage 15: Ivrea–Como, 232 km
Stage winner: Dario Cataldo
Pink jersey: Richard Carapaz

At the start, I head to the Team Ineos bus where I see Dave Brailsford. We talk about the contrasting fortunes for his two young riders. Tao Geoghegan Hart crashed and pulled out of the race a couple of days ago having seen his Russian teammate Pavel Sivakov begin to come into his own. Sivakov, the son of two former professional riders, Alexei Sivakov and Alexandra Koliaseva, is up to eighth overall. Eddie Dunbar has also impressed although the much-heralded Iván Sosa has been quiet.

'These lads put so much pressure on themselves,' says Brailsford. 'The team here has such a different feel to it and part of our job has been to maintain the overall framework of the team but hand the responsibility for the culture to the lads. This is not G or Froomey's team, it's their team.'

I ask about the decision to put so many of the younger riders together as a group for the Giro without an established leader. It feels a bit like Manchester City picking a young side for FA Cup matches, I say, although there's no sign of them winning 6-0 yet.

'Yeah, I suppose it is,' says Brailsford. 'You've got to give young people the space to see what they can do. If there was an older rider here going for sixth or eighth would we be able to give the lads the chance to work things out for themselves or would we fall for the pressure of trying to defend that place? We've got Christian Knees, who sets the tone and keeps them calm, but really we want to see what they can do.'

I have a quick conversation with Team Ineos's Ecuadorian rider Jhonatan Narváez, who is 22 and riding his first Grand Tour. He can only guess how big the news that Carapaz is in pink will be back home but he talks eloquently about how the cyclists in Ecuador take inspiration from the success of riders from neighbouring Colombia.

Richard strolls over and before we move on, Brailsford takes a step closer, lowers his voice and says, 'You know we've signed Carapaz for next year.'

It's a juicy gem but, when it comes to transfer gossip, I am wary of being a pawn in the game. A deal to take Carapaz from Movistar to Ineos may or may not have been agreed in principal but we're reluctant to break the news for two reasons. If it turns out not to be true it'll be a repeat of Richard's much-heralded 'Geraint Thomas to BMC Racing' rumour. Alternatively, having the news out there might be Brailsford's way of applying pressure to Movistar, or Carapaz's agent. We decide to sit on it for a few days and mull over our options.

The final 70 kilometres or so resemble the classic Giro di Lombardia course, with the climbs of the Madonna del Ghisallo and the Sormano to tackle before the Civiglio and the run-in to the shore of Lake Como.

All hell breaks loose in the final hour of racing. Roglič suffers a crash and a mechanical, or is it two crashes? Standing outside the Jumbo–Visma bus all I know for sure is he's crossed the line 40 seconds behind Carapaz. His Giro is going downhill faster than an Olympic ski jumper. (Come on, there had to be one!)

Details are sparse at first but after his crash he took his teammate Antwan Tolhoek's bike. Riding an ill-fitting bike, he was unable to respond properly when the other favourites started attacking. I'm standing with other journalists trying to piece together what's happened.

It turns out that at Roglič's moment of need, the Jumbo–Visma team car was nowhere to be seen. They'd stopped because their sports director Jan Boven needed a wee. Both Boven and his fellow sports director Addy Engels are sheepish at the finish, reluctant to reveal all the details. Then, to add to the drama, it emerges that Movistar's Max Sciandri had picked up Roglič's bike, loaded it onto the roof of the team car, and took it to the finish.

In the podcast, Daniel is aghast that the team car would stop to answer a call of nature. 'They're not children!' he says. 'Couldn't they have waited?'

'But if you've got to go, you've got to go,' I say.

I suggest that Boven perhaps should have gone in a bidon, but as he was driving that probably wasn't practical.

'The thing is,' says Richard, restoring some sanity to the debate, 'it probably didn't make any difference anyway. Roglič took Tolhoek's bike because it was the quickest thing to do. If he'd waited for the team car, he'd have lost more time.'

'But he could have got his spare bike a few kilometres later,' I suggest before saying, 'Oh, I don't know…'

And that's the truth of it. We'll probably never know.

by Richard Moore

Monday, 27 May

Rest day, Fonteno

I wake up early to grey skies and rain in what feels like a monastery on a hill – in fact it's a 17th-century farmhouse – and grab a quick breakfast from the slightly austere dining room where we'd eaten the previous evening. First task of the day is to drive Lionel to the airport, Malpensa, an hour away.

When I return it's still early enough for a second breakfast. What a way to honour Lionel on the day of his departure.

After breakfast No.2 Daniel and I hatch a rest day gameplan. We plan to go to some team hotels, starting with Bora–Hansgrohe and CCC, then on to Jumbo–Visma, Trek–Segafredo and Groupama–FDJ. It's chucking it down. Not just raining, but sheets of water cascading from the skies. Perhaps the weather is partly to blame but the Bora–Hansgrohe and CCC hotel is truly depressing: an Italian motel with no real common area other than a tiny breakfast room. The riders sit on their turbo trainers on their tiny verandahs, pedalling away like hamsters, looking glum.

The glamour of professional cycling.

From the riders' hotels in grim, wet Zingonia – which on the podcast Daniel describes as 'the Compton of greater Bergamo', upsetting Marco Pinotti, who lives locally – we drive into the hills of Lombardy to our hotel. Oh, how I wish we'd sacked off the team hotels. The Hotel Ristorante Panoramico is a *hacienda* perched on a ledge overlooking the magnificent Lake Iseo. The rain has now stopped and low, thick cloud hangs over the water; on the other side of the lake, we can discern disembodied parts of mountain. Patches of dark land and rocky peaks appear and disappear in the gloom. It's ghostly and beautiful.

We record our *Press Conference* episode on the verandah, a world away from the terrible hotels in rotten neighbourhoods where the teams are staying. We briefly ponder the injustice of this. But only very briefly, because the owner appears with two beers and a large bowl of crisps.

Four cats materialise, slinking out of the bushes. They are sleek and graceful as they rub against our legs, jump effortlessly onto the table, scratch their mouths on the edge of my laptop – and make for the crisps! I grab the bowl but trying to stop them getting at them, especially once we start recording the episode, is, well, you know the line. When one of our feline friends – I'm not sure whether it was Dario *Cat*aldo or Mattia *Cat*taneo – is successful in sneaking off with a crisp. I describe the scene for the listeners, perhaps with some embellishment.

This provokes an email from a listener:

Hello,

I'm a big fan of the podcast. I've been a Friend for two or three years (and am waiting for my name to be read out).

BUT...

There I was, out on my bike, listening back to the Press Conference (episode 55) on the second rest day of the Giro, with Richard and Daniel stuck inside with a horde of cats. All very lovely, UNTIL YOU DECIDED TO TIP YOUR CRISPS ON THE FLOOR AND LET THE CAT EAT THEM.

Take it from me, I'm a veterinary surgeon: cats should not eat crisps.

You guys have done an amazing job to build a platform, with a growing audience and industry recognition. That means you have influence – and with that platform and influence comes responsibility. So when you jokingly talk about a cat noisily eating your crisps while you are recording, you're forgetting that cats are obligate carnivores, will struggle to digest potato crisps, and really shouldn't have such fatty, salty food. Considering that a cat weighs less than 4kg and you weigh around 80kg (just guessing – the cat is probably lighter), that means one crisp for the cat is equivalent to 20 crisps for you. So about one crisp for the cat = a whole packet for you. How many crisps did that poor cat eat?

Please, pretty please, with a cherry and all, could you alert your listeners to the fact that cats really should not eat crisps? Or, at the very least, please think carefully before putting feline dietary ideas into the heads of your legion of devoted listeners.

Of whom,
I remain,
Your loyal Friend,
Adi.

I reply:

Hi Adi,

Thanks for the email and kind comments about the podcast – very much appreciated.

We had a few comments about the 'cats eating crisps' episode (cat-crispgate), though none from as qualified an authority. I have to respond to try and set the record straight. I think one of the (four) cats sneaked a crisp, but I can assure you that we did not feed the crisps to the cats – on the contrary, we did EVERYTHING we feasibly and physically could to keep cats and crisps apart. It was like herding cats away from a large bowl of crisps – impossible.

In suggesting in the podcast that the cats were happily scoffing our crisps we may have been guilty, I am afraid, of exaggerating for comic effect. We soon had cause to regret this. As I say, one of the cats did manage to steal a crisp, but that was the extent of it.

That said, I would be lying if I claimed that my concern at the time was with the health of the cats. The truth is that it had been a long day and I really like crisps.

And I know that crisps are not good for humans, even those of us who weigh 80kg (give or take 18kg).

Thanks again and best wishes,
Richard

Tuesday, 28 May

Stage 16: Lovere–Ponte di Legno, 194 km
Winner: Giulio Ciccone
Pink jersey: Richard Carapaz

With the cloud having more or less cleared we can appreciate the view from our hotel at breakfast. The restaurant feels like a glass box suspended above the lake, over which a few wisps linger like the smoke from a recently fired gun.

On Twitter I post a picture of the stunning view from my room, artfully framed (in an effort to dispel Daniel's outrageous claim that I am 'not a visual person') by the window and the chair on my terrace.

'Podcasting pays well, eh?!' responds Joe Dombrowski, the EF Education First rider, which reminds me of our conversation about our hotels versus the riders. (For the record, our hotel was cheaper than Dombrowski's, but much nicer.)

Beneath Dombrowski's reply, someone else writes: 'Where are the cats?' Enough about the cats.

We almost miss the start after whizzing past the turnoff from the main road, then having to drive through a long tunnel before doubling back. We have to park high up in the village and walk to the start – it doesn't look far on Google Maps, and it isn't, but what Google Maps doesn't adequately convey is the extremely steep hill.

Following the start Daniel discloses that he's left the hotel with his room key. The people were so nice that we feel duty-bound to return. This means we almost miss the finish, too.

The clear weather is the very definition of a false dawn. The dark clouds return with a vengeance and the stage is almost a washout. It had already been shortened, with the decision taken on the rest day to avoid the Gavia due to the risk of avalanches. It still leaves the Mortirolo close to the finish and it's dark and raining heavily as the riders tackle this monster, giving us some dramatic images, especially as Vincenzo Nibali does what he does so well – attacking in swashbuckling style. His legs glisten in the rain and water drips from his beak-like nose. The big surprise is that the rider able to counter and bridge up to The Shark of Messina is the Lanky Lancastrian, Hugh Carthy.

It's wet and dark at the finish and Daniel and I huddle beneath an umbrella generously shared by Thomas Dekker, the former rider working for Dutch TV. Watching the race on a small television, Dekker dissects it in forensic and fascinating detail. He feels that Roglič, perhaps through inexperience, hasn't formed enough alliances in the first week or so; he could have joined forces more fruitfully with Nibali, for instance, to gain time over Carapaz and Movistar. Then again, Nibali seemed a more likely rival than Carapaz at the start of the race.

Perhaps a subtext to Dekker's critique is that Roglič rides for the latest incarnation of Dekker's old team (Rabobank), an experience that came to a bitter end when he tested positive for EPO.

Rumours are swirling around Carapaz and his future with Movistar, meanwhile. Today, *Gazzetta dello Sport* write that he could join Team Ineos at the end of the season. In fact, we mentioned this very possibility in the previous evening's podcast. Our source? Dave Brailsford. He mentioned casually to Lionel and me at a stage start a few days earlier that Carapaz would be joining Ineos in 2020. 'Movistar don't know yet,' he added.

Lionel and I had walked away scratching our heads. Why had Brailsford told us? We concluded that he could only have done so because he *wanted* the news to be made public. The fact he had prefixed it with, 'Keep this to yourselves, lads' was the giveaway. *He was using us*, we decided. Well, we wouldn't be used. We'd sit on it.

Until, well, I felt I couldn't sit on it any longer, particularly when I got wind of the fact that others – presumably journalists Brailsford had also 'confided' in ('Pssst, keep this to yourself, Ciro, but…') – were preparing to go public with the story.

Wednesday, 29 May

Stage 17: Commezzadura–Anterselva, 181 km
Winner: Nans Peters
Pink jersey: Richard Carapaz

In the morning I interview Larry Warbasse of Ag2r about his team's failure to win a stage in the Giro since 2011. Thus it is inevitable that an Ag2r rider will win today: Nans Peters, perhaps the least fancied rider in a large break that also includes Esteban Chaves and Davide Formolo, who are second and third respectively.

At the Jumbo–Visma bus at the end of the stage, Daniel is in the vicinity of a Slovenian fan hectoring Addy Engels, the team's sports director. 'I'm first Slovenian to drive around the world,' says the man. 'I'm Ironman. I'm cyclist. 'Rogla' is national hero and champion but please, he needs your help. He is alone. I know cycling. With Ineos he will be two minutes ahead of everyone. He needs help.'

Engels stands nodding politely, presumably biting his tongue.

We drive to our mountain hotel in the German-speaking part of Italy – always such a discombobulating experience that I think I comment on it every year, and imagine that I will carry on doing so. Because the people don't just speak German: they *are* German. They are certainly not Italian (yet they *are* actually Italian).

Tonight, we are hoping to be joined for dinner in our hotel by colleagues Caley Fretz of *CyclingTips* and Hannah Troop, press officer for EF

Education First. Both are staying nearby and say they'll drive over.

'The kitchen will close at 8.15pm,' we are told by the lady at reception as we check in. It is 8.05pm.

'But, can we…'

'No.'

Thursday, 30 May

Stage 18: Valdaora–Santa Maria di Sala, 222 km

Winner: Damiano Cima

Pink jersey: Richard Carapaz

'This is the story of cycling,' Francesco Pelosi, the suave, young general manager of Nippo–Vini Fantini, tells Daniel as he walks from the finish to the buses in Santa Maria di Sala. Pelosi is breathless. His rider, Damiano Cima, has just won the stage, justifying – well, justifying everything, really. It is a contrast to the start of their Giro, when one of their Japanese riders, Hiroki Nishimura, didn't make the time cut in the time trial in Bologna and was eliminated before the Giro had properly started.

That's what Pelosi means when he says it is the story of cycling. One day you're the cock of the walk, the next you're a feather duster, as Piers Morgan would say (of course, Nippo–Vini Fantini journeyed in the other direction).

Not sure we were ever the cock of the walk, but today we are definitely feather dusters. On our way to our hotel – more of a large B&B – Daniel phones to confirm everything: rooms, dinner (what a bonus: it has a restaurant). Normally these calls are routine and brief. This one isn't.

'*Cosa?*' said Daniel. '*No, stai scherzando!*'

He repeats words like this several times, hands fluttering and jabbing, while he gets louder and more aggressive until in the end he is shouting, red in the face, colouring the air blue.

'Problem?' I ask as he ends the call in a flurry of Italian swear words (nothing gets past me).

'She's overbooked.'

He immediately concludes that after accepting our booking and then learning that the Giro is in town our landlady realised she could hike up her prices. So she has reallocated our rooms but neglected to tell us. She tells Daniel she can make space for one but not two. She has taken the liberty of booking another room in a hotel around the corner. She will make it up to us, she promises: dinner is on her.

We decide to record the day's podcast there before I go and check into my hotel (which turns out not to be around the corner but 10 minutes' drive away). We sit on the terrace but there is music leaking from tinny speakers. Daniel asks the lady to turn it down. 'No problem!' she says, before appearing with a large bowl of crisps (I scan the area for cats). There follows a complimentary bottle of Prosecco, icy cold. She can't do enough for us. And dinner, which is good, is on the house.

All of which confirms Daniel's theory. The lengths to which she is going to appease us means that she definitely reallocated our rooms on realising she could let them out for considerably more money.

Friday, 31 May

Stage 19: Treviso–San Martino di Castrozzo, 151 km
Winner: Esteban Chaves
Pink jersey: Richard Carapaz

The stage starts outside the original Pinarello shop in Treviso, where the bike company is still based. Other famous brands that call this place home include Benetton, Geox and Diadora, to name a few. After the start, as we drive out of Treviso towards San Martino di Castrozzo, we pass a succession of ugly, modern, box-like buildings – factory outlets for these and other brands.

Daniel and I speed past them, including a dark grey box with 'Patagonia' on the wall. We drive on for about three minutes before Daniel breaks the silence: 'Shall we go back?'

It's a bit of a detour, up to the next roundabout, all the way round, all the way back, all the time thinking about all the lovely Patagonia gear we're going to buy at bargain prices. When the dark grey box reappears we turn into the small car park.

Closed for lunch.

We are in the Dolomites for a stage that promises much but delivers little, unless you are an Esteban Chaves fan (and let's face it, who isn't?). Chaves wins the stage.

We record the podcast at the Astana team hotel and, in a hushed voice, I suggest that one of the stories of this Giro is how disappointing they've been. For a team that has been on fire, winning stage races left, right and also centre, and having sent a very strong team here, they've been a bit of a shambles.

For those wanting to topple Carapaz – who, as we near Verona, appears surprisingly resolute for someone so inexperienced in this position – there isn't much time or road left. The Giro, as Daniel puts it in tonight's podcast, has 'whimpered towards its conclusion'.

Saturday, 1 June

Stage 20: Feltre-Croce d'Aune–Monte Avena, 194 km
Winner: Pello Bilbao
Pink jersey: Richard Carapaz

When I read Daniel's Giro hotels itinerary, the B&B Hemingway in Bassano del Grappa jumped out, as it would. I confess that Bassano del Grappa didn't ring any Hemingway-related bells, though it should have done. On my book-shelf I have *A Farewell to Arms* and *Across the River and Into the Trees*, both set when Hemingway was stationed in Bassano del Grappa during the First World War. In fact he stayed in the same street as us, hence our B&B's name. The building in which he lived, a few doors along, is now a Hemingway museum.

The opening passage from *Across the River and Into the Trees* describes the scene from my window: 'In the late summer of that year we lived in a house in a village that looked across the river and the plain to the mountains. In the bed of the river there were pebbles and boulders, dry and white in the sun, and the water was clear and swiftly moving and blue in the channels…' It continues with a beautiful description of the soldiers marching along the road, kicking up clouds of dust that 'powdered the leaves of the trees'.

Much to Daniel's (faux) horror I make it my mission to ask Larry Warbasse, a man from the Midwest like Hemingway, to recite the passage in full for the following night's podcast (not the first time Larry has played Hemingway on the podcast, having also done so at the Tour of the Basque Country in 2016).

I love Bassano del Grappa, partly for these tangible connections with Hemingway but also because the place itself is gorgeous, boasting Italy's second most famous and beautiful bridge, Ponte Vecchio (or Ponte degli Alpin), among other charms. Daniel and I go out for dinner to a restau-rant by the side of the 'clear and swiftly moving and blue in the channels' Brenta River, eating on the terrace but surrounded by empty tables and chairs. Where is everyone? Watching the Champions League final, explains our waiter. Afterwards, we go to a bar by the bridge and drink grappa. When in Bassano del Grappa etc.

Bassano del Grappa, and wallowing in a bit of Hemingway nostalgia, is certainly the highlight of the day. The stage was disappointing, the main talking point being Miguel Ángel 'Superman' López accosting a fan after he was knocked off his bike when the fan, and some others, got too close on a climb. In Glasgow parlance, Superman properly lamped him – though in Glasgow you might not encounter many assailants in turquoise lycra and cleated shoes.

Some observers cheer at the fan getting his comeuppance while others think López should be punished severely, even thrown off the race. Surprisingly, there is no retribution for Superman. Maybe the officials feel that he has suffered enough already in this Giro.

Sunday, 2 June

Stage 21: Verona–Verona time trial, 17 km
Winner: Chad Haga
Pink jersey: Richard Carapaz

A relaxing morning in Bassano del Grappa – exploring the Hemingway museum, in my case – before we head to Verona for the afternoon time trial.

En route to our Airbnb apartment – handily placed on the course of the time trial – we call in at at the stage start, where the buses are parked and the riders warm up. We have a couple of interviews to do, and I have Larry Warbasse to ambush. I set off for the buses with a copy of *Across the River and Into the Trees* (purchased in the museum) under my arm. He performs the task with aplomb. I bet Larry was – or could have been – the star of his high school plays.

I also want to see Mikkel Honoré, the 22-year-old Dane riding for Deceuninck–Quick-Step, one of several riders who'd ridden the Baby Giro only two years before making their debut at the senior race. The others are Pavel Sivakov (1st in the 2017 Baby Giro), Jai Hindley (3rd) and Scott Davies (4th); Honoré was 12th.

I don't have to wait long. Honoré steps off the bus and walks in the direction of a couple of girls standing near me. One, very tall (she's a basketball player), is his Italian girlfriend. Honoré stands chatting to the girls, looking content and happy. Fans approach and, although I wonder whether they can name him, ask him for a photo. He obliges, smiling for the picture. He must feel like the bee's knees.

And why shouldn't he? He's 22. He rides for one of the best teams in the world. He's about to finish his first Grand Tour and he's standing talking to his girlfriend, with whom he is clearly smitten (he mentioned earlier in the race that he was working hard to improve his Italian to be able to converse with her parents). If, in these circumstances, you can't allow yourself to feel happy with your lot, when can you? Who says he shouldn't enjoy the moment?

Rik Van Slycke, that's who. The grizzled Belgian, one of the Deceuninck–Quick-Step sports directors, pops his head out of the bus and squints his eyes as he scans the vicinity, clearly looking for someone. He spots Honoré and yells: 'Mikkel!... Mikkel! Here! Now!'

Honoré's face registers first shock then embarrassment and he beats a hasty retreat, scurrying into the bus. He is late for the team meeting. A team meeting for a time trial? What, to discuss tactics?

My sense is that teams work quite hard at keeping young riders in their place and their feet on the ground. Some of the more old school directors appear especially wary of young riders who, like Honoré, are bright, active on social media and good at talking to the media. Occasionally it looks like a deliberate attempt to humiliate, but I guess we can't argue with Deceuninck's results (though they've had a stinker at the Giro, which might also explain Van Slycke's grumpiness).

From the start we wriggle through Verona to our apartment, dump our bags, but then I go off-piste. I don't go near the press centre and I avoid the mixed zone. Instead I climb the crumbling old steps of the Roman amphitheatre, an edifice that dates back to the first century. The finish line is outside it, but after finishing the riders are diverted through the arena, along a pink carpet that leads to a stage, where some are interviewed before drifting away, their Giro over.

It has to be said that this Giro has been an underwhelming race. As Homer Simpson said, the key to happiness is low expectations. And perhaps the problem here is that our expectations were sky-high, based on the field assembled. It looked far stronger than the Tour de France: Tom Dumoulin, Simon Yates, Primož Roglič, Vincenzo Nibali, Superman López, Mikel Landa. A hell of an array of talent. But, for various reasons, the race was a bit of a damp squib. At least, that's how I feel on the final day in Verona before I climb into the arena and take my place among the Ecuadorian fans.

They don't have an area, as such, but up high in the 15,000-seat arena I find a concentration of yellow and blue – confusingly, this makes them difficult to distinguish from the Colombians, who are a more familiar presence at bike races. I sit with these happy, excited people. They sing, they chant, they cry; one girl I speak to, who has travelled from Barcelona, shakes with the emotion of it all.

Having gone into the arena just to get a flavour of the atmosphere, I find that I don't want to leave: this is where the action, or at least the emotion, is.

I stay for the rest of the stage. The real story of the Giro is here. I speak to more Ecuadorian fans: they have travelled to Verona from all over Europe. Some have come from Ecuador. There are men and women, young and old, teenagers and young children, all in yellow and blue. A friend who follows South American affairs closely (as a journalist who covers the region) texted: 'There's a video message for Carapaz from President Moreno... phenomenal story. In Ecuador's press there is talk of virtually nothing else. Giant screens erected all over the country. Incredible.'

Carapaz's win has kind of sneaked up on us but with the moment here its meaning becomes apparent. His ride today is 23 and a bit minutes of gradually rising anticipation. To be with the Ecuadorian fans as they await his arrival, and accept with every passing minute that he is going to do it, it is impossible not to be swept along. It reminds me that even if this has felt like a lukewarm Giro that never really sparked into life, that won't matter one iota to Ecuador. The history books recording the first major win by one of the country's cyclists won't dwell on the fact that all the big favourites, with the exception of Nibali, melted away.

It feels moving and profound to stand with Carapaz's countrymen and women, to bathe in their unrestrained joy and to get a sense of what this success must mean to a small country best known in recent years for accommodating the fugitive Julian Assange in its London embassy.

2019 WOMEN'S TOUR

by Orla Chennaoui

The 2019 Women's Tour was the second featuring daily coverage by Orla Chennaoui, Rose Manley and Richard Moore for The Cycling Podcast Féminin. *As in 2018, Orla's 'Stories of the Stage' were sprinkled with cultural references inspired by a local writer or other artist. Her daily summaries are reproduced below, alongside her diary entries for the six-day race.*

Settling down to dinner on the eve of The Women's Tour is a success in itself. Rose and I had flown into Stansted hours earlier, me from my still relatively new home in Amsterdam, Rose from a hen party in Poland. The member of our trio with the least distance to travel, Richard, was having the most difficulty getting there.

A message pinged on my phone when I landed: 'Stuck in traffic. Might be a bit late picking you up.'

'Oh no,' I replied, 'accident on the M11?'

'No idea,' came Richard's response, 'I'm still trying to get over London Bridge.'

Something tells me that Richard had been a little optimistic with his timing but fortunately our colleague from the *Telegraph*, Tom Cary, happened to be approaching the airport and took a kindly detour.

As we finally got on the road, I worried about the cultural limitations of this year's Women's Tour route and podcast journey. Starting once again in Suffolk, and finishing in Wales as it had the year before, I felt I had exhausted all the Shakespeare, Ed Sheeran and Tom Jones references in my 'stories of the stage' from the previous race. What new discoveries could we share while cutting once more across the belly of southern Britain?

'Did you bring the willy straws?' I ask Rose as we order our drinks at a rather lovely Indian restaurant, the only one serving food late on a Sunday evening in Beccles.

'I'm afraid not,' she says. 'We used them all up in Kraków.'

'What's a willy straw?' asks Tom.

'I had to Google this when Rose said she would bring some,' says Richard. 'I didn't know either.'

We explain what they are. 'Oh, right,' says Tom. 'Thank goodness for that. I thought it was a stripper with a straw on his…'

I look around the otherwise empty restaurant. 'I think you've got the wrong idea, Tom, about either hen parties, or Suffolk. I'm not sure that would be acceptable for either.'

Perhaps this was going to be quite the cultural journey after all.

Monday, 10 June

Stage 1: Beccles–Stowmarket, 157 km
Winner: Jolien D'hoore
Green jersey: Jolien D'hoore

Orla's Story of the Stage

I was going to base this around John Milton and his famous poem *Paradise Lost*, which tells the story of Adam and Eve. I was waiting for some sort of pandemonium or redemption, and I was going to deliberately/mistakenly name Manon Lloyd 'Mammon', one of Satan's followers. But we didn't see her very much in the race, and I thought it was a bit unfair.

Besides, the poem follows the epic tradition of starting *in medias res* – in the midst of the race – with the background following later, but there wasn't much of a background and nothing much happened at the start of the race, so I thought, 'sod that, sod Milton' – sorry John Milton.

I've gone for John Peel instead, because he lived near here and there's a John Peel arts and culture centre nearby. For anyone who doesn't know him, John Peel was a famous DJ, Radio 1 principally, who started off on Radio Caroline, the pirate radio station.

I've thrown in some John Peel song references. See how many you can find.

As I said, the stage was relatively uneventful for the first part, so no anarchy in the UK. The heavens opened shortly after the race left Beccles in the morning, making for not the nicest of days on the road, but it didn't stop the good vibrations. We had the usual fantastic crowds, schoolchildren lining the roads with flags, teenage kicks and older fans alike. I just love that about modern racing in the UK. It's become quite common, people, hasn't it? No matter what the weather, the fans turn out and I love that. Not a happy day of cycling though for Anna Trevisi of Alé–Cipollini: she had a crash early on and didn't finish.

The intermediate sprint went to last year's winner, Coryn Rivera of Sunweb, so quite a groovy feeling for her to know she's coming into form when it matters. The Sunweb riders were thick as thieves in the second sprint, with Rivera, Susanne Andersen and Leah Kirchmann taking the points. Then Christine Majerus showed she had plenty of mountain energy to take the first queen of the mountains points.

We spent much of the first 135 kilometres, no less, with the bunch mostly together, battling through that rain, then with 22 kilometres to go, out of this wild darkness emerged Abby-Mae Parkinson with the first attack. The Drops rider built up a lead of one minute 40 at one stage and got to cross the finish line first, but only on the first time across the line in Stowmarket.

She was caught before the final crossing, and awarded the combativity award for her brass neck, quite rightly so. Maybe a bit of whiskey in the jar for their team DS, Bob Varney, tonight. I think he might be celebrating that one.

We had a bunch sprint in the end. They say love is a drug but winning is a drug for Jolien D'hoore, getting her second opening win in a row at the Women's Tour, and in East Anglia once again. Amy Pieters, her Boels–Dolmans teammate, finished second with Lisa Brennauer of WNT in third.

So, this evening, the jerseys go to Coryn Rivera of Sunweb, who takes the sprint jersey; queen of the mountains goes to Christine Majerus of Boels–Dolmans; the points jersey goes to Jolien D'hoore, as well as the green jersey of overall leader. The best British rider is Ellie Dickinson of Trek Drops, and the best team is Boels.

That's how we're looking at the end of stage one, but who will have what when Saturday comes?

Tuesday, 11 June

Stage 2: Cyclopark (Gravesend), 62.5 km
Winner: Marianne Vos
Green jersey: Marianne Vos

We gather for breakfast in our hotel on the edge of the motorway, near Gravesend. Tom orders Eggs Benedict. 'You're so stage three,' says Rose. 'Stage three?'

'Henley, the posh stage.'

Our hotel is very much stage two. Rose's words, not ours, and she's allowed to say that, she's a local lass. To give it its due, our lodgings are impressively faithful to the era in which they were built, the 1970s. The paper cloths on the restaurant tables are at least new, though the steel-framed, velour-padded chairs have definitely borne witness to one stationary convention too many. 'They look like they should be set out in a row for Alan Partridge to walk in and launch a book,' suggests Rose.

The previous evening, I had ordered breaded chicken with chips, surprised it wasn't dressed up as Chicken Maryland, and a Diet Coke which arrived in a pint glass. I was going to ask if I could have a can instead, but didn't want to seem pretentious. The restaurant had a corner seemingly permanently set up for breakfast, with cereal ready to be poured from plastic dispensers and off-white coffee cups stacked on saucers. We knew we had no choice but to return for a second meal the following morning.

'I made a mistake', says Rose at breakfast. 'I ordered soft-boiled eggs but I think it's going to come with a lot of crap I don't want. Like bacon.'

'I made a mistake', says Richard, 'booking this place.'

Orla's Story of the Stage

This is Charles Dickens country and Gravesend, where we are now, featured in *David Copperfield*.

We did have great expectations for the stage, but alas the old curiosity shop of life doesn't always offer up its finest wares. Stage races often tell a tale of two cities but it all took place in one location today, the Cyclopark in Kent. Twenty-five laps of a 2.5 kilometre circuit, and once a rider was lapped, they were taken out of the race. Hard times for anyone who couldn't keep the pace, although they weren't eliminated – they still get to start tomorrow.

The first rider dropped was Hannah Payton of Drops, so it was the best of times, it was the worst of times for our mutual friend Bob Varney after Abby-Mae Parkinson's heroics yesterday.

There was an early attack from Alice Barnes and another at 12 kilometres – pictures from Italy this time with Elena Cecchini, also of Canyon–SRAM. She got a lead of 30 seconds in a solo break lasting 10 kilometres. Other than that, it was only really the intermediate sprints that broke up the stage.

If any team had been hoping to push this race from the front, well, procrastination is the thief of time and it came down to a sprint finish, Marianne Vos winning comfortably in the end, ahead of Lizzie Deignan and Sarah Roy of Mitchelton–Scott, with Coryn Rivera fourth.

We only discovered afterward that Marianne Vos had a puncture. It happened at just the right moment as there were no cars on the route, so the riders had to go into the pits. She was able to get a change fairly quickly and get herself back in the race again.

Wednesday, 12 June

Stage 3: Henley-on-Thames–Blenheim Palace, 146.5 km
Winner: Jolien D'hoore
Green jersey: Lisa Brennauer

Stage three. The one we've all been waiting for. The posh stage. We whoop as we arrive in the car park of our beautiful lodgings in Hambleden, where the TV programme *Midsomer Murders* is set. I'm not sure whooping is the done thing in the English countryside but that's what happens when you let the riff-raff in.

Luckily for me, the riff-raff are also used to staying in surroundings more in keeping with their station in life, thus I've taken to packing a hot water bottle everywhere I go. I hadn't had need of it before now. While the cottage adjacent to our hotel is beautiful, it is absolutely freezing. I comment on the temperature to my friend who lives in the area the following morning.

'Posh people don't like to put the heating on,' she says.

'Do they not like phone reception either?' asks Richard.

'It's so the poor people can't contact us.'

As we wander around the team buses in Henley, someone remarks that today's stage includes the longest continual climb in the UK. 'Bullshit!' I say. A woman taps me briskly on the shoulder. 'I thought I recognised you. You're from the podcast, yes?' Bugger. I've done it again.

I am relieved when we get on the road. I have nothing against poshness per se, but it has always made me quite uncomfortable. As does the kind of countryside idyll that English people seem so found of – rolling hills, quaint stone buildings and perfect fences. There is something about supposed perfection of any kind that makes me deeply uneasy. As we sit down to a mid-stage refreshment stop, in the most charming tea room you could imagine, Richard comes up with a theory: 'You're uncomfortable with posh, because you are posh.'

'What? I'm not fucking posh!' I protest. The actual posh ladies in the teamroom bristle. I need to get out of here. In the car, on the way to the finish, we listen to the perfect antidote to our surroundings, the *Dear Joan and Jericha* podcast. It consists of two actresses pretending to be uptight, middle-aged women who are actually outrageously politically incorrect. It gets us talking about men's waxing. 'I used to get my back waxed,' says Richard, 'when I was single.'

'Why specifically when you were single?' I ask, against my better judgement.

'Because in those days, they liked to see the back of me.'

Like a gentrified huntsman he'd laid the trap and I had walked straight in.

Orla's Story of the Stage

The reference tonight is Dusty Springfield, because she has a gravesite in Henley, and her ashes were scattered between Henley and the cliffs of Mulhern, County Clare, in Ireland.

We had a very early categorised climb, giving queen of the mountains points after just nine-and-a-half kilometres, with Christine Majerus again taking full points.

Almost immediately after that, Anna Plichta of Trek–Segafredo reckoned that if you go away early enough you can stay a while out front, so that's what she did.

We stopped off in the middle of nowhere just before the second categorised climb and saw Plichta with a lead of just under a minute, so no surprise that she held on to the second queen of the mountains and took maximum points over Majerus.

Then, when we were building up to the second sprint of the day, disaster. Marianne Vos was being led out by her CCC teammates when one of them hit a pothole; her hands came off the handlebars, and a lot of riders hit the deck. It sounded absolutely horrific. We heard almost immediately that Trixi Worrack of Trek had abandoned and then came the news that Vos was also out.

Anyone who had a heart would feel for the Dutchwoman. She started the day in the leader's jersey and finished it in hospital, getting stitches to her face. We're all hoping she gets better soon.

The race was neutralised for about 40 minutes while riders received medical attention. It finally restarted, and Plichta, who had a 55-second advantage before the crash, managed to build it to one minute 40.

It can't be easy, I always think, keeping that momentum, building on it. Goodness knows what goes on in the windmills of the mind when you're waiting for the race to restart, but she did a great job, though she was finally caught with 41 kilometres to go.

And then, with about 30 kilometres to go, another crash, which we only learned about at the finish. Ashleigh Moolman Pasio was caught up in that, so was Lizzie Deignan and several others. Fortunately, all of those riders did at least finish the race.

Then it came down to a sprint finish, Jolien D'hoore winning her second stage, the Belgian beating Lisa Brennauer, with Demi Vollering third, just a fraction of a centimetre ahead of Roxane Fournier.

Thursday, 13 June

Stage 4: Warwick–Burton Dassett, 158 km
Winner: Kasia Niewiadoma
Green jersey: Liane Lippert

By the time we reach the start of day four we have covered some 350 miles in the car. That's over 560 kilometres, with Richard's optimistically packed bike in the boot all the while, untouched and unridden. He had planned to recon some of the route as we went along, but the British summer hadn't been favourable.

Time and road were running out, but he had committed over dinner the previous evening to taking on the finishing circuit in Burton Dassett Country Park today, come what may. 'It's raining heavier than ever. Am I really going to ride this?' he asks, trying to elicit sympathy as we dry off en route from the soggy start in Warwick.

'Maybe you could do it Dutch style, and ride with an umbrella?' I suggest. We don't have an umbrella.

'How am I going to dry myself after?'

'Maybe there will be a hand dryer in a nearby pub?' I suggest. 'You could do a limbo dance under it.'

'What if it's one of those that you stick your hands *into*?' Richard asks, determined to find an escape route.

'You could always insert body parts one by one. Perhaps a toe at a time.'

I don't envy him. It has already been the kind of day when you huddle by the team bus exhausts for warmth, and the rain is only getting heavier. Neither Rose nor I are doing much to rally the spirits.

We arrive at the top of the climb and ask directions to the media facilities. The rain is now slicing through the air sideways.

An official with two layers of rain hood, neither of which are covering her head or helping her mood, glumly points us in the direction of the press compound. Oh my goodness. Our shelter on the first summit finish of the Women's Tour is a single, open-sided, three-peaked tent, with two freestanding Portaloos for comfort. It occurs to me that cycling journalism isn't much more of an inspired career path than that of a rider: 'Cycling is a shit job,' as Rose observed moments earlier. But at least they would be moving to keep warm.

Shunning the flapping canvas of the Tour Village, Rose and I find a nearby pub in which to station ourselves for the day while Richard assembles his bike and sets off. There are already mid-morning half-pints on the go in the Red Lion, with a police chase programme playing on the huge TV in the corner. As the pub fills up through the day, word spreads about the bike race nearby.

'Apparently there's something called a broom wagon,' I overhear one man say.

'I saw that,' replies his female friend. 'I actually saw it. It was sweeping all the way across the road with this big broom on the back of it. It was really impressive.'

I'm not sure how many pints she's had, but I sincerely hope Richard won't end up being swept off the road. It is too wet to go and save him.

Orla's Story of the Stage

We did Shakespeare when we were in this area last year, so I thought I'd do something a little bit different.

This is very different: we're going to play 'guess the reference' between two literary greats of Warwickshire – is it Philip Larkin or is it Daniel Friebe?

I think it's fair to say that we feel like we've been a little bit disappointed with the first half of the race in terms of the lack of attacks. We've been looking forward to today, but then, always too eager for the future, we pick up bad habits of expectancy. Something is always approaching; every day, till then we say…

Well, today it is then. It's the first summit finish in Women's Tour history: we're sitting in a pub at the foot of the climb. Burton Dassett climbs from the Red Lion pub like aroma from a kitchen, its wisp of road rising slowly and serenely towards the summit, one kilometre away.

The race did a circuit of Burton Dassett Country Park, three laps to finish the longest stage of this year's race. Sarah Roy made the first move, with a whole 128 kilometres to go. She started the day fifth overall, just six seconds down, so it was a bit of a surprise that she got to go and build up such a lead in the end.

She was joined by Femke Markus of Parkhotel Valkenberg and Charlotte Becker of FDJ, and between them they took both intermediate sprints and built up a lead of eight minutes 20 seconds at one stage.

Trek–Segafredo and WNT finally did start to lead the chase with about 75 kilometres to go, and by the time we got to Burton Dassett for the first time it was quite difficult to see through the sheet rain. But you know, a brutal day like this on the road is like death, it's no different whined at than withstood, is it? It's about who can withstand it best that really matters.

Through the gloom, a blink of light suspended between the twin strobes of a car's headlights, Roy leading Markus, with Becker dropped and Elisa Longo Borghini, Kasia Niewiadoma and Liane Lippert of Sunweb not far behind. Roy and Markus were caught, Roy having been out front all day long, but being brave lets no one off the grave.

By the time they came up the climb second time, it was Niewiadoma, Lippert and Longo Borghini in front. They were caught by the chasing group on the next lap, which included Lisa Brennauer, who had been the race leader at the start of the day, and Lizzie Deignan.

So we had a charge of about 25 for the line.

We were standing just by the finish by that stage. With the pouring rain everyone was taking shelter where they could and then, out of the gloom, two eyes blaze, two shoulders sway, two lips pursed, two thighs thump, pound and pummel: Kasia Niewiadoma took the win in front of Liane Lippert, with Lizzie Deignan third.

Friday, 14 June

Stage 5: Llandrindod Wells–Builth Wells, 140 km
Winner: Lizzie Deignan
Green jersey: Lizzie Deignan

Into Wales for our penultimate stage and I forgot how significant the portions of food are here. It must be something in the Celtic genes. It reminds me of home.

Day five starts with the best breakfast of the trip. Indeed, it is one of our best meals. There might not be much to draw the eye to the Greylands Guest House from the outside, but I will certainly be drawn back by my belly. The extensive menu ranges from the traditional fry-up to modern twists on old favourites. I order the cheddar and bacon porridge cakes with homemade orange bread, and they are as fresh, filling and delicious a meal as you could hope for.

Which is fortunate, since I was spending the day in the Canyon–SRAM team car and it turns out they survive on adrenaline alone. By the time we get to our evening meal in an old pub near Builth Wells, recommended by our friend Alun who is joining us for the evening, I am ready to inhale everything the menu has to offer.

Forgetting temporarily that we are no longer in England, I order the steak and ale pie with a side of onion rings and chips. What I receive is a huge bowl of stew with a puff pastry lid, 16 rings of deep-fried onion and at least three large sliced and fried potatoes.

Over dinner we get chatting about what song we'd like to be played at our funerals. Richard surprises us with *Candle in the Wind*. As we later squeeze into the car to drive back to our hotel, it occurs to me that his song choice could have been subconsciously inspired by the extra onion rings I'd been pushing his way over dinner, and so I wind down the window just in case.

Orla's Story of the Stage

We're going for Roald Dahl today as he's Welsh and there's a housing estate near us named after him, so that will do.

The Queen Stage of this year's Women's Tour promised much and mercifully it delivered. We had an intriguing situation at the start of the day, with Liane Lippert in the race lead, but on the same time as Kasia Niewiadoma, with Lizzie Deignan just three seconds back.

So the question was, was it going to be the great mouse plot, a case of nibbling away at time bonuses with the sprints, or going all-in for the stage win?

Well, we had a breakaway go early in the stage, which suggested that it wouldn't be a day to take time with sprint bonuses. There were 10 riders in that break, and you could say that Ellen van Dijk, Leah Kirchmann and Sheyla Guitiérrez were maybe the gremlins in there, their presence as well as the sheer number of riders probably dooming it. Lisa Klein was instructed by Canyon–SRAM to sit up and come back to the bunch as they figured they needed the numbers around Niewiadoma to work together.

The break was brought back and the inevitable attacks followed, including riders like Amalie Dideriksen, Erica Magnaldi and Soraya Paladin. A group formed and got four-and-a-half minutes before Canyon–SRAM and Sunweb did the work to bring them back in for the big climb of the day, the enormous crocodile of a bunch swallowing up the break on that climb.

Canyon–SRAM and Sunweb did things perfectly, but Sunweb didn't do much to capitalise, and instead it was Niewiadoma and the two Trek riders, Lizzie Deignan and Elisa Longo Borghini, who got away. They had to work together to keep that break, and Niewiadoma really had to outfox the other two by going solo before the dash for the line. She didn't, and had to take on the two Trek riders in the battle for the finish.

So, no tales of the unexpected for the would-be Fantastic Mister Fox, and instead Niewiadoma was the filling in the Trek sandwich, with Deignan champion of the world, Niewiadoma in second, and Longo Borghini third.

That result meant that Deignan took the leader's jersey from Lippert, and held a one-second lead over Niewiadoma, a dream ending to two fables for her, both the story of the stage and that of the overall. No, wait there's more; Deignan has four, what a score. Sorry, revolting rhymes there, but as well as the stage and the overall she keeps the jersey of best overall British rider and is now the leader of the points competition as well.

No overall for Niewiadoma, but ah, sweet mystery of life, she does take the queen of the mountains jersey. Coryn Rivera keeps the sprint jersey, and gets a kiss-kiss on the stage from our Dusty Springfield competition winner, Fiona Prue, as you do, a dream come true, she said. Sorry, another rhyme stew.

And that was day five, we've had dirty beasts of stages in the last few days, now just one more to go.

Saturday, 15 June

Stage 6: Carmarthen–Pembrey Country Park, 125 km
Winner: Amy Pieters
Green jersey: Lizzie Deignan

Orla's Story of the Stage

Dylan Thomas was buried in Carmarthenshire, so we're going on a Dylan Thomas literary adventure. Strap yourselves in.

To begin at the beginning, we had a really strong breakaway go early, a group of 11 riders that included last year's winner Coryn Rivera, Grace Brown, Chantal Blaak, Hannah Barnes, Ellen van Dijk and Leah Thomas among others.

That breakaway then split into three, with a group of five becoming seven, with Rivera, Barnes, Van Dijk, Thomas, and Janneke Ensing being joined by Chantal Blaak and Grace Brown.

Now from our country and green mountain, Black Mountain loomed and they all took on the Black Mountain together, but they were caught, those seven, after the descent.

We were wondering how much the intermediate sprints would matter in the grand scheme of things. Rivera had taken the first intermediate sprint so she secured the sprints jersey with that, Lizzie Deignan took a single second for third in the second intermediate sprint, which left her with a two-second lead over Kasia Niewiadoma in the overall.

There were more attacks in the final 25 kilometres, with the former race leader Liane Lippert and Lizzy Banks trying to get away, and they were joined by Martina Alzini and Charlotte Becker.

They never built up much of a lead, and as the race rushed towards the Welsh coast came the prospect of sea and a sprint finish, with Amy Pieters eventually taking the win and a bonus 10 seconds. That wasn't enough to overturn Lizzie Deignan's lead. And so she took her first overall race win since becoming a mother. It's a phenomenal comeback for her, a true warrior – soldier comes home if you like, this being a British race. No rider has ever won the Women's Tour twice and the ghosts of the past rose up to interrogate Deignan: could she make history? Yes, she could, the first to win the race twice, a legacy that will last as long as forever.

Kasia Niewiadoma and her Canyon–SRAM team gave it all, all, and all to finish in second. Am I to understand Canyon–SRAM led her out for an intermediate sprint, only for her to finish fourth? We think that might be the case. Pieters finished third overall. Christine Majerus was fourth, with Demi Vollering fifth: an adventure and a work in progress for her; it really feels like we're seeing the arrival of a force to be reckoned with on the world stage.

As for the jerseys, Deignan took the points jersey as well as the overall, Niewiadoma took queen of the mountains, Rivera the sprints, and Deignan the best of British as well. Trek–Segafredo won the best team, and Sarah Roy won the overall combativity prize.

Of the 156 riders, 27 of them failed to start today, and really from the first declension of the flesh it felt like they were dropping like flies at one stage, but we did have a strong field to finish in the end, and a wonderful battle.

Driving into Carmarthen Velodrome, Richard and I spot the children's playpark at the same time. 'Decent,' is his verdict, 'that would kill a good hour with Maxime,' referring to his two-year-old son.

My instinct is that it is more of a 10-40 minuter, until I spot the adjacent climbing park for older children and concede that it falls into the chunkier end of the child-occupying scale. This is what parenthood does to you. Even when your children aren't in the same country, they're always with you in some way.

It's a day to reflect on parenthood and what it is to try to combine this gypsy lifestyle with having little ones at home. When I speak to Lizzie Deignan, the overall race winner, moments after crossing the line, the Trek–Segafredo rider – who'd given birth less than a year earlier – has the glimmer of a tear in her eye.

'I'm sorry, it's just I've been trying not to think about Orla all week,' she says, referring to her baby daughter. With my daughter now four, and my son still only five months old, what Deignan has achieved almost brings me to tears myself, as does the deep, visceral longing for my own children.

It strikes me that athletes will always have their titles and medals to point to as a reason for their absence. I have a few podcasts. It can sometimes be difficult to justify that need to sometimes be away from home when you love your job as much as we do.

Before recording our final podcast, Richard and I remind each other that it is still, however, a job. The fact we enjoy it should be a bonus, not a source of guilt.

Our last podcast of the Women's Tour is recorded sitting on the grass in Pembrey Country Park, near the finish line. The rain has stopped and, for an hour, we are just three friends sitting in the evening sunshine chatting about bike racing. There are certainly worse ways to earn a living.

We travel back to London in the fine company of Elton John and Billy Joel, among others, stopping briefly for a service station dinner and WH Smith present raid for the kids. Phil Collins has joined us now, with his *Invisible Touch* taking us back along the M4. The blue sky is broken up by streaks of light grey, pink cloud, in that wannabe summer way that's all too familiar in the UK. The setting sun flashes through the treeline as we speed back home, and Phil gets to a key change. In that lapse of time between the end of one thing and the start of another, when real time is suspended as you travel to where you belong, there is satisfaction that all is as is should be, and of a job well done.

2019 TOUR DE FRANCE

by Lionel Birnie

Friday, 5 July

And so to Brussels for the start of my 17th Tour de France, and the seventh since we started *The Cycling Podcast*. The first episode was recorded on Richard's iPhone while sitting on the grass in a London park a week or so before the 2013 Grand Départ in Corsica. Richard and Daniel flew off for the opening weekend of the race and I went to the Glastonbury Festival, joining them in Nice for the team time trial. I remember listening to the episodes they made without me on the flight to the south of France and on hearing 'Ciro' for the first time wondered if the podcast might be stopped in its tracks before it got going. I knew Ciro Scognamiglio was a cycling correspondent for the august Italian newspaper *La Gazzetta dello Sport*, but who was this quirky comedic character? I was convinced 'Ciro' was actually Daniel putting on a stereotypical Italian voice. But no, Ciro was genuine and – to date – the only fictional characters on *The Cycling Podcast* remain US Marketing Guy (remember him?) and Gianni Savio.

Our arrival in Brussels is a reminder of how the podcast has grown since those early days. We are reunited with François Thomazeau and head to an independent brewery and bar called the Brussels Beer Project. In the spring, Eoghan Walsh, a Friend of the Podcast, invited us to speak in the bar on the eve of the Tour and so here we are.

When we arrive, the place is buzzing. There's already a big crowd in and we're not due on for an hour so we retire to the restaurant across the road to plan what we're going to talk about. When we return to the bar every seat is taken and it's standing room only at the back. I get the sense they've been enjoying the punchy Belgian beers and so when I'm offered one I opt for the gentler Cyclist Saison rather than the Eddy Merckx-strength IPA called Cannibal with its ABV percentage to rival the lower, slower slopes of the Muur.

With practice, I have become more comfortable speaking to an audience but there's still an element of self-doubt that creeps in, especially on occasions like this when I see how close we are to the audience. When you can see the whites of people's eyes it's immediately apparent if a joke falls flat or if interest is waning.

I need not have been anxious. The lights go out suddenly just before we're about to start and there's a big, boozy cheer, which settles my nerves. It turns out to be a brilliant, fun evening. François delivers his catchphrase 'Bull-sheet' with perfect timing, Richard's zingy one-liners must surely be down to having consumed a large glass of Cannibal, and I get to talk about two of my passions – *cassoulet* and the 1989 Tour de France. Midway through we are joined by Jonathan Vaughters of EF Education First, who has been at an event just down the road launching his memoir, then by Orla Chennaoui and, fleetingly by Ciro, whose spritely presence never ceases to bemuse and amuse. In the audience I see Seb Piquet, the voice of Radio Tour, and Hannah Troop, erstwhile co-host of our Explore series. It feels like *The Cycling Podcast*'s family is all here. At one point there are not enough mics to go round so I take a back seat, figuratively speaking, and just listen and laugh along. It gives me a moment to reflect on what *The Cycling Podcast* has become in six years and a sense of pride washes over me that I've had a hand in it all. However, I know that a good part of it has been down to serendipity and a gradual evolution that has occasionally taken us by surprise. After all, if I'd sat down in June 2013 and tried to imagine all this, I'd have dismissed the idea as totally fanciful.

Saturday, 6 July

Stage 1: Brussels–Brussels, 194.5 km
Stage winner: Mike Teunissen
Yellow jersey: Mike Teunissen

The serious business of the Tour de France begins. Our hub for the Grand Départ weekend is the Palais des Exposition, amid the imposing buildings constructed for the 1935 and 1958 World's Fairs. There's an almost Soviet austerity to the hall built for the 1935 expo and I'm initially worried we've been stuck up on this glorified industrial estate away from the hubbub in Brussels.

However, this turns out to be a Grand Départ with a difference because we spend the weekend travelling everywhere by Metro and on foot, which makes a nice change and connects us more directly with the Tour experience. We get to feel the atmosphere build over the afternoon.

Our walk to the Metro station takes us past the striking and shiny Atomium structure, built for the 1958 World's Fair, when there was peak excitement for the atomic age. I also cannot pass the Heysel football stadium without thinking of the tragic violence that marred the 1985 European Cup final. The stadium has been revamped and renamed – it's the King Baudouin now – but as I tread the pavements outside the ground my mind conjures up news footage of the chaos, the ambulances and the casualties.

Everywhere we look there are reminders that Brussels has been chosen to host the Grand Départ to honour Eddy Merckx, the greatest cyclist of all-time. This is the 50th anniversary of the first of his five Tour victories. Merckx pulled on the yellow jersey in Paris on 20 July 1969, the same day Neil Armstrong set foot on the moon.

One quirk of that 1969 Tour was that it started with a prologue time trial in Roubaix and the next day there was a road stage to the Brussels suburb of Woluwe-Saint-Pierre (or Sint-Pieters-Woluwe, as it is known in Flemish), the town where Merckx grew up. In the afternoon, there was a team time trial, which his Faema squad won, and Merckx pulled on the *maillot jaune* for the first time a decent stone's throw from his family home.

Merckx's career and legacy bamboozle me. It's before my time and so I find the sheer volume and scale of his victories difficult to process and contextualise. It's impressive, of course it is, and we'll never see another rider capable of winning from the season's start to end year-after-year the way he did. His appetite for victory and the way he, metaphorically, devoured his opponents earned him the nickname 'Le Cannibale'. And yet I feel coldly detached from his brilliance in a way that I don't when I consider some of the other greats. Perhaps it's because there were so few signs of weakness, so few athletic flaws to Merckx, or perhaps it's because I find the stories of his dominance slightly – dare I say it – boring. As a result I am drawn to tales of the ones that got away. One of my favourite Merckx-related quotes comes from his Faema teammate Guido Reybrouck, who Merckx helped to win Paris-Tours in 1968. 'Between us, we won everything,' Reybrouck said. 'I won Paris-Tours, Eddy won all the rest.'

Despite the temporary graffiti 'Are you R'Eddy?' that's sprayed all over the walls and pavements, we forget about Merckx for a little while and head to the team buses where I debut an exciting new segment for the podcast called 'Outside The Team Bus', in which I plan to interview a rider from a different team each day.

'Aren't all your interviews done outside the team bus?' asks Richard.

'That's not the point,' I say.

The point is to broaden out the conversations a bit and, over the course of the Tour, hear from riders on teams we wouldn't necessarily make a beeline for. My first 'victim' is Alex Dowsett of Katusha–Alpecin. Admittedly, Dowsett is someone we'd almost certainly speak to at some point during the Tour but I want to get some relatively easy runs on the board early on so that Outside The Team Bus has a chance of making it beyond the opening weekend.

The riders head off in the direction of the Muur in Geraardsbergen and we head for lunch, making a point to enjoy this relative calm before the Tour picks us up and carries us off round France.

To get to the finish line, we have to cut across the corner of the Parc de Laeken, the biggest green space in the city, and we watch as a crash disrupts the finish and brings down one of the favourites for the stage, Dylan Groenewegen. He hits the ground with around a kilometre-and-a-half to go but despite the loss of their main man the Jumbo–Visma train is not derailed entirely. His teammate Mike Teunissen is able to take a deep breath, recalibrate and then summon the strength to pip Peter Sagan and Caleb Ewan on the line. As shock results go, this is a big one and a reminder that the Tour always has the capacity to surprise.

In the evening, we head to Aux Armes de Brussels, the restaurant François has booked. It's a traditional brasserie once favoured by the city's other famous son, the singer Jacques Brel. François goes for the local favourite *anguilles au vert*, or *paling in 't groen*, or – once more for the English-speakers – eels in a herby green sauce. Eels are one of the few foodstuffs I won't eat but François raves about them. Apparently the dish originated from the days when the eels would be scooped out of the Belgian canals and the sauce would be made from whatever herbs and greenery could be picked nearby. I decide not to tell François that the canals are too polluted nowadays and the farmed eels are considered too fatty by connoisseurs because he seems to be enjoying his water snakes too much.

Sunday, 7 July

Stage 2: Brussels–Brussels, 27.6 km team time trial
Stage winners: Jumbo–Visma
Yellow jersey: Mike Teunissen

With the team time trial not getting underway until well into the afternoon, there's a chance to pop into the Rapha cafe for a coffee before enjoying a pleasant lunch and finally taking the Metro up to Heysel and the expo centre.

Because of the crashes during the finale of yesterday's opening stage, Team Ineos are first to roll down the start ramp.

'I reckon Team Ineos will set the best time here,' I say, and they do, not least because there isn't a time to beat yet. It's this sort of recurring humour that I like to think keeps morale high in *The Cycling Podcast* team car during a Grand Tour.

The more serious question is whether anyone can beat them. The Team Ineos line-up features five riders who have been their country's national time trial champion at some time or other – Geraint Thomas, Egan Bernal, Jonathan Castroviejo, Michal Kwiatkowski and Dylan van Baarle – so it's no surprise when their time stands for almost the entire afternoon.

The first team to push them close are Katusha–Alpecin, who get within six seconds. Shortly after that come Deceuninck–Quick-Step, who look set to depose Ineos until the final kilometre when it begins to slip away from them. They hit the line less than a second slower. Yves Lampaert yells his frustration as they cross the line. In the end, the disappointment at their near-miss is eased when Jumbo–Visma scorch round the course and blow everyone away. They are 20 seconds faster than Team Ineos. Over 27.6 kilometres that is a comprehensive win.

Team time trials always interest me because there is more than one way to skin a cat. Seeing how each squad tackles the same challenge is interesting. Received wisdom is that anyone who finishes with all eight riders still together is clearly not trying hard enough – although it could equally be that they're trying to protect a climber in their ranks, as is probably the case with UAE Team Emirates and Dan Martin. Seeing the point at which teams shed riders can be instructive too. With the full line-up of eight taking between 20- and 30-second turns at the front, the recovery time for each rider can be between two minutes and 20 seconds and three-and-a-half-minutes. But as riders drop off that recovery time reduces and the load on those who remain increases. It means the race is a test of judgement as well as strength because seemingly small mistakes made early on can have significant repercussions later on.

There can be no doubt that Jumbo–Visma's work over the winter has paid off. They were the strongest team and they made the fewest mistakes and they fully deserved to win the stage and keep Teunissen in the yellow jersey for another day.

This weekend we've been staying with Charlotte, a friend of Richard's and a Friend of the Podcast who occasionally sends us WhatsApp messages correcting our pronunciation of Flemish names. (It's Tom *Bo-nen*, not Tom *Booo-nen*). The house is actually just outside the city limits and technically stands on Flemish soil. With the fields adjacent to the house, it's difficult to believe we're just a few minutes from one of Europe's capital cities.

We record the podcast in Charlotte's garden and her dog Ruby makes a guest appearance with a well-timed bark in between gnawing on a punctured football. Then we sit round the table and eat homemade chilli con carne and drink wine, and for an hour or so I forget that we're even covering the Tour de France. We've been here three nights and we've not moved yet but that all changes in the morning.

Monday, 8 July

Stage 3: Binche–Épernay, 215 km
Stage winner: Julian Alaphilippe
Yellow jersey: Julian Alaphilippe

Today will go down as a vintage day in more ways than one. Last November we had a live event at the Clapham Grand in south London and after the show a man named David Hesketh introduced himself to François and I as the UK managing director of Laurent-Perrier. With the Tour due to visit Épernay – which, along with Reims, is one of the towns at the heart of the champagne-producing region – David invited us to visit Laurent-Perrier to learn more.

Before that we had a stage of the race to watch, of course. At the start in Binche, Matt White was asked if he thought the finish would suit Julian Alaphilippe.

'Suit him?' said White, 'I reckon he designed the route himself.'

The final 50 kilometres of the stage turn out to be breathtaking stuff.

Lotto–Soudal's Tim Wellens, who has been in the early break, goes clear on his own but by the time he reaches the Côte de Mutigny, he is starting to suffer. Alaphilippe's attack from the slimmed down group of favourites is brutal. He powers across to Wellens, pauses briefly and then leaves the Belgian standing.

The sight of the Frenchman riding through the vineyards on the narrow country roads is the Tour at its beautiful best. It's a little like the race used to look in the 1980s when I fell in love with it watching Channel 4's highlights.

Out at the finish line, among the crowds, it's noticeable that Alaphilippe's style has captured the imagination. This is the sort of panache the fans – particularly the French fans – swoon over. Alaphilippe wins the stage and takes the yellow jersey.

Behind him the tricky final climb and the aggression in the last hour or so of racing means there are small splits everywhere. When we see the final result of the stage we note that Egan Bernal has finished five seconds ahead of Geraint Thomas, hopping above him in the overall standings, and we speculate whether that has any bearing on the pecking order at Team Ineos.

There's a fascinating dynamic between the defending champion and the youngster. In the podcast I mention that I'd been slightly underwhelmed by Bernal's performance at the Tour of Switzerland, despite the fact he won the race, and Thomas's form is a little unknown because he crashed out of the same race on the fourth day. After six Tour victories in seven years as Team Sky, I sense there's less certainty about Team Ineos this year.

We head to our hotel, where we are met by David and a bottle of Laurent-Perrier, which we enjoy while recording the episode. I feel slightly under pressure because dinner is scheduled for 8.30pm at the Château de Louvois, which is a good 20 minutes away by taxi. We wrap up recording earlier than I can remember.

On the way, I type out the text for the podcast's episode description on my phone. Richard points out that I've been spelling Mike Teunissen's name incorrectly for the past couple of days, inserting a rogue 'h' into his surname. It's probably because I remember the Dutch climber from the late 1980s, Gert-Jan Theunisse. That's my excuse anyway.

Just before I send the text to our producer I spot that autocorrect has spelled Thibaut Pinot as Thibaut Pinky.

'Thibaut Pinky,' chuckles François. 'I like it.'

The taxi pulls off the main road and makes its way up a long drive towards the glorious château. We are greeted by Nicole Snozzi, who has worked as a brand ambassador for Laurent-Perrier for many years. We are shown into a beautiful drawing room where tasting shall commence. There are four glasses laid out for each of us and over the next hour we taste and listen to Nicole and David talk about the history of Laurent-Perrier, the production methods and how the cellarmasters know when they have a good vintage on their hands. It is particularly moving to hear Nicole talk about how the spirit and passion of Bernard de Nonancourt, who ran the company for decades until his death in 2010, is kept alive. De Nonancourt was awarded the Croix de Guerre for his service in the Second World War. In 1945, his unit recovered more than half a million bottles of wine from Hitler's Eagle's Nest retreat in Bavaria. The impression he left on Laurent-Perrier's staff is quite something. Champagne production is not a profession – it's a passion, much like podcasting.

I'm recording for our *Road Trip* episode and so I try to relate the world of champagne to professional cycling by asking whether it's accurate to say that champagne is the Tour de France, the leader in its field, and prosecco and cava, the Italian and Spanish equivalents, are pretenders to the throne. Nicole's reaction suggests that the words 'prosecco' and 'cava' are simply not to be uttered on Laurent-Perrier's premises. They're not the same thing at all.

Dinner is remarkable, as much for the service as the food. We start with a beautifully fresh swordfish tartare, which sparkles with citrus and coriander, followed by guinea fowl. Both dishes are delicate enough not to overwhelm the champagne. We serve ourselves – clumsily in my case – from platters held at our side by waiters, who then return to the kitchen, tidy up the food on the platters and present them again for seconds a little later.

It's a formal but not stuffy occasion, although I must admit feeling a slight sense of imposter syndrome. My passion for the food and wine that France has to offer us during the Tour is probably apparent, but I put myself in the category of enthusiast rather than expert. I feel slightly concerned that Nicole feels her expertise is being wasted on me, as well as bemused, though delighted, that my job talking about cycling has led to an invitation to enjoy such an experience. As François says, David has offered us the chance to witness a side of French culture and history that very few are privileged to see.

As we arrive back at our hotel, I say to Richard, 'How do we top that? Not with sandwiches from the petrol station, that's for sure.'

Tuesday, 9 July

Stage 4: Reims–Nancy, 213.5 km
Stage winner: Elia Viviani
Yellow jersey: Julian Alaphilippe

After speaking to Mike Teunissen about his stint in the yellow jersey and Jasper Philipsen, the youngest rider in the race, Outside Their Respective Team Buses, I feel the day has got off to a flying start. Philipsen of UAE Team Emirates hails from Mol, the same town as Tom Boonen, and emerges from the bus covered in a few bandages after crashing towards the end of yesterday's stage. He also has a scarcely concealed desire to win a Grand Tour stage sooner rather than later. For the moment, though, Philipsen is learning the ropes as a lead-out man for Alexander Kristoff, the latest 30-something sprinter to be written off as a fading force by *The Cycling Podcast*. See also Greipel, A.

I've arranged to interview David Walsh, one of the journalists who was instrumental in bringing to light Lance Armstrong's doping, for an episode of *Kilometre 0* and so we leave the pressroom in Nancy and find a quiet cafe. Armstrong's downfall is a well-documented story, told in newspaper articles, books, documentaries and even a film, but I want to focus on the 1999 Tour itself, the first of Armstrong's seven redacted Tour titles. Walsh is such an engaging storyteller, blessed with a deft turn of phrase, that almost an hour slips by without me noticing. Richard and I decide to make the episode of *Kilometre 0* a two-parter so we can tell the story as fully as possible.

After the stage we head to our Airbnb on the outskirts of Nancy. François has booked a table for us at the Brasserie Excelsior so we need to head into the centre of town. We must also record the podcast. Plan A is to take the tram into town but when we arrive at the stop we find there's a 16-minute wait for the next one. Although it's a 25-minute walk to the town centre we decide to set off on foot, knowing we can stop to record en route if we spot a suitable bar.

There's the odd boulangerie and a barber's shop but no bars so when the tram catches us, we let it take us the rest of the way. As we trundle into town, François coins a joke about Arkéa–Samsic's lead-out tram, as opposed to train, and we all laugh, although I accept it's probably one of those where you had to be there.

We take a table outside the Cafe Leffe, in the opposite corner of the square from the Excelsior, and set up our recording equipment. We're keen to start recording but we'd like to order a drink first. The waitress is world-class at avoiding eye contact. Two, three or four times she walks past our table, timing her glance away to perfection.

'Unbelievable,' I mutter, as she passes a fifth time without stopping to take our order.

'If podcasting doesn't work out, you could always get a job here,' Richard tells me, 'You'd be brilliant at that.'

Once the podcast is in the bag, we head across to the Excelsior and join Tour de France royalty in the queue of people waiting to be seated. There's Seb Piquet and the doyen of *L'Equipe*'s coverage, Philippe Brunel, who is one of the most recognisable figures in the pressroom. With his shoulder-length black hair and uniform of black v-neck T-shirts, black jacket, tailored black trousers and black suede boots, he has a striking presence. He also wears his Tour de France press pass not on a gaudy lanyard like the rest of us but on an elegant silver beaded chain.

Continuing his fascination with dubious things fished out of water, François opts for sea snails. I go for the local speciality of Quiche Lorraine – which arrives slightly singed round the edges, I have to say – followed by a platter of pork meat on a bed of sauerkraut. I know we're not in the Alsace region just yet but it leapt out at me from the menu and it was very good.

Wednesday, 10 July

Stage 5: Saint-Dié-des-Vosges–Colmar, 175.5 km
Stage winner: Peter Sagan
Yellow jersey: Julian Alaphilippe

I arrive back from my morning run just as Richard is returning from the supermarket with our breakfast. We sit in the garden, which is a cool, pleasant space with a wrought iron table and chairs and billowing shrubs and plants that are just the right side of overgrown.

I'm obviously still a bit flushed from running in the early morning sunshine because as I arrive François says, 'Ahhh, it's Lionel Pinky.'

We set off for the start early because Richard and François are to interview the Tour's race director, Christian Prudhomme, about La Planche des Belles Filles. This has come to be known as Prudhomme's climb because it's one he introduced to the race in 2012. Tomorrow's visit will be the Tour's fourth in eight years. On each occasion up to now, the man in yellow at the top of La Planche des Belles Filles has gone on to win the Tour. Bradley

Wiggins in 2012, Vincenzo Nibali in 2014 and Chris Froome in 2017. This year, the race will go beyond the 'old' finish line and tackle an extra gravel section.

While the other two are off with Prudy, I fill the Skoda with petrol, park up and find a cafe. I order a coffee and a mineral water and I'm somewhat taken aback when the bill is €8. I query it with the waiter, who shrugs and says something about the Tour de France.

In Colmar, Peter Sagan gets his first stage win of the race and the 12th of his career, drawing him level with Gino Bartali, Mario Cipollini, Miguel Induráin, Robbie McEwen and Erik Zabel in the all-time list. He's unlikely to get close to Mark Cavendish's 30, let alone Merckx's record of 34, but the stage win puts him 47 points clear of his closest rival in the race for the green jersey and a different record.

Sagan has made the green jersey his own since his Tour debut in 2012 and – although this is venturing into dangerously speculative territory – I'm willing to bet my house that he will win a record seventh in Paris. That would put him one ahead of Erik Zabel, who won six in a row from 1996 to 2001.

I get my abacus out to calculate that no one has worn more of the Tour's three main leader's jerseys than Sagan. Merckx's record of 96 days in the yellow jersey won't be toppled any time soon. Chris Froome would have to win another two, probably three, Tours to get close. Richard Virenque has a collection of 95 polka-dot jerseys. Sagan's tally of green jerseys already stands at 109 (and will rise to 125 by the end of the Tour). Even taking into account 2017 when he was disqualified for his part in the crash that took Mark Cavendish out of the race in Vittel, Sagan has worn almost three-quarters of the green jerseys presented since the start of the 2012 Tour.

'Is there any point to the points competition at the moment?' I ask.

'There is for Sagan,' says Richard.

'But surely they should mix it up a bit? Change the way the points are scored?'

'What's the point?' replies Richard. 'However they do it, Sagan will still win.'

Richard makes a good point. (I'm using the word point too much now).

The points competition has never been designed solely for the pure sprinters. Despite his 30 stage wins, Cavendish only won the green jersey once, in 2011. It has always been a competition that has favoured consistency over pure speed and no one can argue that Sagan is not the most consistent rider. He can score on more or less any territory. In fact, if Christian

Prudhomme was ever tempted to shun the high mountains of the Alps and Pyrenees one year and set a Tour course for the all-rounders, Sagan would be in with a shout.

Our hotel in the chocolate box town of Kaysersberg has a Tour de France link. The Hotel Chez Hassenforder was opened by Roger Hassenforder, a winner of eight stages in the 1950s, shortly after he retired. Hassenforder, now 89, had the honour of presenting the yellow jersey to Julian Alaphilippe on the podium after today's stage, and in the restaurant there are a few photos of him in his prime.

For some reason, I end up ordering the same meal as last night – Quiche Lorraine followed by sauerkraut topped with pork knuckle, pork belly, frankfurter and other German-style sausages. It proves to me that you really can have too much of a good thing and I'm not even sad when I fail to pierce a final piece of particularly slippery frankfurter and it flies off my plate and skids over the floor towards a small dog that has been watching me intently while I eat. It strikes me that to the dog I'm a bit like Peter Sagan: devouring all the meat (points), showing no inclination to share, while he's waiting for a small consolation to bounce his way.

Thursday, 11 July

Stage 6: Mulhouse–La Planche des Belles Filles, 160.5 km
Stage winner: Dylan Teuns
Yellow jersey: Giulio Ciccone

The Cricket World Cup semi-final between England and Australia is on and England have made a brilliant start – or rather, the Aussies are having a shocker. While I wait for the riders to emerge from their buses I spot Matt White and show him the score on my phone.

Daniel is is standing in earshot.

'I thought you were Irish now?' he says.

'Only when it suits him,' says Daniel's ITV cameraman.

'Hey, that's harsh!' I say, 'I'm as Irish as Dan Martin.'

'So not at all, then?' says Whitey.

For the record, Martin's mother is the sister of Dublin-born Irishman and 1987 Tour de France champion Stephen Roche, which makes Nicolas Roche his cousin. Nicolas Roche is as French as he is Irish, of course, because his mother is French. Nationality in international sport is a pretty fluid concept and yet many riders have to declare for one over another.

Having the first mountain-top finish of the Tour midway through the first week is something of a double-edged sword. On one hand it's great to have a proper battle for the general classification so early on, but on the other there's always the risk someone takes a strong hold on the yellow jersey and squeezes the life out of the race.

Opinion is split about the final kilometre-long stretch of gravel that comes after the familiar finish at La Planche des Belles Filles. There's an increased risk of a puncture ruining the Tour for one of the main contenders but there's no disputing it's a stunning spectacle, especially when the gradient hits 21 per cent.

The battle for the stage is between Dylan Teuns and Giulio Ciccone, both Tour de France debutants. The Belgian Teuns wins the stage and Ciccone, who won the king of the mountains competition at the Giro in May, has the more-than-adequate consolation of pulling on the yellow jersey. It was a smart, aware piece of riding by the Italian because he won the strategically placed time bonus at the top of the penultimate climb, the Col des Chevriers, which together with another time bonus on the line is enough to give him the *maillot jaune*.

Behind them, the first riders to be eliminated from the overall picture are Alejandro Valverde and Romain Bardet but, to my relief, the race is still very much alive because the time gaps are relatively small.

Alaphilippe rides with verve and although he doesn't manage to cling on to the yellow jersey, it is his aggression that teases out Geraint Thomas and Thibaut Pinot and forces the gaps to open. Thomas's strength surprises me, as does Bernal's frailty – there's been a 14-second swing between the two Team Ineos leaders – but we agree in the podcast that La Planche des Belles Filles is probably not the ideal sort of climb for Bernal.

Who do we see strolling around the pressroom hoping to be noticed? Gianni Savio, the man who signed Egan Bernal for Androni Giocattoli–Sidermec in 2016, when he was just 18 going on 19, on the basis of an impressive VO2 Max test result. I speak to Savio for a few minutes about how he found and signed Bernal and ask him if he thinks it's too soon for him to win the Tour. 'Maybe next year,' is Savio's verdict.

Whenever the Tour has visited La Planche des Belles Filles, we've always struggled to find decent accommodation. This north-eastern corner of France is not a tourism hotbed and on all three previous occasions we've ended up staying in Lure, which I have previously described as a sort of economic downturn theme park. One year, my non-smoking hotel room was so thick with stale smoke I had to sleep with the window open. I moved my bed as close as I could to the open window so I could breathe fresh air and woke up in the morning with a cold, wet head because it had started raining. Then there was the infamous guesthouse a couple of years ago where our host, who – I couldn't help noticing – was missing a finger, offered to barbecue us some meat on what looked like an open fire in the garden.

This time Richard thinks he's struck gold with an eco-friendly hotel next to a lake. The price tag is a bit punchy, they decline to refund us for François's room (he's off to work for ASO for the day tomorrow), which is fair enough because we've notified them at short notice, and the restaurant is closed but apart from that it sounds great.

Friday, 12 July

Stage 7: Belfort–Chalon-sur-Saône, 230 km
Stage winner: Dylan Groenewegen
Yellow jersey: Giulio Ciccone

A noise wakes me in my eco-chalet at about six in the morning but I think nothing of it and go back to sleep for another hour or so. When I reawaken, I notice a little bag has been placed in the doorway.

Trying to ignore the fact someone has been in my room to deliver the bag while I was asleep, I get up to investigate and find it contains what can generously be described as an eco-breakfast. There's a mini pain au chocolat, a mini crossant and a tiny bread roll, a small pot of apple and strawberry compote, a little carton of juice and a micro pot of jam.

I go for a run to work up an appetite for my bijou breakfast and as soon as I return my phone rings. It's Richard, calling from the eco-chalet next door.

The chalet is so eco I can hear him twice – through the walls and, a fraction of a second later, down the phone line.

('Is there any milk?') he says from next door. 'Is there any milk?'

I search the contents of the bag and the fridge.

'Doesn't look like it.'

('How does the coffee machine work?') 'How does the coffee machine work?'

'I don't know.'

The longest stage of the race is also the most boring. The two breakaway riders are Stéphane Rossetto of Cofidis and Yoann Offredo of Wanty–Groupe Gobert, who also happen to be close friends who train and holiday together. The peloton is content to let them continue with their leisurely touring holiday to Burgundy.

It takes them three-and-three-quarter hours to cover the first half of the stage. They're averaging about 31 kilometres per hour.

'I could probably keep up with them today,' I say.

'On a bike?' says Richard, an incredulous tone to his voice.

'I'm not surprised they're going at a snail's pace on the day they go to Burgundy,' I say.

Silence.

'Eh? Snail's pace? Burgundy? Oh come on, that's a good one.'

There's quite a lot of snail on offer at the buffet laid on for the press. I have to be vigilant because the chewy little blighters are lurking in everything.

With a good three hours of racing still remaining, I walk into town to find a laundrette figuring that I can do enough laundry now to see me all the way to Paris. It's an unconventional strategy but one that will leave me with both rest days free.

I get everything washed, dried and folded in time to get to the team buses to watch the finish. The sprint is messy but Groenewegen gets his first stage win of the race (and Jumbo–Visma's third). It's also the second day in a row that a rider named Dylan has won the stage, leaving Van Baarle of Team Ineos as the only Dylan in the race without a victory.

With all the Dylan-related excitement, I completely forget to drop my snail's pace gag into the podcast when we record at our hotel.

Saturday, 13 July

Stage 8: Mâcon–Saint-Étienne, 200 km
Stage winner: Thomas De Gendt
Yellow jersey: Julian Alaphilippe

At the start in Mâcon, we present the first *Pédaleur de Charme* award of the Tour to Denmark's Michael Mørkøv and I ask him about his work setting up the sprints for Elia Viviani. He admits he watched with frustration from the sofa as his Italian teammate came up short time after time at the Giro d'Italia. Mørkøv recently won the Danish road race championships and so is wearing the red jersey with a white cross on it.

A couple of years ago – having pronounced his name as More-Cough for a while – I asked him how the Danes say it. Merr-Coo, he said. So I started calling him Michael Merr-Coo, only to be picked up by the Danes for saying Michael the English way rather than the Danish way. So I ask him for clarification this morning and he says he's pretty relaxed about the whole thing, which is generous of him.

Falling foul of the Pronunciation Police and their fiendish chief inspector Rob Hatch is an occupational hazard on *The Cycling Podcast*, and I make as many mistakes as anyone, although it's not for a lack of effort. We always make a serious attempt to get the names of people and places right but we also try to bear in mind we are broadcasting to a mostly English-speaking audience so it's important people know, first and foremost, who we are talking about. For the accomplished linguist like Daniel I understand why he gives French, Italian, Spanish and German names an authentic flourish, but he doesn't do the same for the languages he doesn't speak, such as the Flemish Belgians and Dutch.

Mind you, there are inconsistencies everywhere. Why say Ah-Jay-Deu-Zairr for Ag2R but then Cough-uh-diss instead of Coh-fi-dee? And if the Deutschland Tour starts in Munich, do we say Munich or München? Does the Tour finish in Paris or Paree? And if it's the former, why do we say Paree-Roo-bay?

One of the things that first attracted me to the world of professional cycling was that it sounded exotic and so I'd resist attempts to anglicise everything. I remember when the Giro d'Italia and Vuelta a España were routinely called the Tour of Italy and Tour of Spain in the written press and we certainly don't want to go back to that, but by the same token, should I get annoyed when Ciro calls me Lee-oh-nel instead of Lionel? Or should I just accept it's the way he says it in his accent?

Anyway, there's a race on, and it's a humdinger, although I come close to missing a big chunk of it because I can't resist leaving the pressroom, in the Stade Geoffroy Guichard, home of Saint-Étienne – les Verts, the greatest football team in France (sorry François) – to have a nose round the stadium. I find a staircase that is closed off by cones and then push at an open door and find myself in the upper tier, looking down at the green pitch and all the green seats. It's only when I try to retrace my steps that I realise the door has been locked. Unsure what to do, I wait a while until I spot a security guard and he shows me back to where I should have been all along.

The stage is won in impressive style by the breakaway specialist Thomas De Gendt. At a Lotto–Soudal training camp a couple of winters ago I asked De Gendt for his secret to getting in the breaks and he made it sound pretty simple. If at first you don't succeed, try, try and try again. As De Gendt pointed out, the success rate for the *barroudeurs* is pretty low. He might get in 10 breaks for every shot at victory. But today he is extraordinarily strong – and he has to be because the stage drags the riders across the grippy terrain of the Massif Central. They cover 200 kilometres and take in almost 4,000 metres of climbing. When De Gendt powers away from Alessandro De Marchi, the last man capable of staying with him, the Italian has no reply and there's an almost admirable edge to his resignation.

Behind De Gendt there is further drama. Geraint Thomas and his Ineos teammates skid across the road on a sweeping downhill corner and mount a furious chase to avoid losing any time. Then Alaphilippe and Pinot attack on the penultimate climb and steal a few seconds on the rest. In Alaphilippe's case, the bonus seconds at the top of the climb and on the line are enough to give him the yellow jersey again. I don't want to make out I'm some sort of tactical genius but I did predict this in last night's podcast. Mind you, it didn't take a genius to see the opportunity was there for the Frenchman.

Before we leave our hotel the following morning, I can't resist challenging François to a game of babyfoot. One team's little wooden players are wearing white with blue trim, the others are in green so we decide the match is Olympique Marseille versus Ireland. As a child I once reached the semi-finals of a babyfoot tournament held on a French campsite before losing to a Dutch boy who had mastered some sort of Johan Cruyff-inspired version of Total Babyfoot. François's skill at the game betrays a youth spent in French bars. He also quotes all sorts of unwritten rules about how you can and can't score goals, which contradicts his frequent assertion about cycling that the rules have to be in black and white if they are to be respected. It doesn't matter much, anyway, because I'm no match for François and the final score is OM 4 (Cascarino 4), Ireland 1 (Cascarino 1). The result puts a little bounce in François's step, which he usually reserves for those occasions when he's made fun of the British.

by François Thomazeau

Sunday, 14 July

Stage 9: Saint Étienne–Brioude, 170 km
Stage winner: Daryl Impey
Yellow jersey: Julian Alaphilippe

It is kind of funny that for most of the past decade, every time the Tour de France course has been announced by Christian Prudhomme in October at the Palais des Congres in Paris, a few of my foreign colleagues have complained that it had been designed for a Frenchman to win. Whatever the number of climbs, the length of stages, the amount of time trials, those colleagues seemed convinced that Prudhomme's main goal in life and as a Tour de France director was to see a French rider bridge the 34-years gap since Bernard Hinault last won the Tour in 1985. Well, Christian is not a very good planner then!

And he got it very wrong again if, as was said in October, this year's Tour had been designed for Romain Bardet. All the odds seemed in favour of the man who finished on the podium in 2016 and 2017: shorter distances, high altitude finishes, fewer time trials. And a stage even ended in Bardet's birthplace of Brioude, an obvious sign of favouritism.

Well unfortunately, by the time we did reach Brioude, at the beginning of the second week, Bardet had almost already lost the Tour, trailing compatriot Julian Alaphilippe by 3:20 at that stage. On the final stretch to his hometown, he tried briefly to break clear of the main pack, but reached the finish in the anonymity of the bunch. It was an anti-climax for the local favourite, and a summary of his most lacklustre Tour de France since his 2013 debut.

As early as the Pau time trial, five days later, his Ag2R team manager Vincent Lavenu told me that something had gone wrong in his leader's preparation and that they would have to review what it was exactly. While Bardet salvaged some pride with a consolation polka-dot jersey in Paris – in arguably his worst Tour as a climber – there was no hiding a bitter disappointment. Lavenu even confessed that Bardet called him a few days after the finish in Paris to tell him he had considered giving up the sport altogether. It would have been a waste, but part of the problem might arise from that very French obsession with the Tour. In a way, Bardet has been plagued by his early success in the race and by the subsequent claims that he might be the best-placed rider to break the French jinx. Since his pro debut, he only rode the Vuelta once and has yet to take part in the Giro! His consistently good results in Liège-Bastogne-Liège, his second places in Strade Bianche or at the Worlds in 2018 have shown what a versatile rider he could be without his Tour de France monomania.

Sources within the team hinted at diet problems, themselves resulting in a general weariness about trying so hard to no effect. But Bardet is a clever young man and he will hopefully be able to reinvent himself as a cyclist and find new goals and motivations. The Tour might not be one of those.

Adam Yates may also be affected by the same Tour jinx. Since his fourth place and white jersey in 2016, he has been marked out as Mitchelton–Scott's GC man for the Tour. The first of the two Yates twins to shine in the pro ranks, he has since been repeatedly overshadowed by brother Simon and he failed yet again in this edition, finishing just inside the top 30, like in 2018. While Adam had not lost his GC ambitions in Brioude, the stage win by teammate Daryl Impey – and what a deserved victory it was – was the first of four by the Australian outfit, two of them by Simon (see below) and the last by Matteo Trentin.

The transition from a team going for stage wins into a GC team is not an easy one. Mitchelton–Scott made a first step in that direction when Simon Yates won the Vuelta in 2018. But they showed they retained other options too and they should probably keep it that way.

It was the second time in three years that we came to Bardet's region of Aubrac and it again turned out to be one of the most beautiful parts of the country. *The Cycling Podcast* team spent the night in the glamorous village of Lavoûte-Chilhac, surrounded by a buckle of the Allier, and celebrated Bastille Day on the town's main square overlooking the river. Simple, tasty, solid food, strong organic wine and a friendly, relaxed atmosphere on a large terrace, a band murdering 1980s hits and spectacular fireworks – every once in a while it kind of feels good to be French! That is why I accepted to croon a sort of lounge version of *La Marseillaise* for the pod.

Monday, 15 July

Stage 10: St Flour–Albi, 218 km
Stage winner: Wout van Aert
Yellow jersey: Julian Alaphilippe

I unwittingly broke some illusions in this Tour de France by revealing to most *Cycling Podcast* members and listeners that we French never ever use the word echelon to describe a split in the peloton caused by crosswinds. Echelon is an English word and what's wrong about it?

In France, we use the word *bordure* and that is exactly what happened in this windy stage to Albi, when some of the GC contenders – Thibaut Pinot, Jakob Fuglsang, Richie Porte, Rigoberto Urán, Vincenzo Nibali and Mikel Landa – found themselves trapped at the back.

There was no stopping Julian Alaphilippe at this stage of the Tour and after taking the yellow jersey, leading out Elia Viviani for a stage win, breaking away with Thibaut Pinot, he was again the man who started the echelon by speeding as the pack split at a roundabout, with his Deceuninck–Quick-Step teammates on his heels. It was a brilliant move, which left all the riders who had chosen the wrong side of the road forced to chase unsuccessfully until the finish.

Among the most dejected riders on the line was George Bennett, who had chosen the very moment when the *bordure* started to get to the back of the peloton to collect bottles. Great team work indeed. Sitting fourth overall at the start, the New Zealander was seen as ideally placed to seize the yellow jersey should Julian Alaphilippe crack in the first Pyrenees stage. But Bennett reached the finish line 9:41 behind Belgian teammate Wout van Aert, handing their Jumbo–Visma outfit their fourth stage win in 10 days. Hardly a consolation for Bennett, who now describes himself on his Twitter account as a '10speeder/water boy getting bottles and pushing pedals for @JumboVisma_Road…'

Van Aert obviously did not need a bottle from Bennett to win a bunch sprint in his first ever Tour de France. At 24, the three-times cyclo-cross world champion belongs to that new generation of riders seeming to produce more astounding talent than we have seen for decades. In a year when we celebrated the 50th anniversary of Eddy Merckx's first Tour de France victory in 1969, it is also exciting that two of the most promising riders in the bunch, Van Aert and Remco Evenepoel, are Belgian.

We ended a prolonged first week – the first rest day was unusually scheduled for Tuesday – in the charming small town of Gaillac, renowned for its wines. At the lovely Au Fil des Saisons restaurant, our dinner came with two bottles of L'Origine by Domaine de Brousse. Highly recommended.

Tuesday 16 July

Rest day, Albi

I was caught in the echelon at breakfast on Gaillac's Place de la Liberation where *The Cycling Podcast* team started answering questions submitted by our dear listeners for the press conference held on every rest day at the Grand Tours. Lionel announced he had made arrangements to have lunch with Jonathan Vaughters in Albi. I had no intention to have lunch with the EF Education First manager and I was not invited anyway. As it turned out, the chat was great but the meal pretty bad, so I did not miss much. Richard also had plans to talk to Jakob Fuglsang at the Astana team hotel, also in Albi, for which I had no interest whatsoever. Had I decided to do some work on the rest day, I might have gone to Thibaut Pinot's press conference, but it was never discussed so I gave up without even asking.

As a result I was left behind in Gaillac, forced to look after everybody's laundry, not unlike George Bennett when he was ordered to go for bottles in the previous stage while the action was unfolding. Luckily there was a washing machine in the flat we were hiring and I could spend most of the day listening to the machine running while I was checking everything was going smoothly from the dining room sofa.

My task was interrupted around midday by my sudden urge to go for lunch, which I did on the same Place de la Liberation at a great little place called Vigne en Foule. It has become quite a cliché for some of my British colleagues (namely Daniel) to claim that French cuisine reached its peak in the 19th century and is now outrageously overrated. Well I'm glad they think that actually, as it leaves those great spots where young chefs – often women – rejuvenate our food heritage rather tourist-free. It was nearly perfect at Vigne en Foule with a great simple salad with fresh home-grown and tasty tomatoes and a perfectly cooked *filet de dorade* served with the compulsory glass of Gaillac. Nice, subtle and pretty affordable. Long shall we keep those joints unknown to Trip Advisor.

I loved the place so much that we returned in the evening when my team leaders finally made it back from Albi and had dinner next to the full Eurosport France team and their consultants Jacky Durand and David Moncoutié, both former Tour de France stage winners. My little plastic mascot Doraemonpoulidor was quite pleased he could take a selfie with Jacky.

Wednesday, 17 July

Stage 11: Albi–Toulouse, 167 km
Stage winner: Caleb Ewan
Yellow jersey: Julian Alaphilippe

There is a discreet man in the press peloton called Jean-François Quénet. 'Jeff' is the typical behind-the-scenes man and one of the best-informed journalists in cycling. Non-descript, intense, bespectacled, he speaks perfect French and Italian, excellent English and fluent Spanish and provides the official live feeds for the Tour as well as the Giro, the Dauphiné and several other smaller races all over the planet. His flat in Angers is the place where countless foreign riders, most of them Australians, settled down when they set foot for the first time in Europe in search of a pro career. Jeff is almost never there, spending most of his time in his other flat in Kuala Lumpur or in frequent flyer lounges in airports all over the world. It would be much easier to cite the Aussie riders whom Jeff did not help make a career in Europe than to list those who did. But one of the riders dearest to his heart is certainly Caleb Ewan. I remember Jean-François telling me about him as early as 2012 or 2013 as one of the most promising sprinters in the world. Ewan actually stayed with Jean-François in Angers in 2011 to discover European cycling. In October of that year, Jeff even took him to Paris for the Tour de France presentation and stopped his car on the Champs-Élysées on the very spot of the traditional finish line of the final stage of the Tour. 'One day I'll win here,' said Ewan, who was only 17 at the time.

It took him eight years to keep his word but he did in this Tour, and I could not help sending a text of congratulations to Jeff when the Australian raised his arms after winning his first Tour de France stage in Toulouse. Ewan went on to win two more, including the Paris one for the Belgian Lotto–Soudal outfit he joined this season after his former team – now Mitchelton–Scott – unexpectedly kept him out of the Tour in 2018.

While this first half of the Tour was rather erratic, with 10 different stage winners out of 10 stages, the only thing to seldom change was the name of the riders in the morning breakaway. The best of friends in real life, Stéphane Rossetto and Yoann Offredo might not be quite strong enough to win a Tour stage but they apparently decided at the start of this edition to make sure that one of them – and sometimes the two of them – would be at the front everyday. This time it was Rossetto, and he came pretty close to making it as he was still leading the way with Aimé De Gendt when the Belgian attacked him with 10 kilometres to go, angering the Frenchman, who claimed they could have made it together. The row earned Rossetto television time at the end of the stage, which was the aim of the game after all. While the two Parisians – Rossetto is Offredo's daughter's godfather – might not have the best tactical skills, they obviously work hard on their speeches and have become media favourites as great quotes providers.

We recorded the podcast on the terrace of a brasserie as dusk was falling on the huge Place du Capitole in the centre of Toulouse. Lionel had *cassoulet*. Just okay, he said. As we finished recording, a crowd of cyclists suddenly invaded the square and started riding all around it. Scores of kids, families, older folks, men and women, a multi-coloured flock of smiling people in the saddle. This is also the Tour.

Thursday, 18 July

Stage 12: Toulouse–Bagnères-de-Bigorre, 202 km
Stage winner: Simon Yates
Yellow jersey: Julian Alaphilippe

The first day in the mountains – OK, we had Planche des Belles Filles, but in the mind of the peloton the race really goes up a gear when we reach the Alps or the Pyrenees – is always slightly different. The atmosphere at the buses is tenser at the start. Riders just nod or stare vaguely at your silly questions about the hardships of the stage, as if they needed being reminded how much they are going to suffer. Sports directors crack jokes in a lame attempt to pretend that this is just another day in the car. And you secretly hope there is going to be action, attacks, attempts, failures and bonks while actually fearing that the GC contenders will take it easy with a crucial individual time trial the next day.

Unfortunately, the second option prevailed, which at least made it possible for a breakaway to succeed. Simon Yates's attitude since the start in Brussels suddenly became much clearer. The Briton had been dropped repeatedly in the first week and lay 97th overall, one hour and eight minutes behind Julian Alaphilippe. It should have been seen as a warning from the 2018 Vuelta champion: no GC ambitions equals stage wins. Any suggestion that he might be off form was gradually ridiculed as he led the way up Hourquette d'Ancizan and all the way down to Bagnères-de-Bigorre to outwit Pello Bilbao and Gregor Mühlberger on the line.

With all due respect to Simon, his victory was not exactly what the journalists scrumming around the buses at the finish line were interested in. Early in the stage, the word had spread that time trial world champion Rohan Dennis had given up and the rumour was that he had gone missing. For the Australian to call it quits the day before the individual time trial that was his only goal in this race came as a real shock, made much worse by the fact that nobody at Bahrain–Merida seemed to have any idea what the problem was. Dennis finally reappeared at his team bus without saying a word before a few team officials came to talk to the press without saying much more. It was hinted that the Australian was unhappy about the TT bike Bahrain–Merida had provided, that he was leaving the team or that his mental health was fragile. We were actually left clueless as we started queuing for the press buffet, traditionally held in the headquarters of the local fire brigade.

After recording on the main square of a small village along the way, we spent the night – and the next – in a great B&B just outside of Pau in Serres-Castet. I slept in the 'yellow room' to keep in line with the Tour. We booked in what appeared to be the best restaurant in town only to find out that the chef was actually trying too hard to play in a league where he clearly did not belong. Like a sprinter tackling l'Alpe d'Huez in the leading group. And the more the dinner went on, the more the gaps increased between the dishes. We made it back home way outside the time cut.

Friday, 19 July

Stage 13: Pau–Pau, individual time trial 27 km
Stage winner: Julian Alaphilippe
Yellow jersey: Julian Alaphilippe

The Alapmania spread all over France in July but it probably culminated with the Frenchman's unexpected victory in the only individual time trial of this Tour in Pau. I will not elaborate again on Pau's presence on the Tour map, as it has now become a prerequisite. What do we know before the route is announced? The Tour will finish in Paris, go to the Alps and the Pyrenees, and most certainly to Pau. Every team has their own favourite hotel in town, every journalist their traditional dinner of *foie gras, confit* or *cassoulet* and Jurançon or Madiran in town. Pau stages are thus quite predictable – you'll go talk to Team Ineos DS Nicolas Portal the day before because he lives there – but this one was not.

The absence of TT specialists Tom Dumoulin, Chris Froome or Primož Roglič – and the still puzzling absence of Rohan Dennis – had already made it an undecided stage but Alaphilippe's name was certainly not among the ones mentioned at the start. That he should beat Geraint Thomas, Rigoberto Urán or Richie Porte certainly came as a surprise and one that raised questions. Was the Frenchman going to keep the jersey in the Pyrenees? Could he win the Tour? Everything now seemed possible for the man who had already won Milan–Sanremo, Flèche Wallonne and Strade Bianche and had the season of a lifetime. While 'Loulou' kept repeating he still had no GC ambitions, his extraordinary performances also raised eyebrows from those of us still tempted to see the shadow of doping behind every exceptional feat. A few stories in the French and the Dutch press rediscovered ketones, food supplements which might enhance performance but are not banned, substances *The Cycling Podcast* already mentioned at length in an episode a few years ago.

Another controversy arose from the edition of La Course, held on the same course as the men's time trial and won as expected by Marianne Vos thanks to a brilliant last-gasp effort. Our dear colleague and friend Peter Cossins found himself on his own in the van used by ASO for press conferences close to the finish line and tweeted a picture of it implying that no journalist was interested in Vos's victory. I was myself in the press centre a few miles away and I can confirm that many colleagues, and certainly all our Dutch colleagues, attended the broadcast press conference and asked questions to one of the country's most celebrated champion, while several other hacks, including Richard, actually talked to Vos on the finish line without getting in the van.

Which certainly did not answer the lingering question about the future of women's cycling and ASO's part in it. The Tour organisers have been repeatedly attacked for not doing enough – which is certainly true even though they still organise three of the main events on the women's calendar, La Course, Liège-Bastogne-Liège and Flèche Wallonne – and they are aware of it. A prominent ASO official told me before the Tour that 'like it or not', they had no choice but to launch a major stage race for women, if only to protect their image, knowing that it probably would not be profitable, at least in the short run. But a women's Tour de France remains out of the question, unless it was held at some other time in the season. Of course, a women's Tour coupled with the men's looks great on paper, but this is not Wimbledon or the Olympics, static events held in purpose-built facilities. To think a women's Tour would be possible at the same time as the men's is to ignore the logistical demands of the race. When would the women race? Before the men, running the risk of being caught by them? After the men, running the risk of catching them? All together as in most marathons? Meaning the podium ceremony would be held until everybody has finished? More jerseys, more time in the mixed zone, more press conferences. And probably twice as much staff working around the clock, many more policemen and *gendarmes* on the road, longer hours for everyone involved especially as the hotels during the Tour are already full with the men's event only. To add a women's Tour to the whole thing would probably force some Tour people to sleep more than 100 kilometres away from the next day's start. Or should the women's race be held the day before, or the day after? It would require double staff for ASO as this is a moving event, making the whole operation a financial disaster.

I am convinced we will know sooner rather than later about ASO's plans and let us hope they manage to create the great stage race women's cycling deserves.

Saturday, 20 July

Stage 14: Tarbes–Col du Tourmalet, 117 km
Stage winner: Thibaut Pinot
Yellow jersey: Julian Alaphilippe

Oh my Merckx (sorry I'm an atheist), what a great victory by Thibaut Pinot this was! I have never been chauvinistic or even a proper fan. I have not had a favourite rider since childhood (it was Hennie Kuiper at the time) and I really try not to get carried away by a bike race, whatever happens. But this was slightly different because I could really appreciate it as an achievement, the end of a long journey to the top. I was lucky to discover Pinot in 2010 when he was crowned the best climber of the Tour de Romandie after only a few months as a pro. Thanks to my friendship with FDJ team director Yvon Madiot, I had first-hand access to this young man and his incredible potential. That year in Romandie, he was literally flying in the mountains with such a natural elegance that he really left the rest of the peloton dumbfounded. I never quite saw Pinot look as airy, light and carefree in the climbs ever since until this year on the Tour. As if hard work had finally turned him back into what he was from the start. The Frenchman seriously looked a class above the rest of the bunch in this stage and in the next to Foix. He certainly was better, stronger than Egan Bernal and Geraint Thomas those two days. Whether his form would have lasted in the Alps had he not been injured once again is just speculation. But the promises shown in the Pyrenees made his withdrawal even more frustrating for every lover of the sport. It was not only the rider himself. Everything within the Groupama–FDJ team had seemed more professional, more efficient, if only the way Pinot was handed a jacket after each stage to avoid catching a cold. For once, manager Marc Madiot was left with playing his own exuberant and sometimes embarrassing part on the finish line and talk to the press while his brother Yvon was brought back to the role he relishes, that of the man in the shade. Philippe Mauduit, hired this season from UAE Team Emirates after stints with Saxo Bank, Lampre and Bahrain–Merida, brought serenity and experience into the whole operation. With all these men around him, and his brother Julien as his faithful and trusted coach, Pinot seemed poised to give his very best in this Tour. Unfortunately hard luck struck again as he was forced out through injury in the ill-fated stage to Tignes (see stage 19, below).

I was among the journos flocking like vultures around the Groupama–FDJ hotel when a team car brought him up there to face the press and spend the night before going home. Since Thibaut speaks little English, I interviewed Mauduit in the car park while Pinot was talking to my colleagues in the lobby. When I had finished, I decided to return inside the hotel to maybe catch a few of the last questions to the Frenchman. I rushed in by a side-door, opening on a corridor with a lift at the end of it. I pressed the up button. When the door opened, Pinot was there, his back to the mirror, crying like a baby. Next to him was press officer Marion Gachies, vainly trying to comfort him. It was an unexpected vision. And one of the most moving moments of my career as a cycling reporter. I only managed to mumble a few words in a trembling voice.

'I can tell you that we're all sorry Thibaut. The press, the fans, every one of us. We all wish you the best. And don't worry, it'll work out soon.'

'Thank you,' he sobbed while Marion was patting my arm.

I left them at the next floor to step into the empty lobby, feeling stupid and rather sad.

Ah well, it's only cycling, isn't it?

The night after Le Tourmalet was still a moment of celebration as we headed for Le Viscos, my favourite hotel and restaurant at the foot of the pass. We had far too much to eat as usual. I thought I had played it safe by ordering fish in advance. Little did I know that chef Alexis had received a six-kilo turbot the day before. I had almost half of it on my plate. I also probably should have turned down the second starter (or was it the third?) and the Armagnac. One of us was DNF at the end of the meal. You will never guess who it was.

by Richard Moore

Sunday, 21 July

Stage 15: Limoux–Foix (Prat d'Albis), 185 km
Winner: Simon Yates
Yellow jersey: Julian Alaphilippe

Thought I'd ride my folding bike up the Prat d'Albis, the new climb just above Foix that the Tour is visiting for the first time. Apart from anything else, it will be a good way of working off the meal (or meals) we'd eaten in Le Viscos the previous evening. My goodness. The food, in quality and quantity, was astonishing. Most remarkably, it defeated Lionel, who did a Rohan Dennis and went missing without explanation some time between the second and third helpings of *porc noir*.

'We are confused,' says a spokesman for *The Cycling Podcast* when asked about Birnie's disappearance. 'Let's say I am disappointed with what happened with Lionel today because we expected a big effort from him tomorrow. It was his decision to stop at the feed zone. For sure it has nothing to do with his physical condition.'

Birnie declines to comment.

Alas, the best laid plans… after getting my folding bike out of the car at the pressroom and plotting my route on Google Maps, it starts raining. Plan B is to watch by the team buses in Foix, where we see Simon Yates take his second stage win while behind him there is, yet again, little to separate the GC favourites, even if Pinot looks the most impressive.

Whether by accident or design – let's give Christian Prudhomme and Thierry Gouvenou the benefit of the doubt and say design – these weekend Pyrenean stages have been brilliantly teasing. They have offered clues without giving away the ending. They have provoked the GC contenders without forcing them to fully reveal their hand.

There are two entirely different ways of reading Alaphilippe's performance over the two days. Either they provide evidence that he is close to his limit and on the brink of collapse, or that he might have enough in the tank to hang on. Over the two days he loses 1:22 to Pinot and 56 seconds to Bernal, but he gains three seconds on Thomas. Currently Pinot appears to have the momentum but he is still almost two minutes down on Alaphilippe. Bernal is unconvincing: he hasn't taken time where we expected him to. Thomas looks solid but unspectacular.

It is tantalising and difficult to recall a Tour being so evenly balanced and difficult to call with only a week's racing left.

Monday, 22 July

Rest day, Nîmes

We wake up in cool, overcast Foix to drive across the south of France to Nîmes, where we make straight for an ugly complex of cheap hotels on the outskirts of town, where Lionel has arranged to meet Matt White. All of France's worst hotels are here, clustered around a Courtepaille, the French equivalent of Little Chef, but much, much, much, much better.

After dropping off Lionel, François and I park and walk the 150 metres or so to the Courtepaille. We almost don't make it. The heat, as we step out the car, hits us like a punch to the face. It almost floors us. Our movements are exaggeratedly but necessarily slow. Any more effort and we'll collapse. It's brutal.

We stagger into the air-conditioned Courtepaille and fall into a booth. We can barely speak, managing only, as if they are our dying words: '*Un verre de vin rosé, s'il vous plaît.*'

This is the heatwave which is set to accompany us over the next couple of days as we head towards the Alps. We muse over how this might affect Thibaut Pinot, who apparently, in what is maybe just another myth about the mercurial Frenchman, doesn't like the heat. 'In that case he's in luck,' says François, 'because it's going to be 10 degrees and raining in the Alps. They're expecting storms.'

Pah! In the 40-degree heat of Nîmes, such a forecast seems – dare I say it
– fanciful.

Tuesday, 23 July

Stage 16: Nîmes–Nîmes, 177 km
Winner: Caleb Ewan
Yellow jersey: Julian Alaphilippe

It's so unusual to have a stage of the Tour that starts and finishes in the
same place, especially so deep into the race. Today feels like a second rest
day in Nîmes. To wake up and go back to bed in the same bed – albeit a
Kyriad – is such a glorious luxury. Plus, Nîmes is a lovely place to stop, even
in this stifling heat.

The heat might be affecting even the most laidback of people. The previous evening, François's anger flared, most unusually, when we sat down outside a pub to record our *Press Conference* episode. Once seated, and having set
up recorder and mics and got ourselves comfortable, the owner came and
told him and Lionel to move because the tables were reserved for eating.

I was inside at the time ordering drinks. François came in to tell me that
we were moving on. I tried to cancel the beer but the barman reacted with
irritation and demanded we pay. I didn't want to but François tossed a €10
note in his direction and stomped out – actually, a much cooler, more effec-
tive form of protest.

'This is typical of the south,' said François as he stomped away. 'I hate to
say it because I am from the south, I live in the south, I love the south, but I
have seen this attitude too many times.'

'It's bullshit,' he added.

Wednesday, 24 July

Stage 17: Pont du Gard–Gap, 200 km
Winner: Matteo Trentin
Yellow jersey: Julian Alaphilippe

For the second year in a row Team Ineos (formerly Sky) have a rider sent
home for violent conduct. Last year it was Gianni Moscon for throwing
a punch, this time it is Luke Rowe, who gets involved in a scuffle at the

front of the peloton with Tony Martin of Jumbo–Visma towards the end of an otherwise routine stage. Martin is sent home too, depriving two of the strongest teams of two of their strongest riders.

A yellow card would have been proportionate, Dave Brailsford says when Lionel calls him. Brailsford feels a straight red is 'very, very harsh'.

Perhaps it is a question of optics: the fact that Rowe and Martin have their altercation right at the front of the bunch, and that it is caught on camera, possibly dooms them. It looked as though Martin tried to run Rowe off the road, apparently after Rowe had lifted a hand to Martin. It is, we all agree, a case of 'beef' followed by 'afters' – though Lionel argues that it is not real beef but 'vegetarian beef'.

'Quorn,' I suggest.

Lionel notes that each rider is their team's road captain; François points out that they are more than road captains, more like bodyguards, protecting their leader and also fighting for position and space on their behalf. Which probably explains the altercation that led to their expulsion.

Thursday 25 July

Stage 18: Embrun–Valloire, 208 km
Winner: Nairo Quintana
Yellow jersey: Julian Alaphilippe

At this Tour Matt White has resembled someone who has played the lottery and lost the jackpot but won the lucky ball. While Adam Yates has, for the second year in a row, been posted missing in his GC quest, his brother, Simon, has won two stages and Daryl Impey has won another. Then, yesterday in Gap, Matteo Trentin won a fourth.

Impey's success seemed particularly sweet for White. When he got back to the team bus and gave a few interviews, he was crying.

I go to see White at the start today to ask him why that win meant so much. I have to wait a long time because he is chatting with some Australians, who have given him a couple of bags filled with biscuits and other goodies from home. 'Anzac biscuits, mate,' says White. 'Amazing biscuits. Here, try one.'

Idiotically, I then press record and begin my interview. This interview never makes it on to the podcast – nobody wants to hear the sound of two men talking with their mouths full of biscuits.

Fortunately, I do make out what he says as he talks about his special bond with Impey, the last rider signed when the team was launched in 2012. The South African had been a journeyman. He was on the books of three teams in 2011, having originally signed for Pegasus, an Australian team that went kaput before they even raced. At Mitchelton–Scott he has found a secure home and they have developed a strong, highly versatile and selfless rider capable, as he showed in Brioude, of winning.

White's demeanour changes when talking about Trentin. The Italian had shown his class the previous day, I suggest, in attacking from such a strong group, powering over the climb and winning alone. White shrugs, looking completely unimpressed: 'He did what he's paid to do.'

Pointedly, he adds: 'You know, that was only his second win for us.' It seems a little harsh, though Trentin, signed on a big contract from Quick-Step last year, is reported to be moving on again in 2020, to CCC. The politics and dynamics of teams always fascinates me. To most outsiders, Trentin would be – as Daniel would put it later – the first name on the teamsheet for his strength and versatility. But a rider's physical talent is only one component of what makes him a good teammate.

Tonight is our most challenging evening of the Tour. François's forecast has come true. The weather has spectacularly turned: the rain tonight, as we drive up the mountain to our Airbnb accommodation, is lashing down, in a storm of biblical proportions. Our apartment is part of a goat farm, above a cheese shop in which we shelter when we arrive. The apartment is perfectly nice but has no bedding or towels. Marie, the owner, says that she emailed to tell me this two days earlier: one of many emails I have not opened. Not that there was much I could have done about it. And I had emailed her in January to tell her we would be travelling with the Tour de France.

It doesn't matter, she says with a smile. Once we have checked in she sends her son out in the storm with some essentials. He arrives at the door looking bedraggled but at least he has managed to keep our bedding dry.

After this palaver, we drive a few hairpins up the mountain to try and find somewhere to eat. It is an out-of-season ski resort: there is one restaurant open but it is full, we are told after sprinting across the car park through torrential rain, ducking inside and shaking the excess water off like dogs clambering out of a lake.

At the other end of the car park is a pizzeria. We return to our apartment and pass a very pleasant evening in our mountain apartment, eating pizza from boxes and drinking wine.

Next morning we tidy up and leave, but Marie, so pleasant the previous evening, clearly isn't impressed by our failure to bring bedding and towels, or by our clean-up operation (or perhaps both). She leaves me a brief but quite stinging review on Airbnb: 'Un peu déconnecté du contexte.'

Ouch.

Friday 26 July

Stage 19: Saint-Jean-de-Maurienne–Tignes Col de l'Iseran, ~~126.5 km~~ 89 km
Winner: ?
Yellow jersey: Egan Bernal

This has long been in my diary as the day I go up in a helicopter, courtesy of Skoda, who sponsor *The Cycling Podcast Féminin*. They ran a competition during the Women's Tour, with listeners invited to predict the winner of stage one. Several guessed correctly (Jolien D'hoore) and the winner, chosen at random, was a chap called Stephen De Souza.

Stephen's prize was an all expenses paid trip to the Tour de France, including travelling ahead of the race in one of the Skoda VIP cars, then popping up in a helicopter for a bird's-eye view of the peloton, followed by a picnic by the roadside and a seat in the VIP stand at the finish. I'm not quite sure why but the deal was that I had to tag along too.

'I personally wouldn't go up in a helicopter,' says Lionel as we drive to the start. 'They're very unsafe.'

'There has never been an accident involving a helicopter at the Tour de France,' I say. 'We'd have heard about it.'

'But you know what this means?' pipes up François from his nest. 'That the chance of there being one increases a little every day.'

For the rest of the journey, whenever it goes quiet, Lionel makes a choppy noise that – I assume – is meant to sound like a helicopter's rotors.

In the *Village Départ* I meet Stephen and we are introduced to our driver, Tim Harris, the former British road race champion with jet-black hair and a mahogany tan. Tim is a great raconteur and entertaining company. It promises to be a good day.

We leave 20 minutes or so before the start, racing ahead to meet Stephen's wife and two kids. Having won his prize, he'd arranged a family holiday in the area. They have a brief reunion before we zoom ahead again to meet our helicopters. First, around 40 kilometres into the stage, we watch the Tour pass from the roadside. It's a short 126 kilometres stage, steadily climbing pretty much all day before the monster Col de l'Iseran, but we are standing by a roundabout, where the road is flat, and you'd have thought, from the way the riders are going, that this was a sprinters' stage. There is an air of chaos, an atmosphere of anarchy. It is a big old mess: Dan Martin and others off the front, the group behind stretched in a long, fractured line, and finally, cast adrift and clearly struggling, one rider with a teammate... is it Thibaut Pinot? A few minutes ago I had been talking about Pinot to my companions as the most likely winner of the 2019 Tour de France.

What is going on?

There is no time to find out. We are running, Anneka Rice-style, to our chopper, with our pilot mentioning, just as we clamber aboard, that this will be her first time flying in the mountains. 'I normally fly tourists over Paris,' she says.

I am so preoccupied by the fragments of the race that we've just seen that I have no time to worry about this. Up we go. Disgracefully, I spend much of our time in the air refreshing Twitter, trying to get updates. Here we are in a spectacular valley, mountains towering over us on each side, hovering over the race, but just far enough away to not be able to make out who is who or – more to the point – who is where. Three TV helicopters buzz around beneath us, 50 metres over the race. We are 150 metres above them. And many more hundreds of metres above us are the planes receiving the images and transmitting them. The logistics of it all – not to mention the cost and the fuel burned every day – is mind-boggling.

The helicopter ride is wasted on me. I feel too disconnected. I want to get back to Earth as quickly as possible.

We land at the foot of the Iseran, meet Tim, jump back in our car and speed away. Up the mountain we go: green, scraggy and empty, apart from thousands of fans. We crest the summit and plummet – Tim is a very fast, very skilful driver – until, at the 30 kilometres to go banner, we pull off the road to park in a little clearing. There is a caravan and an awning and trestle-style tables and chairs – and, a little incongruously, Andy Schleck.

The chef is in the caravan, and he emerges brandishing bowls and plates of simply sensational food, using ingredients sourced locally (he makes different dishes every day).

But, again, I am glued to my screen, and the race. I'm not the only one. I prop my phone up on the table and Tim and I watch Egan Bernal attack. Pinot by now has dropped out in tears, suffering from an injury to his leg he'd suffered in a seemingly minor crash a couple of days earlier. Now

Alaphilippe is beginning to struggle, perhaps cracking. Here, then, is the decisive point of the race: Bernal riding into crowds of fans on a benign day of blue skies (so much for François's prediction of storms!).

We finish lunch and pose for a group photo. While saying 'Cheese!' I feel a dollop of rain. The air cools dramatically and suddenly, as though a new weather system simply replaces the old one. We dash for the cars. I keep watching the race on my phone. Having stopped for lunch we are only 30 minutes or so ahead of the riders. Tim, whose daily challenge is to keep just ahead of the race, steps on the accelerator and we carry on descending. The sky turns dark grey. Proper rain begins to fall, rapidly turning into hailstones. Not hailstones – that doesn't do them justice. They are like mini-boulders. That's what they sound like as they ricochet off the car. I fear for the car. We enter a tunnel and the noise is turned off – what blessed relief. When we come out the other side we are met again by the same crescendo – a noise so deafening that we can't hear each other shout. The road on this side of the tunnel is white: the hailstones have congealed, turning it into an ice rink. Most of the Tour vehicles travelling ahead of the race have now stopped by the side of the road. 'We can only keep going because we're in a 4x4,' says Tim. 'Look, watch this,' he brakes hard and we skid.

On the screen, meanwhile, Bernal is now with Simon Yates and they are approaching the summit, still in perfect weather. Yet here we are, only a few kilometres ahead, in a completely different universe – the kind of hellscape that might feature in a Cormac McCarthy novel. We crawl along, but what will happen to the race? Only one thing can happen, surely: it has to be stopped. They can't send them plunging off the mountain into this. To stop the race will seem absurd to the riders and to everyone watching. But to those of us ahead of the race it is clear. It has to be stopped.

Tim slams on the brakes again, before we pile into some stopped cars. Before us, crawling across the road, is a giant, muddy, rocky tongue: a land-slide. Among the first to the scene is Dag Otto Lauritzen, a professional rider from the 1980s who now works for Norwegian TV: he has his camera crew with him and is the first to broadcast from the scene. Then the land-slide begins to move, as if it was coming to life. The air fills with the sounds of panic. We scamper back to our vehicles.

The route to the finish in Tignes is blocked. But Tim has a look and sees an alternative road, which we take. Meanwhile Radio Tour crackles into life with the familiar but now urgent voice of Seb Piquet: 'Attention! Attention!' The stage is cancelled. All riders and teams are to stop at the summit of the Iseran. Arrangements are made to transport them to emergency accommodation in Val d'Isère; Seb relays some detailed instructions over several minutes.

There is confusion in our party. If there isn't going to be a stage finish then there is no need to go to Tignes at all. The Skoda hotel is in a different valley, in a different direction. The message is conveyed to our car: we should head there now. 'What about me?' I ask. I am not staying in their hotel.

'Oh shit, yes,' says Tim. 'What will we do with Richard?'

Looking at Google Maps I can see that we are almost at the foot of the climb to Tignes. I know Lionel and François are at the top, where the finish was supposed to be, and that they will have to come back down this road. 'Just drop me here,' I say.

I am dropped off and the first people I see – or who see me – are podcast listeners who give me a friendly, morale-boosting reception. They have been here for hours waiting for the Tour and so are obviously disappointed, but there is a strange, almost giddy atmosphere, which you often find when things have taken a spectacularly unusual turn.

Our attention is drawn by a throng of cheering people moving at walking place towards us. Loud music is emanating from the throng and horns are blaring, and at the centre of all the commmotion are two Deceuninck–Quick-Step people carriers. Sitting on the passenger seat of one of the cars, still in his yellow jersey, is a smiling Julian Alaphilippe. The sunroof slides open, the music gets louder and then Alaphilippe rises up on the seat and emerges from the car, like Jesus Christ, or the Pope. He waves and everyone cheers: a moment of jubilation and joy in the madness. It's also the last time anyone will see Alaphilippe in a yellow jersey at this year's Tour.

I wait for Lionel and François at the Deceuninck hotel and when they arrive we record our episode as, all around us, Belgian TV set up a makeshift studio to broadcast their evening show. Finally, and very late, we set off, along with Simon Gill, who was at the summit of the Iseran taking some wonderful pictures of a strange, surreal day. He had been there as the race was called off and the riders and teams gathered at the top in an atmosphere of chaos and confusion.

For the second year in a row we are put up by Friend of the Podcast Simon Lund, and this time he is here to welcome us. It is almost 11pm when we arrive in a pretty frazzled state and close to midnight when we sit down to tuck in to the food and drink that Simon has generously laid on. It isn't ideal, then, that an argument then develops which gets so heated that poor Simon and his friend retreat, spending far longer than seems necessary washing dishes.

It kicks off when Lionel remarks that it was very unusual that everyone simply went along with the decision to stop the stage. 'But there was no choice,' I say. I am surprised that Lionel is surprised. Earlier, I had listened to his interview with Richard Plugge, the Jumbo–Visma manager, and noted, also with surprise, that Lionel seemed sceptical when Plugge said that he believed it was the right decision.

'Of course it was the right decision!' I say.

Maybe I assert this a little too forcefully – let's upgrade that to 'probably' – Lionel is, to use the parlance, triggered – and an argument develops. A pretty silly one, which owes much, no doubt, to the fact that we are close to the end of three weeks of spending almost every waking hour in each other's company; that it has been a long, stressful day; that it is now very late; that we are all tired, and that the table contains [insert a respectable number here] empty wine bottles. I also think that on a deeper, perhaps even subconscious level, we are all a little traumatised by what has happened – that such a 'weather event' could strike so suddenly and with such violence.

Eventually civility is restored. Simon and his friend return to the room with another bottle of wine. The conversation moves on.

But for the record, I was right. Haha, only joking, Lionel. As difficult as it is to write the following – deep breath – in Lionel's defence, his main point was that it was extremely unusual, perhaps unprecedented, for there to be such consensus, especially when the rules about what should happen in such circumstances are not entirely clear. On this point I suppose he was right, dammit.

It has been a strange, unsettling day.

Saturday, 27 July

Stage 20: Albertville–Val Thorens, ~~130 km~~ 59.5 km
Winner: Vincenzo Nibali
Yellow jersey: Egan Bernal

Thick clouds smother the Alpine valleys, visibility is down to about 10 metres, and all morning there are rumours about today's stage being cut or cancelled altogether. Initially ASO announce that it is drastically reduced to just 59.5 kilometres, leaving Val Thorens as the only real climb, albeit a long 'un.

We drive towards Val Thorens in a fog of our own, half-expecting to have to make a detour for Paris at any point. It feels like a wet Sunday or the day after Christmas.

The stage does go ahead but, being so short, everyone feels a little short-changed. After two-and-a-half weeks of tremendous racing and entertainment, it is a shame to see the race stutter to its conclusion. But it is what it is, as Bradley Wiggins might say.

Vincenzo Nibali wins, reminding us that he's still in the race, but we spend much of today still discussing the previous day's events. The debrief continues over dinner in one of the hotels in Val Thorens, where Seb Piquet, the voice of Radio Tour, joins us.

Seb, who sits near the front of the race in a car with the *chief commissaire* and *directeur de course* Thierry Gouvenou, had a key role, of course, and he tells us who said what when, and how the decisions were made. The fact that such a thing has never happened before makes it seem all the more strange, dramatic and alarming. It also makes the swiftness and clarity of the decision-making – as well as the hasty drawing up of contingency plans – all the more impressive. Seb reflects on the fact that the Tour, and the riders, were extremely lucky.

'Imagine if the storm had broken as they descended the Col de l'Iseran… if Bernal had ploughed into the hailstones and ice... or if the landslide had hit a vehicle or a rider… when you consider what might have happened, it doesn't bear thinking about.'

Sunday 28 July

Stage 21: Rambouillet–Paris, 128 km
Winner: Caleb Ewan
Yellow jersey: Egan Bernal

A big old schlep to Paris is in front of us as we wake up in François's friend's apartment in Les Menuires, 15 minutes down the mountain from Val Thorens. I am doing an interview with Radio 5 Live at 9am. Arranging it for then was safe, I had thought.

The plan is to leave immediately afterwards but as 9am approaches I begin to feel guilty because we are more or less ready to go – I sense that my radio interview is only delaying our departure.

If I didn't already feel bad, Lionel does a good job of making me feel worse. At 8.30am he appears in the kitchen/living area that Simon Gill and

I are sharing. He seems unusually chipper. 'When's your interview? 9am?' he asks, rhetorically.

'Five Live isn't it?' he adds, rhetorically again, before adopting a generic radio voice and performing a parody that sounds suspiciously rehearsed: 'Should dogs drive cars? Dave in Sheffield's on the line: he says his dog can drive. But Linda in Hartlepool says of course dogs shouldn't be allowed to drive.

'Now over to Richard in the Alps – what do you think, Richard, should dogs be allowed to drive cars?'

At 9.08am we leave the apartment, head into the mist and join the long line of cars still driving off the mountain. None of them, as far as I can see, are driven by dogs.

We haven't had breakfast and are keen to stop at the first service station for a croissant and coffee. Unfortunately the first service station is closed. So is the second.

The drive goes fairly quickly but all the time we save by only stopping a couple of times is lost upon entering Paris. Our hotel is close to the Place de la Concorde but getting there is enormously complicated. Security in Paris around the final stage of the Tour has been getting tighter and tighter over recent years and we drive in circles for an hour or so. There is a minor road rage incident when a car blasts its horn then cuts aggressively in front of us, narrowly missing the wing of our car. With a manouevre that Peter Sagan would be proud of, I get us back in front. It means we are two metres further ahead than we would otherwise have been.

Eventually we use our accreditation to get through a roadblock, hoping we can wriggle our way to our hotel. Instead we are spat straight onto the course. It is like going into a wardrobe and entering Narnia. Here we are, driving up an empty Rue de Rivoli, heading to the Champs-Élysées, crowds spilling over the barriers, positively humming with a sense of anticipation and excitement that *The Cycling Podcast* Skoda does not really live up to.

We don't want to be here. We aren't even sure we should be here. What a way to end the Tour. I grip the wheel so tightly that I can actually feel my fingers turn white. And then, as we approach the Place de la Concorde, there is an opening: to our right, a gap, for vehicles to enter the course. I steer towards it with utter conviction – looking like we know what we are doing is key at this point – and the *gendarmes* step aside to let us through. We re-enter the Paris congestion about 300 metres from our hotel.

It's our first time in Paris for the final stage in a few years and I don't see a second of the race. We spend it in and around the team buses on the

Place de la Concorde, recording our final podcast, going from team to team and assessing their Tour, before arriving at the Lotto–Soudal bus just in time to watch the final kilometre. This is serendipitous, because they're one of the few teams to have a TV screen embedded in the side of the bus. It is also serendipitous because Caleb Ewan wins and we are able to capture the reaction of the team's staff and guests and riders' partners.

We interview a few riders as they arrive back at their buses but these are always a bit awkward because they want to see their partners and families and celebrate with their teammates. My attempt to interview Nils Politt about the mid-Tour birth of his daughter falls particularly flat.

When it's all done we are once again grateful not just for François's easy company but also for the ease with which he can find a fantastic place to eat anywhere and at any time. It is after 10pm when we sit down in Brasserie Mollard, where we eat well and toast a fine Tour, one of the best any of us can recall.

In some respects, though, our final dinner mirrors the race: starting strongly and getting better and better before a dessert that doesn't quite live up to the high standards of the entrée and main course and constitutes a bit of an anticlimax.

2019 VUELTA A ESPAÑA

by Lionel Birnie

Saturday, 24 August

Stage 1: Salinas de Torrevieja–Torrevieja, 13.4 km team time trial
Stage winners: Astana
Red jersey: Miguel Ángel López

I'm on the 6.45am flight to Alicante to meet *The Cycling Podcast*'s Head of Winning Behaviours, Jonathan Rowe, who has driven the Skoda to the Costa Blanca for us. With the team time trial kicking off in the early evening, there's time to check in to our hotel, which is a petrol station, cafeteria-style bar and hotel all in one.

The time trial course starts at Salinas de Torrevieja, close to the salt lagoons. I learn that the lake is pink thanks to a combination of a certain type of bacteria and algae that thrive in the salty water. I also learn that even putting a toe in the water is prohibited to avoid contaminating the water. This, I imagine, must be frustrating for Instagrammers who visit.

The start ramp is chiselled-out salt and flanked by large salty dunes. On their way to the start, the riders roll through an arch that has also been neatly carved out of the salt. Salt is very much the star of the show. The team buses are parked outside the warehouse where pallets are stacked with bags of salt. The lagoons of Torrevieja are one of the primary salt producers in Spain, incidentally.

I do a lap of the team buses before heading to Torrevieja to watch the riders come in. Team Jumbo–Visma have a shocker. One of their young

Americans, Sepp Kuss, has a mechanical problem early on although they manage to overcome that setback well enough. Then they crash en masse taking a left-hand corner. It's a strange one because the road appears to be going slightly uphill. Primož Roglič and Steven Kruijswijk are among the fallers and when they cross the line it's clear they're not in the mood to talk because they do an abrupt 180-degree turn and ride off to their team bus. Only Tony Martin stops to talk to the media and he explains that the crash happened when they unexpectedly hit a wet patch of road. I'm confused by this because it's been a hot summer's day without a drop of rain. It later turns out that someone's hosepipe burst, spraying water all over the road.

Jumbo–Visma's misfortune has consequences for Deceuninck–Quick-Step, who are the only team to seriously threaten the best time set by Astana. They come round the corner and have to slow to get past a Jumbo–Visma team car that had stopped to help their riders. That disrupts their rhythm and they cross the line two seconds slower than Astana.

Miguel Ángel López, who crossed the line at the head of Astana's formation, pulls on the first red jersey of the Vuelta. I am a bit puzzled by this too, because the common convention is that the teams engineer it so one of the faithful foot soldiers gets to lead the race, rather than put a genuine contender for the overall classification into the spotlight on day one. But what do I know?

I record an unconventional solo podcast before heading for dinner at an Indian restaurant. Curry on the Costa Blanca. Welcome to the Vuelta.

Sunday, 25 August

Stage 2: Benidorm–Calpe, 199 km
Stage winner: Nairo Quintana
Red jersey: Nicolas Roche

I'm slightly disappointed that the start of the opening road stage doesn't take us into the heart of Benidorm. I'm curious to see what it's like. It was a little fishing village until the first tourism boom in the 1950s, which was sparked by the town's young, go-getting mayor Pedro Zaragoza, who was 28 when he came to office and set about laying the foundations for the holidaymakers' behemoth it is today. He travelled all round Europe selling the idea of sun, sea and sangria. He sent gifts to prime ministers and heads of state. And he lifted a ban on women wearing bikinis. Then he encouraged the building of high-rise apartment and hotel blocks, and the final piece of the jigsaw was the expansion of Alicante airport in 1967, which opened the doors to millions of visitors. At a certain point I can't help feeling they should have put a limit on the development because some of the tower blocks look a bit J.G. Ballard to me.

I'm willing to concede that I'm too pasty to enjoy a sun-worshippers' holiday and when I travel abroad I like to sample more than home comforts and Happy Hour, so I know Benidorm is not really trying to appeal to me.

The opening road stage of the race takes the riders through hilly countryside that is familiar to many of them. Calpe is a popular base for team training camps, with Deceuninck–Quick-Step among those to spend several weeks of the winter in the region.

Nevertheless, the final climb of the Alto de Puig Llorença catches out plenty of riders, notably almost all of Team Ineos, and sets up an enthralling finale.

The team buses are parked on a long straight stretch of road a couple of kilometres from the finish line and the race passes on the opposite side of the road. I'm watching on my phone but the images are slightly delayed so I'm surprised when all of a sudden Nairo Quintana comes flying past. He is being chased by a group containing Rigoberto Urán, Nicolas Roche, Primož Roglič and, amazingly, Fabio Aru, who seems to have rediscovered some form to be in this company.

Quintana holds on to win the stage and Roche takes the red jersey. There are jubilant scenes at the Team Sunweb bus when they get confirmation their man is in red and sports director Luke Roberts talks about the dilemma they faced when they knew both the stage win and the race lead were there for the taking. It's important not to be too greedy, he says.

The mood at the Team Ineos bus is very different. Their sports director Nicolas Portal is characteristically candid about their shortcomings. Only David de la Cruz and Salvatore Puccio made it into the second group. Tao Geoghegan Hart and Wout Poels lose almost 10 minutes. What was it, I ask, poor positioning going into the climb? Portal declines the ready-made excuse and says it was more to do with not having the legs at the crucial moment.

Monday, 26 August

Stage 3: Ibi–Alicante, 188 km
Stage winner: Sam Bennett
Red jersey: Nicolas Roche

With the Vuelta zigzagging along the Costa Blanca for a few days, we can stay in the charming little hillside town of Altea for a couple of nights. The whitewashed, cobbled streets are a far cry from the full English breakfast and lager bars on certain stretches of the coast.

I've made it my mission to find the best *pan con tomate*, which is popular for breakfast in large parts of Spain. It's very simple stuff – toasted bread topped with fresh tomato sauce and then a drizzle of olive oil – but like many simple things it's also very good. Some places seem to add a bit of garlic or salt to liven it up a bit. This morning's offering is the best so far, mainly because it's not too watery so it doesn't sink into the toast and make it soggy.

My other mission is to get to the finish in Alicante early so I can head to the technical zone where Eurosport's outdoor studio is set up. My task is to speak to Bradley Wiggins, who is growing into his role as a strident pundit, before he goes on air.

Just before this year's race started, the Union Cycliste Internationale, the sport's governing body, confirmed that Juan José Cobo had been stripped of his 2011 Vuelta title, making Chris Froome – not Wiggins – Britain's first Grand Tour champion. Richard is speaking to Froome, who is still recovering from his horrible crash while checking out the time trial course during the Critérium du Dauphiné in June, on the phone. The plan is to put our conversations with Froome and Wiggins together for an episode of *Kilometre 0*.

I spot Wiggins strolling down the finishing straight towards me. It's not so much a stroll as a swagger. There's always been a touch of the Liam Gallaghers about him. He's vaping as he walks and at one point almost disappears in a huge white cloud of – what is it? It's not smoke, so it's gas, I guess. Initially I am taken aback by the size of him but when I think about it, this is probably a normal, healthy build for a man who stands well over six feet tall. This is Wiggins after his brief flirtation with rowing, not the skeletal figure stripped down to the bare minimum for the Grand Tours. The contrast startles me slightly.

I take Wiggins back to 2011 and his second season with Team Sky. Having won the Dauphiné in June, he crashed and broke his collarbone a week into the Tour de France and the Vuelta was not only his comeback from injury but the first time he had shown over three weeks that his fourth place in the 2009 Tour de France was not a one-off. Froome and Wiggins finished second and third to Cobo and I ask him how different things might have been at Team Sky going into 2012 if Froome had won that Vuelta. Would Wiggins have won the Tour? It could all have been different, but it's a question we can't possibly know the answer to.

Tuesday, 27 August

Stage 4: Cullera–El Puig, 175 km
Stage winner: Fabio Jakobsen
Red jersey: Nicolas Roche

At the start in Cullera, I see Marc Sergeant, the softly spoken contender for the title of cycling's friendliest man, standing on the grass a little way from the Lotto–Soudal bus. I cross over to him and offer my condolences for the loss of their young rider Bjorg Lambrecht, who died after crashing at the Tour of Poland earlier in the month.

It's clear that Sergeant and the team's riders are still coming to terms with what happened. Sergeant was on holiday with his children and grand-children when he got the call telling him Lambrecht had died. He says that talking to Lambrecht's parents was the most difficult conversation he's had in his long career in cycling.

I wonder how the riders carry on in such circumstances, knowing that danger lurks around every corner, accepting that crashing is part of the job. Sergeant explains that Lambrecht was spectacularly unlucky to collide with a concrete culvert – a little gully built into the edge of the road for drain-age. The riders were given the choice of whether to race on or take a break. Some of Lambrecht's closest friends asked to be taken out of the line-up for the BinckBank Tour so they could attend the funeral. Two of them, Tiesj Benoot and Jasper De Buyst, returned to racing at the Tour of Denmark a week or so later and they each won a stage.

'Cycling is a way of life for us,' says Sergeant. 'The riders race because it's what they do and their way to honour Bjorg is to keep racing and keep trying to win. But it's difficult and if a rider comes to me and says, "I can't go on," I would understand and let them take their time.'

Sergeant also admits that the most difficult times are perhaps to come, when the racing season ends and there's time to reflect. Even the thought of removing Lambrecht's name from the list of riders on the team bus at the end of the year is too much to face at the moment and, he says, the team will continue to honour his name in some way.

At the finish in El Puig, I meet up with Orla Chennaoui and we discuss the race so far – and the fact that yesterday's stage saw an Irish stage winner, Sam Bennett, and an Irishman in red, Nicolas Roche. I kick myself later when I realise I've missed the opportunity to call the segment 'Irish Corner'.

Bennett loses the opportunity to win back-to-back stages by going the long way round a roundabout on the run-in. Despite slipping out of position he fights back strongly to force a photo finish. If it had been another 100 metres to the line, Bennett would surely have won, but the Dutch champion Fabio Jakobsen nicks it.

Most of the general classification contenders have a quiet day, although Primož Roglič loses a crucial teammate. Steven Kruijswijk, third overall at the Tour de France last month, has been suffering with a bad knee since crashing in the team time trial on the opening day and he pulls out in the first 50 kilometres. EF Education First's Rigoberto Urán also hits the deck although his teammates do a sterling job to get him back to the peloton. At the team bus, Mitch Docker holds his hands up and takes responsibility for the crash. It's a *domestique*'s worst nightmare. A moment's inattention, a touch of wheels and your team leader is on the ground.

Just a brief mention for the paella – and variations on paella – on offer at the pressroom buffet. The Valencian version with rabbit is excellent but the dish with black pudding and chickpeas in it is sensational even if it might have the traditionalists up in arms.

Wednesday, 28 August

Stage 5: L'Eliana–Observatorio Astrofísico de Javalambre, 170 km
Stage winner: Ángel Madrazo
Red jersey: Miguel Ángel López

The climb to Javalambre is a bit like a mini Mont Ventoux, especially with the rocky landscape stretching beneath us and the domed roof of the observatory at the top just past the finish line.

When I reach the top and check on the race situation, three riders are almost 12 minutes clear. They are Burgos BH teammates Ángel Madrazo and Jetse Bol and Cofidis's José Herrada, whose brother Jesús briefly led the race last year. I look at the run-in to the bottom of the final 11-kilometre climb and give them no chance of surviving to the top. The road is net uphill almost all day.

As the intrepid trio reach the start of the climb, they still have eight minutes but I still reckon it's not enough to hold out if López, Quintana, Valverde, Roglič and the rest decide to turn it on.

I'm wrong, of course, because what we witness is an astonishing display of rope-a-dope riding by Madrazo, who has already been on the attack a lot in this Vuelta and has the white with irregular-sized blue polka-dots jersey as king of the mountains to show for it. Three times he is dropped and three times he claws himself back up to the others as Bol plays the policeman's role, sitting on Herrada's rear wheel and refusing to help.

Madrazo, who endeared himself to British fans at the 2013 Tour of Britain by winning both the mountains and sprints titles while riding for Movistar, refuses to lie down and, having seemingly been dropped for good with four kilometres to go, he returns to the two leaders inside the final kilometre and then pushes clear of Herrada.

Between big gulps of air, Bol cannot contain his delight at having pulled off the victory. Yes, they outnumbered Herrada two to one but Burgos BH are a small team.

Behind, the favourites get close but not close enough. López attacks and regains the red jersey. This gives Daniel the opportunity to use López's nickname, Supermán, pronounced with a roll of the Rs and with the emphasis on 'man'.

As nicknames go, it certainly divides our audience. Later that evening we receive an email from a listener. One says, 'Finally, just say "no" to Superman.' Another says: 'Please, please, please stop saying SuperrrrMAN.'

Cycling is a sport of unwritten rules, as you are all by now aware, and it seems that some nicknames are good while others are bad. Where is the line drawn and who's drawing it? I'm not sure but I can say with certainty that Daniel would have plenty to say about it if we suddenly started referring to G and Froomey in the podcast. The justification seems to be that the exuberant Colombian radio reporters say Supermán and Nairoman all the time, but your guess is as good as mine.

Dinner at our hotel in Rubielos de Mora features a lot of truffle, a local specialty. It's not as nutty or woody as some truffles I've had but it goes very well with each of the dishes.

Daniel and I record a final segment of the podcast attempting to add some context to the overall battle. I embark on a slightly laboured analogy which compares Movistar and their bemusing tactics to truffle hunters. It strikes me that while Quintana has three truffles and Valverde has one, Valverde seems intent on pinching one of Quintana's truffles to make it two truffles each, while López and the rest are off unearthing fresh supplies of truffles. It doesn't really work in the podcast and it doesn't really work in print either but for the next few days I receive messages asking me for an update on Movistar's truffle status so it must've resonated with some people.

Thursday, 29 August

Stage 6: Mora de Rubielos–Ares del Maestrat, 198 km
Stage winner: Jesús Herrada
Red jersey: Dylan Teuns

I drive from my hotel in Rubielos de Mora to the start in Mora de Rubielos, frustrated that I am unable to get to the bottom of why these towns around 30 kilometres apart have such similar names. Was there some kind of argument over the name and this is the compromise?

I'm making an episode of *Kilometre 0* about *soigneurs*, partly inspired by the knowledge that Thomas De Gendt hasn't had a post-race massage for years. I ask one of the Lotto–Soudal *soigneurs* if he knows why De Gendt doesn't bother with the traditional leg rub in the evening.

'He's a special guy, uh? You better ask him yourself,' is the reply.

So I do. De Gendt explains that he simply doesn't feel the benefit and would prefer to have an hour extra to himself in the evening. 'Don't your legs hurt?' I ask. 'Everybody's legs hurt,' he says. He also says that when he was at Quick-Step they more or less forced him to have the nightly massage. Old school, is his verdict.

Whenever I observe the *soigneurs* at the start of a stage they seem to be the ones who have time on their hands. They're often joking among themselves or leaning on the bonnet of the team car watching the world go by. But that's because this is a rare hour or so of downtime for them, a pause between their other duties. Like the mechanics they work long days. They're up early to make the race food, mix up the drinks bottles, load the musettes. During the stage they go to the feed zone and then they rush to the finish line to greet the riders with a cold drink or a warm jacket. And finally, they do a couple of hour-long massages in the evening. And if they have any time to spare they cover for others or help with the laundry. As they say, a swanny's work is never done.

I drive the course to the feed zone and watch as they hand the musettes – cotton bags containing lunch – out to the riders as they pass. 'Have you ever dropped one?' I ask one of Deceuninck–Quick-Step's *soigneurs* – who is called, delightfully, Peter De Coninck – as he heads back to the car.

'You can't call yourself a *soigneur* if you drop the musette,' he says.

'I guess you can't leave this team now, not with your name.'

'No, I guess my job is safe for now.'

He runs across the road and I dash back to my car and follow the convoy of team cars into the finish at Ares del Maestrat where there is an almighty snarl up. The police officers who are trying to clear the jam look stressed. They wave at me to back up but there's nowhere to go, so they wave at the guy coming down the road towards me to back up instead, but there's nowhere for him to go either. Somehow – I have no idea how – after a good 20 minutes of frantic arm-waving the jam eases itself and I manage to squeeze through.

The race is turned on its head by an 11-man break which might have been caught but for a terrible crash in the bunch. Rigoberto Urán, Nicolas Roche and Hugh Carthy are among those who are forced to abandon the race while up ahead Dylan Teuns and David de la Cruz are in a move which helps them rocket up the overall standings.

With 10 riders still out in front but spread all over the place in the final 50 kilometres, it's one of those races that changes every time you look away from the screen. On the last climb Teuns gets away with Jesús Herrada and the pair ride hard to the line. Teuns finds himself in the opposite position to the one he was in at La Planche des Belles Filles during the Tour. He's in a two-man break knowing he stands to take the race lead so he gives it everything knowing his companion will win the stage. Herrada is grateful for the opportunity to succeed where his brother José fell short yesterday.

Teuns now leads De la Cruz by 38 seconds in a race he was uncertain of starting. A freak accident on his sit-on lawnmower in August left him needing stitches to a wound in his head. Apparently the thing stalled suddenly and he hit his head on the steering wheel. Only in Belgium.

I couldn't get a room at Daniel's hotel so I'm staying 20 minutes away in a rather inferior place. We record the podcast in the gardens of Daniel's hotel and I head back to my place for a very strange meal. The waiter gives me the hard sell and persuades me to order the barbecued mixed grill. What arrives are chunks of unidentifiable meats that manage to be both charred and undercooked. At one point a flying beetle lands on my shirt and falls on the table and I can't be absolutely certain it's not escaped from the plate.

There follows a very uncomfortable night. The walls are thin and as I try to doze off I hear the man next door engage in a long phone call. If I thought that was bad, my neighbours on the other side arrive back just after midnight and – how shall I put this delicately? – begin some pretty vigorous practice for the Indoor Mixed Madison Championships. Fortunately it seems they are practicing for the sprint event rather than the full Olympic distance and at last I manage to fall asleep.

Unfortunately, I'm up again a couple of hours later with a very nasty case of mixed grill's revenge.

I shouldn't complain, but sometimes, when you're hugging the toilet bowl at 3am, covering the Grand Tours can be a lonely business.

Friday, 30 August

Stage 7: Onda–Mas de la Costa, 183 km
Stage winner: Alejandro Valverde
Red jersey: Miguel Ángel López

The finish at Mas de la Costa is a belter. I remember the climb from three years ago when Matthias Frank won from a long escape as Chris Froome, Nairo Quintana and the rest battled their way past the remnants of the break-away. This time, perhaps remembering how passing riders on the narrow roads had complicated matters, it's all together at the bottom of the climb. The big four come to the front on the steep slopes and at one point, just when the gradient is at its worst, Alejandro Valverde, Primož Roglič, Miguel Ángel López and Nairo Quintana are side by side across the full width of the road.

It's the picture of the Vuelta so far and for a brief moment it's impossible to say who looks the most likely champion in waiting. If I had to pick, I'd say Miguel Ángel López.

And yet, when push comes to shove it's Valverde in his world champion's rainbow jersey who surges away to win the stage, with Roglič right on his wheel. Then there's daylight to the two Colombians, López and Quintana. Mind you, this is a finish that's made for a man who has won on the Mur de Huy at Flèche Wallonne five times.

Despite faltering slightly, López is back in red as the game of pass the parcel continues with the leader's jersey. Teuns is dropped with about 25 kilometres to go and slips to 18th overall.

Roglič is riding a very different race to way he approached the Giro and my sense is he has more in the tank for the second half of the race than he had in Italy. Certainly there's an intensity to him that manifests itself in monosyllabic responses to the media. At the Jumbo–Visma bus after the stage he answers one question with a 16-word response then hops on board. Suddenly I'm minded to think that perhaps Roglič is the one who looks most likely to nudge clear of the others.

There's a long drive up to Catalonia before the start of tomorrow's stage and I've decided to get an hour or so under my belt tonight. My hotel promises sea views but when I check in it becomes apparent that it'll require binoculars to get a good look at the thin sliver of watery blue on the horizon.

My hopes of a nice dinner on the seafront are dashed and so I order shrimp croquettes and a pizza in the hotel restaurant, where I eat alone wondering why the staff have rather optimistically laid a long table for 18 in the centre of the room. Just as I am finishing my meal, at close to 10.30pm, a large group of teenagers arrives and fills the long table. My room is next to the lift shaft and, by the sound of it, the group of teenagers take turns to ride in the lift one by one between about midnight and half past one.

Saturday, 31 August

Stage 8: Valls–Igualada, 166 km
Stage winner: Nikias Arndt
Red jersey: Nicolas Edet

Piloting *The Cycling Podcast* team car solo can have its advantages. I can listen to football podcasts (which I wouldn't dare suggest if the Buffalo was with me) and my music, which strays beyond maudlin ballads and *Belle and Sebastian*.

But the very considerable downside is that there's no one to navigate, no second opinion at tricky junctions, and this morning that catches me out. I end up taking a wrong turn and end up on a busy single-carriageway road driving almost 50 kilometres in the opposite direction to Valls in Catalonia. And because the two sides of the road are divided by plastic bollards there's nowhere to turn round for more than 40 minutes. Of course, that means I have to drive another 40 minutes just to get back to where I started making it a race against time to get to the start.

I make it – just – and manage to grab a few minutes with Dimension Data's Ben King for an episode of *Kilometre 0* we're making about the riders who have come through Axel Merckx's Hagens Bermans Axeon development team since it started as Trek–Livestrong a decade ago. King was one of the first and he's been followed into the World Tour ranks by Sam Bewley, Taylor Phinney, Alex Dowsett, George Bennett, Ian Boswell, Lawson Craddock, Joe Dombrowski, Jasper Stuyven, Nathan Van Hooydonck, Tao Geoghegan Hart, Eddie Dunbar, Neilson Powless, Logan Owen, Jasper Philipsen and the list goes on. It's an impressive alumni and another of Merckx's former students, Ruben Guerreiro, features in the shake-up for the stage in Igualada, eventually finishing fourth.

On my way to Igualada, I succumb to the lure of the golden M on the roadside and I pull over to get a burger and fries (something else I'd never do if the Buffalo was around). Who should I see just ahead of me in the queue? TV's Matt Stephens (a former British road race champion, let's not forget) and his Eurosport crew.

'Our little secret, eh?' he says.

'Oh yes. Our little secret,' I say, promising not to tell anyone about the chicken nugget chaser he adds to his order.

At the finish I catch up with Orla in the zona técnica and we discuss a snippet of news announced by Deceuninck–Quick-Step that has caught my eye. They've agreed to sign 20-year-old Belgian climber Mauri Vansevenant when he finishes university next summer. He's the son of three-time lanterne rouge at the Tour de France Wim Vansevenant and he was named after the 1991 Vuelta champion Melcior Mauri. As heroes go, that's quite an offbeat choice.

The rain is heavy in Igualada but Team Sunweb shine in the finale. Martijn Tusveld takes one for the team, getting himself out in front only to fall as he exits a sketchy roundabout, although the result is to take pressure off his teammate Nikias Arndt in the group behind. Arndt delivers the stage win and I'm starting to think the red jersey has been made using some particularly itchy material this year because no one seems to want to hang onto it for more than a day. Nicolas Edet of Cofidis is catapulted into a lead of almost two-and-a-half minutes with Dylan Teuns pogoing back up to second place after they both made the break.

My Vuelta stint is at a close. I drive to Barcelona, where I am reunited with Richard and we record the podcast on a pleasant rooftop terrace as the sun sets.

Just as we wrap up recording, we receive a text from Daniel. He returned to his car in Igualada to find it had been broken into and everything had been taken. Clothes, laptop, everything gone. It's a horrible situation and an inconvenient one because it'll mean scrambling to replace the essentials before tomorrow's mountain stage to Andorra. Mind you, where better than Andorra to replenish his wardrobe? I have visions of seeing Daniel in a duty-free Sergio Tacchini tracksuit and Fila trainers next time we meet. It was no laughing matter at the time, of course but, with the passing of time we can joke about it and I'm dying to ask if the thieves also took his running kit, which would have been drying out on the parcel shelf. Surely not.

by Richard Moore

Sunday, 1 September

Stage 9: Andorra la Vella–Cortals d'Encamp
Winner: Tadej Pogačar
Red jersey: Nairo Quintana

Today starts well, which is ominous. I wake up in Barcelona having had a fabulous meal with Lionel the previous night in a Galician restaurant. The drive to Andorra lies ahead of me. I leave at 9.30am and arrive in Andorra just after midday.

I park in the press area of the large, empty car park vacated for the Vuelta, next to a Eurosport car. Then I wander 15 minutes to Odei cafe, opened by the Australian cyclist Leigh Howard but now owned by another Australian cyclist, Jack Haig. There are a few staff members of the Mitchelton–Scott team inside, but no Haig – he is racing in Plouay – though his girlfriend is running the coffee machine.

Hannah Barnes, the Canyon–SRAM rider and partner of Tao Geoghegan Hart, is here, and I have lunch with her. She talks mainly about her love of American football – favourite team the LA Rams – and a forthcoming holiday to America and Mexico. She has bought some good, healthy food in the cafe and is decanting it into tupperware boxes to give to Tao for the five-hour transfer later to Pau.

My phone rings. It's Lionel. But since I have a mouth full of poached eggs I ignore it. Then he texts. Then Gregor Brown, a journalist on the race, sends me a voice message by WhatsApp. Lionel's message reads: 'Just had a call from the Vuelta saying you've got to move the car. It's parked somewhere it shouldn't be.'

He follows that with: 'Classic Buffalo . ☺ 🐎 🐃'

Then: 'They just called again to say if you don't move it now they're towing it.'

There are no emojis with this one. I sprint down, almost throwing up my poached eggs, to find Laura, who runs the press office, and two other Vuelta officials standing over the car, glaring at me. The Eurosport car has gone and *The Cycling Podcast* Skoda is, I will admit, a little conspicious, surrounded as it now is by team buses.

After the start I drive to the foot of the final climb at Encamp. There is press parking in the underground car park by the cable car; I park nowhere near any Eurosport car then get the cable car to the top, a 20-minute ride to 2,100 metres. Emerging at the summit I can't help but notice that it is very chilly. I don my layers: a thin Rapha jacket over a denim shirt. Insufficient.

As the riders begin to climb up to the finish it starts raining. Then hailing: icy bullets from the sky. It is like stage 19 of the Tour de France all over again as ice forms on the road. The hailstones are lethal: further down the mountain riders are taking shelter in buildings, or in, the case of James Knox, trying to grab umbrellas from spectators, but of course the riders at the front plough on – quite literally, since the climb includes a 'gravel' (dirt) section that is turned by the rain and hail into thick, gloopy mud (Miguel Ángel López and Primož Roglič both fall off).

The hail stops but the bad weather continues after the finish: thunder, lightning, and the only way off the mountain for 90 per cent of the people up there (including the riders) is the cable car.

The riders, many shivering and looking miserable (honorable exceptions: Edvald Boasson Hagen and Yukiya Arashiro), are supposed to go first, followed by the people working on the race, including journalists, and then the general public. The queue stretches for a couple of hundred metres and moves very, very slowly, because the cable cars are overloaded and keep halting. When this happens the cars just hang there, swinging slowly and bouncing lazily in silence – it's as if they have stopped for a breather.

Eventually I reach my car and turn the heating to max. I put the address of my hotel, just across the border in France, in the SatNav: it says I'll get there at 9.30pm. But I haven't had dinner. I figure I'll stop en route. We also still have to record today's podcast. My phone rings as I drive out of Andorra. It's the hotel. And the proprietor is furious. 'Unacceptable! Check-in closes at 8pm. 9.30? No! No! Unacceptable.'

The call goes on for 14 minutes. I persuade him to allow me to arrive at 9.30. Daniel, stuck behind me, isn't so lucky, or persuasive. He is told to find another hotel. I arrive at 9.38. It is a beautiful place – and it isn't really a hotel; it's the angry man's house.

Once I've checked in I go to try and find somewhere to eat in the village, which feels like mission impossible – it's France, it's after 9pm, and it's Sunday. But amazingly the staff in the restaurant of a none too fancy hotel take pity and rustle up a *cassoulet*. I dial up Lionel and we record a very late podcast – me wearing chunky headphones and speaking into a microphone in between mouthfuls of *cassoulet* while the other diners look on, puzzled and perplexed.

When I get back to my lodgings and open the door the man who couldn't accept check-ins after 8pm suddenly materialises. 'So you found somewhere to eat.' He seems disappointed.

A testing day. I finish it with a cup of Nuit Calme tea. I really need something stronger.

Monday, 2 September

Rest day, Pau

Ahead of me is a two-and-a-half hour drive to Pau. First there is breakfast to negotiate. It is the sort of place where, when I move, I hear the floorboards creak elsewhere in the house. When I enter the breakfast room, Monsieur appears from another door at exactly the same time. When I put my knife in the homemade apple and nut jam (very nice, incidentally), he materialises at my shoulder to explain that there is a special spoon for that.

When I go to pay I have a problem. My jacket, with my wallet in the pocket, is missing. I try to explain to the man that I have probably left it in last night's restaurant. He isn't having it. How will I pay, he keeps asking. I say I will have to go back to the restaurant to see if my jacket is there. Only with extreme reluctance does he allow me to go.

I return and there is my jacket, sitting on the back of my chair. I return to pay. Monsieur seems surprised.

It's a relief to get on the road to Pau and once there I head to the EF Education First hotel on the outskirts of town to do a couple of interviews. While waiting I chat to the team doctor, Rick Morgan. Our conversation haunts me late into the evening, and indeed will remain in my thoughts for weeks, because we speak about the death on the eve of the Vuelta of Bjorg Lambrecht, the 22-year-old Lotto–Soudal rider who crashed and died at the Tour of Poland. 'He should have been here,' says Rick.

Morgan had been working at the Tour of Poland, he tells me. He was in the team car as it went past the fallen rider: a routine crash, everyone thought, and for Morgan it was a case of checking that none of his riders were involved and carrying on. This one appeared so innocuous. Morgan thinks that Lambrecht hit something in the road and lost control. It wasn't at particularly high speed. There was no one else involved.

But something struck Morgan as strange as they drove past. Attending to Lambrecht, the first person on the scene, was a doctor from another team, Deceuninck–Quick-Step. And Morgan could tell from the sense of urgency, the frantic ripping off of Lambrecht's clothes, that this was not a routine crash. He heard Lambrecht say, 'Help me.'

I have nothing to say to this. My eyes are swimming in tears.

'You know, I reproached myself for not stopping to try and help,' says Morgan. 'But really, even if he'd suffered that injury [a lacerated liver, followed by a cardiac arrest] in a hospital, nobody could have done anything.'

Morgan says that since Lambrecht's death some of the riders have spoken to him about their fears. But as Morgan says, this was a freak incident. 'I'd say it's more dangerous riding your bike to work in the city than being a professional bike racer,' he says.

I guess rationalising is a human and necessary reaction – necessary certainly if you are going to be a doctor or a professional cyclist. We mourn and move on. But the loss of Lambrecht is so shocking and sad because it seems so impossible to rationalise. He was so young – he looked much younger than his 22 years – and so talented. His career and his life were ahead of him. His parents had just arrived in Poland to follow their son. There are really no words to describe just how awful it must have been – and will continue to be – for them.

'Help me.' Those two words haunt me for a long time.

Tuesday, 3 September

Stage 10: Jurançon–Pau time trial, 36 km
Winner: Primož Roglič
Red jersey: Primož Roglič

Very strange to be in Pau for the Vuelta and not the Tour de France, which visits every year without fail. It's a lovely, understated and unfashionable city – in the sense that it never seems to be in fashion – and a time trial starting in the suburbs in mid-afternoon gives me some time to explore it on my folding bike.

I ride along the Boulevard des Pyrénées, high above the Ousse river, to the Château de Pau, the 14th-century castle that was Henry IV's birthplace and which is now a museum. It's a grand, dazzling place that should be swarming with tourists but isn't, because this is Pau and the tourists are all in Biarritz, Bordeaux or, for different reasons, Lourdes.

Today's is also a strange stage because there is a fear that Roglič might win so decisively that he kills the race at the halfway point. Roglič is inscrutable, a self-contained man of few words and in possession of a steely cool calm. He reminds me of one of these buttoned-up male characters in a 19th-century novel who communicates using only lingering stares and long silences. Is there another side to Roglič? Hidden depths? I don't know, but I attended the Jumbo–Visma training camp in Spain last December and interviewed him there. I got very little out of him – far more revealing was the revelation from the coach, Merijn Zeeman, that they'd had a three-hour meeting the previous day about his race programme for 2019. This, said Zeeman, was unusually long, and Roglič had had much to say.

As with Mr Darcy in *Pride and Prejudice*, there's clearly a lot more going on in there than he lets on.

Anyway, it was a truth universally acknowledged that Roglič would win today's stage and take more than two minutes out of Lopez and Quintana.

Wednesday, 4 September

Stage 11: Saint-Palais–Urdax, 180 km
Winner: Mikel Iturria
Red jersey: Primož Roglič

A beautiful Basque stage that criss-crosses the border between France and Spain, starting in one country and finishing in another. But remaining throughout in 'Basqueland' – as the author Mark Kurlansky calls the seven provinces that make up the Basque Country, four of which are in Spain, three in France, where – until 1981 – it was illegal to teach the Basque language.

In the Spanish part of the Basque Country, meanwhile, the language has been taught as a first language in schools since Spain became a democracy after the death of Franco in 1975. Unlike local languages in some other parts of the world, Basque is not dying but thriving. And it is a young person's language. Quite a few Basques – including Juanma Gárate, the former rider and now EF Education First sports director – are much less proficient in the language than their children, who all speak Spanish as well.

I have been reading Kurlansky's book, *The History of the World According to the Basques*, while at the Vuelta. It offers a new perspective, for me at least, on this fascinating, beautiful and very prosperous corner of Europe (it's my impression that the prosperity is more concentrated in the Spanish part, though as far as Basques are concerned it's all Basqueland: '4+3=1' once being a popular bit of graffiti).

'The Basques seem to be a mythical people, almost an imagined people,' writes Kurlansky, an American who obviously immersed himself in the place. 'Their ancient culture is filled with undated legends and customs. Their land itself, a world of red-roofed, whitewashed towns, tough green mountains, rocky crests, a cobalt sea that turns charcoal in stormy weather, a strange language, and big berets, exists on no maps except their own.'

According to Kurlansky there's a 'Basque type with a long straight nose, thick eyebrows, strong chin, and long earlobes.' These earlobes are often filled with earrings, either hoops, like the Izagirre brothers or Iban Mayo, or black discs, like another Basque rider, Omar Fraile.

For many years, of course, there was a violent separatist movement in the Basque Country, one that kept the Vuelta away for more than 30 years before its return in 2011. But it's a region with a high level of autonomy and a local government that sits in very grand buildings in the political capital, Vitoria.

'The borders around Basqueland endure because they are cultural, not political,' writes Kurlansky.

Fittingly, a Basque rider, Mikel Iturria, on a Basque team, Euskadi–Murias, wins today's stage.

Thursday, 5 September

Stage 12: Circuito de Navarra–Bilbao, 171 km
Winner: Philippe Gilbert
Red jersey: Primož Roglič

Still reeling from the disappointment of last night's meal not being prepared by a Michelin two-star chef (the menu had been 'designed' by him, something the hotel had made, to my mind, rather too much of on their website), I decide to skip the start.

In Bilbao I head off on my folding bike to a climb, the Alto de Arraiz, that comes a few kilometres from the finish and is actually within the city itself. But astonishingly, considering how many bike races are held here, no race has used it before. Someone had written to Javier Guillén, the Vuelta director, suggesting it and when he went to see it, he 'fell in love.'

I can see why. It is steep and narrow and today it is packed with fans, which makes for a great climax to the stage – and a big improvement on the usual bunch sprint, or reduced bunch sprint, that we tend to see in Bilbao. Today it provides a launchpad for Philippe Gilbert to leave his breakaway companions and ride solo to the finish for his sixth Vuelta stage win.

In the evening I head out for *pintxos* and *Txakoli* wine with Eneko Garate, a friend who used to manage the Basque Kaiku team and now runs a publishing company, mainly publishing cycling books in Spanish. I am puzzled when the barman serves the *Txakoli* in normal wine glasses, rather than performing the elaborate ritual of pouring it from a great height into tumblers.

I ask Eneko about this. 'Oh, that's a San Sebastián thing,' he explains. 'Here in Bilbao it's served in wine glassses.' It means that the wine is flat rather than slightly sparkling, as it is in San Sebastián, an hour up the coast. But it illustrates another point made in Kurlansky's book: that although Basqueland has a clear cultural identity, regional variations (including in the language, dialects and sub-dialects) are significant.

Before we leave Bilbao and the Basque Country, a word about my hotel, the Ilunion. A sign on the wall said: 'More than 40 per cent of our employees have some kind of disability,' which I only spotted (the sign, I mean) after noticing, and remarking to myself in one of the internal conversations that rattles around your brain when travellling alone, how charming and helpful the staff were. If you're going to Bilbao I recommend the Ilunion.

Friday, 6 September

Stage 13: Bilbao–Los Machucos, 166 km
Winner: Tadej Pogačar
Red jersey: Primož Roglič

Los Machucos is a classic climb of the modern Vuelta: spectacular or silly, depending on your point of view. The ramps at the bottom – slabs of slatted concrete at an almost impossible angle (the slats presumably to minimise the risk of tyres slipping) – are ridiculous. But it helps to give the Vuelta its distinctive identity and sets it apart from the Giro and the Tour, which probably wouldn't risk such an extreme climb.

Climbs like this create problems for those of us trying to cover the race, too. I linger too long in Bilbao and get stuck behind the race, which means I am late to the foot of Los Machucos, which means I can't drive up. Is it possible ride up Los Machucos on a folding bike, even a carbon fibre one with seven gears? There is an evacuation road, which the riders will come down after the stage. Trouble is, it is as spectacular/silly as the other road, which the race is taking.

There's nothing for it but to commit to the task, pedalling up those slabs of slatted concrete. Riders like to say that they take a Grand Tour 'one day at a time' and my approach to this climb is similar, but more microscopic, in that I'm taking it 'one rev at a time'. I can't think beyond the current, very slow pedal revolution.

After a kilometre or so I see a slate grey campervan parked up ahead of me. As I get closer, I see that it has subtle, discreet décals. It's the Roglič mobile: home to his wife and three-month-old baby as they follow the race. I have no idea why it is parked here, in the middle of nowhere. Eventually I draw level and by the doorway see a pair of flipflops: Mrs Roglič and Baby Roglič must be inside. (When I mention the campervan on the podcast one listener suggests that in addition to Superman and Nairoman we should introduce a new nickname for Roglič: Camperman.)

About 40 minutes in to my ride, as I wobble on up holding my phone on the handlebars, watching the stage on the Eurosport Player (excellent 4G up here), I realise I am not going to make it. I have ridden five kilometres but there are still two kilometres to the top. On the screen, Pogačar and Roglič are three-and-a-half kilometres from the summit. Do the math.

I am back down the hill in what feels like two minutes, in plenty of time to intercept the riders as they arrive at their buses.

I sleep well.

Saturday, 7 September

Stage 14: San Vicente de la Barquera–Oviedo, 188 km
Winner: Sam Bennett
Red jersey: Primož Roglič

One of the riders in today's breakaway is Harm Vanhoucke, a 22-year-old riding his first Grand Tour with Lotto–Soudal. He isn't supposed to be here. The call came only a week or so before the race after the awful death of Bjorg Lambrecht at the Tour of Poland.

Vanhoucke and Lambrecht were best friends as well as teammates. They had grown up racing each other. They were the same age. They raced together 93 times since 2016, Lambrecht finishing ahead of Vanhoucke almost nine times out of 10. On five occasions they shared a podium; both finished in the top 10 in 49 races. One of the most memorable occasions was the 2017 Tour de Savoie Mont Blanc: Lambrecht was second and Vanhoucke third with Egan Bernal the overall winner. At the time, they were three promising 20-year-olds excelling in a senior race against riders much older.

Today Vanhoucke is in the break that goes early and stays out front for most of the stage. As Sam Bennett wins the stage I wait at the Lotto–Soudal bus for Vanhoucke. I'm not sure whether he'll want to talk about his late friend, and the strange and tragic circumstances that brought him to the Vuelta. When he arrives back at the bus he gets off the bike slowly and stretches his back painfully.

Vanhoucke is shy and softly spoken and guarded. But when I ask him whether it was a difficult decision to accept the team's invitation to ride his first Grand Tour in place of Lambrecht, he opens up: 'I first asked his parents if they were good with it. If they really wanted it. They said to me, the only one Bjorg would want to replace him was me, because I was a really good friend of his. We always shared a room. It was a really good feeling to hear that from the parents and, yeah, I do my best here.'

He has done his best today, being out front most of the stage. 'I ride in his place and I want to honour him in the best way I can,' says Vanhoucke. 'I think he will be happy from above.'

Sunday, 8 September

Stage 15: Tineo–Santuario del Acebo, 154 km
Winner: Sepp Kuss
Red jersey: Primož Roglič

I wonder what the atmopshere is like at the Jumbo–Visma dinner table. They have an interesting blend of open and talkative riders – Neilson Powless, George Bennett, Sepp Kuss and Robert Gesink – and stoic, impassive, dare I say monosyllabic ones, like Tony Martin and the overall leader, Primož Roglič.

Perhaps that's unfair on Martin. But at the top of the climb to the finish, in this beautiful, remote part of Asturias, I am given a sharp reminder of just how blunt some riders can be.

Kuss drops his breakaway companions to ride most of Santuario del Acebo alone and take a very impressive win before breezily giving a few interviews. On the podium he's handed a bottle of beer and downs it in two.

Powless, when he appears, stops to describe his day, spent supporting Roglič, at some length and in fascinating detail.

I am standing just beyond the line when Martin appears and stops right beside me. 'Tony, any chance of a quick word?' I say, raising my recorder towards him. He doesn't so much as glance in my direction, staring straight ahead and very slightly shaking his head to indicate no. He reaches down for his bidon and takes a slug while still staring, stony-faced, straight ahead. I don't move. He doesn't move. We stand beside each other in silence for a very uncomfortable minute or so before Martin's *soigneur* appears.

Maybe he's just knackered.

Monday, 9 September

Stage 16: Pravia–La Cubilla
Winner: Jakob Fuglsang
Red jersey: Primož Roglič

Another new climb for the Vuelta. Which is extraordinary. This one feels like entering a secret world.

Only, it's not really like that at all, because it isn't hidden in the back of a wardrobe – it's sitting there right in the middle of the country, or at least Asturias. I mean, how can the Vuelta have avoided it?

It's dubbed the Galibier of Asturias, at least by Daniel. It has that same majestic, epic quality; going on and on, for 17.8 kilometres, on a rough, bumpy road, up into the clouds and among the birds whose enormous wingspans allow them to hover, watching, poised to dive on prey that might include small mammals and humans (for all I know). At the top there's a pretty green plateau before the road deteriorates into dirt track.

When I arrive at the large red inflatable structure that acts as the Vuelta press centre, and which looks like a bouncy castle, Daniel is studying Google Maps, and Apple maps, and Michelin maps, and Waze, and any other maps he can find, trying to figure out whether it is possible to drive down the dirt track and join up with the road, because it will slice over an hour from the journey to León.

As the riders finish, led in by Jakob Fuglsang, I think it'll be interesting to ask a few of them for their impressions of the climb. What they tell me shows that it isn't always easy to tell how difficult a climb is from the car. All seem pretty underwhelmed, apart from George Bennett, who appreciated the beauty. But none of them say it was especially hard. In fact, they all, even riders like Mitch Docker, say it was quite straightforward. Seven or eight per cent is hard. Six per cent is easy, relatively speaking. This one averages 6.2.

Oh well. So much for the Galibier of the Asturias. I am one of the first journalists to leave the pressroom because the drive to León is over two hours and I'd like dinner, thank you very much. There's a bit of congestion but I get there at 9.30pm, entering the hotel lobby to find Daniel, who left a good hour after me, checking in.

He had taken the dirt road, crossing two rivers (he says), before being spat back out on tarmac. All this in a compact BMW SUV (white). I didn't know he had it in him. It's a Daniel I haven't seen before: a risk-taker, a cross between Bear Grylls, Ranulph Fiennes and Jeremy Clarkson.

Tuesday, 10 September

Rest day, Burgos

As with the first rest day, this one involves some driving, from León to Burgos, where I am meeting Orla for lunch. It's pouring and about 10 degrees so before we meet I go shopping for more appropriate clothing. I find a big, comfortable hoodie and put it on in the shop.

Over lunch Orla and I talk about the article she'd written for a recent edition of *Rouleur* magazine, recording our conversation for the next episode of *The Cycling Podcast Féminin*. The article was inspired by the #MeToo movement, with Orla trying to find out whether this sort of behaviour – on a spectrum from inappropriate advances and the abuse of power to physical sexual abuse – was prevalent in professional cycling.

She unconvered some pretty dark stories, one involving a *soigneur* who sexually assaulted a teenage rider. I find the story of this *soigneur*, and how and why he gets away with it, absolutely horrifying. It is society in microcosm, the *soigneur* preying on vulnerable young women who, afterwards, 'constantly question their own role, always thinking, "What have I done?"'

He was sacked from one team but the team didn't want to admit what had gone on, so, as Orla puts it, 'he was allowed to give his version of why he was sacked' and get a job in another team. He still works in women's professional cycling. Surrounding this issue – not just in cycling but in society at large – is the infamous omertà, sustained by victims' fear of the consequences of speaking out.

In cycling, someone who's doing a great job in trying to break this is Iris Slappendel of The Cyclists' Union, a new organisation for female professional cyclists. It's far more than a riders' association. Iris and her colleagues help with contract issues and other problems with teams and individuals in the sport and they can offer advice in confidence. More power to them.

After lunch I head to the Jumbo–Visma hotel on the outskirts of town to meet George Bennett, always one of the most interesting riders to interview. He just says what he thinks. Asked about his team signing Tom Dumoulin for 2020, most would say it was fantastic, it would only make them stronger, a brilliant addition to the team, blah blah blah. Bennett says: 'I found it a curious move in the sense that we're doing well already.'

I tell Bennett that Richard Plugge, the team boss, said that he had consulted with Bennett, Roglič and Steven Kruijswijk before signing Dumoulin.

'Yeah, but I think it didn't matter what I thought,' laughs Bennett. 'It's not like if I'd said I didn't want him to come he wouldn't have come.'

At the start of the interview Bennett fixes me with a look and points to something on the hoodie I'd purchased in Burgos: 'Nice label.'

I look down and can feel it scratching my chin. It is really quite big and very obvious and it's puzzling that Orla, who'd sat opposite me for an hour or so, didn't notice it.

Or perhaps she did.

Wednesday, 11 September

Stage 17: Aranda de Duero–Guadalajara, 219 km
Winner: Philippe Gilbert
Red jersey: Primož Roglič

The best stage in a Grand Tour since…? I'm not sure. George Bennett said the previous day that he was 'shitting himself' about this stage: the longest of the race, high on the plateau, with strong wind forecast.

From Bennett's words I inferred that everybody, certainly the team of the race leader, would be alert to the danger.

Driving to the finish in Guadalajara I can see the wind bending what few trees there are. A feature of the plateau is that it is stark and empty and therefore more or less completely unsheltered. It means crosswinds, of course. Yet, as we learn later, the race apparently splits before they even get to the crosswinds. Like a Formula One Grand Prix, positioning on the grid is all important.

I say 'apparently' because I don't know. The start of the stage isn't televised. We only have the riders' accounts to go by, and these are, to the say the least, unreliable, not through any malice but because nobody can see everything that happens.

Who, in the first three kilometres ('apparently'), lets a wheel go? Don't know. Who is driving it so hard at the front in those first few kilometres? Don't know. You would guess Deceuninck–Quick-Step, who place seven of their eight riders in the 40-man group that goes clear. But Tim Declercq, who I speak to at the finish, insists not.

I don't mind this at all. I like the mystery. The absence of facts and visual evidence leaves a lot of space for guesswork, rumour and intrigue – the very essence of a good story, and this stage spawns hundreds. And what a deliciously thrilling spectacle it is: 220 kilometres of flat-out racing, echelons chasing echelons across the beautiful, barren Spanish landscape: beautiful and enthralling. The gap between the front group, containing echelon king Quintana, and the chasing group, containing Roglič, once stable, hovers between five and six minutes. After a couple of difficult days in the mountains Quintana is dragged back into contention by the huge engines of Deceuninck–Quick-Step. By the end of the day he will be back up to second overall.

After such an exciting day we have no right to expect a great finale but that's what we get. Sam Bennett is the fastest in the front group and the biggest threat to Deceuninck but the Belgian masters of this kind of racing have a plan, of course they do. Declercq puts in an enormous turn on the final rise, setting up Zdeněk Štybar, who attacks with two kilometres to go. There's a chance he will stay clear – it's a good move – but if not, Philippe Gilbert is on standby.

Štybar's attack forces Bennett to make his move early, with 700 metres to go. Gilbert is lurking, and with great cunning and calculation – a 'wily old fox,' as his teammate and roommate James Knox describes him – he waits for Bennett to play his hand and start to fade before pouncing. It is ice cool and completely ruthless.

I stand just beyond the finish line and watch the riders in the front group arrive more than an hour ahead of schedule, all of them flopping over their handlebars as they gulp in some air. I have never seen such shattered expressions. They look exhausted and exhilarated. Some, such as Owain Doull, riding his first Grand Tour, simply cannot believe that they'd ridden like that for 220 kilometres. I bet many of them didn't know they were even capable of riding like that for 220 kilometres.

Perhaps it has changed little but it has been bonkers and brilliant.

Thursday, 12 September

Stage 18: Colmenar Viejo–Becerril de la Sierra, 177 km
Winner: Sergio Higuita
Red jersey: Primož Roglič

Our hotel for tonight, the Box Art Hotel, is a lovely, grand building perched on a hill, with a modern, glass-fronted restaurant below. It's a hotel-come-art gallery, the art on display including sculptures by Javier Benito, paintings by South African artist Andrew Hollis, and some large, abstract canvases by

Angel Garcia, who happens to be the man who owns the hotel and who shows me around when I arrive.

It's a beautiful, relaxing place, and we eat a delicious meal in the restaurant, polished off with a glass of local whisky.

That's right: Spain's only whisky distillery is in nearby Segovia, and an infamous stage of the 1985 Vuelta a España finished outside it, handing overall victory to a local rider (Pedro Delgado) at the expense of – of all people – a Scottish rider (there's a book you can read about this if interested). Destilerias y Crianzas, who once owned a distillery in Scotland as well, produce five whiskies from their premises in Segovia.

Sadly the restaurant doesn't have the 10-year-old single malt, but they do produce a bottle of the DYC blend and big, heavy-duty crystal tumblers (whisky glasses have to be heavy, in my opinion). Once I have removed the ice (come on, guys), and added a splash of water, I have a very enjoyable dram – and, at about 4am, a very dry mouth.

Friday, 13 September

Stage 19: Ávila–Toledo, 165 km
Winner: Rémi Cavagna
Red jersey: Primož Roglič

A rider I have wanted to interview the whole Vuelta is Willie Smit, having read about him in *Procycling* magazine the previous year. His mother was an alcoholic, his father was killed clearing landmines in Afghanistan.

As a young child Smit was taken into custody by the authorities when it became clear his mother couldn't look after him. His grandparents took over his care, but his mother contested that – she and his father weren't married, which complicated things – and there were court hearings.

He loved his grandparents though they lived on a remote farm. The only way he could make friends, and see life beyond the farm, was by bike. This was his introduction to cycling. He gained an education and went to law school. According to Daniel, he also became a very good golfer with a handicap of two.

Now he rides for Katusha–Alpecin, a team with an air of despondency about it because its future looks so gloomy. Smit is a refreshing antidote to the negativity. He produces little films that are invariably positive and upbeat, even a little twee, such as one about a picnic with the love of his life, his girlfriend (now wife), on his birthday.

I had hoped to speak to him on the second rest day but at the last moment Katusha–Alpecin were told by the organisers that they were being moved to a hotel 50 kilometres away from everyone else, and 50 kilometres further from the following day's start. I guess this is the sort of thing that happens to teams about to go out of business. I doubt it happens to Team Ineos.

Anyway. This morning I finally get to speak properly to Smit, whose continued participation is something of a miracle after his crash at the finish in Oviedo. A horrific gash to his knee required 16 stitches and he hadn't been optimistic of finishing the next day, yet here he is in Ávila almost a week later, now confident that he will make it to Madrid despite being on the antibiotics that the team insisted he take to prevent an infection in his knee.

Outside the team bus, around 25 minutes before the start of a stage, doesn't seem like the ideal time to tell a life story, particularly one as complicated as Smit's. But this doesn't stop him. I don't have to ask him many questions as he tells me about his mother, who doesn't speak to him now but for whom he clearly has great sympathy and affection, his beloved grandparents, his late father, who he didn't really know but admires tremendously. He's engaging and likeable as well as tough and resilient.

The adversity he has survived is clearly what drives Smit in his cycling career and to finish his first Grand Tour, which is a hard enough thing to do without having to take medication that you know is draining your energy and sapping your strength.

Saturday, 14 September

Stage 20: Arenas de San Pedro–Plataforma de Gredos, 190 km
Winner: Tadej Pogačar
Red jersey: Primož Roglič

At the foot of the Plataforma de Gredos, as we wait for shuttle buses to take us to the summit, I explore the gift shop and bump into Jeroen Swart. I know Swart from the tests he conducted on Chris Froome following the 2015 Tour de France, when Swart measured the Tour de France winner's VO2 Max among other things.

Swart is a South African former rider, physiologist and coach. He has worked for several years in various anti-doping roles. He is also a medical doctor and this year he was appointed head of medicine at UAE Team Emirates. It was an appointment that surprised me but I've seen him at a few races and he seems to enjoy the role, or at least the opportunity to work on a World Tour team.

At this Vuelta I've spoken to him a few times about Tadej Pogačar, the 20-year-old Slovenian phenomenon who has won two stages, and at the start of today's final mountain stage sits fifth overall.

Back in Pau, when I first talked about him with Swart, I assumed that Pogačar's chances of finishing his first Grand Tour would be about 50:50. It is traditional for such young riders, in their first year as a professional, to do the first 10 days or so and then be withdrawn. Swart wasn't so sure this would happen: he said they'd monitor the rider and if they felt he was too fatigued, or in danger of suffering long-term damage, they would pull him out. But it wasn't guaranteed.

'He doesn't show any signs of tiredness, then,' I say to Swart in the gift shop almost two weeks after the time trial in Pau.

'On the contrary,' says Swart. 'I think he's getting stronger.'

Swart isn't involved in Pogačar's training – his role is strictly medical (UCI rules prevent doctors coaching riders, which makes sense). In essense, Swart is coming to the same conclusion as everyone else: that 'Pog,' as we've taken to calling him, is a physical freak.

Today he proves it, attacking long before the climb to the bleak, deserted Plataforma de Gredos, and riding alone for 38 kilometres to take his third stage win and climb to third overall. In Madrid tomorrow he will finish on the podium of his first Grand Tour. And it is my belief, having studied his face at close quarters while interviewing him a couple of days ago, that Pog hasn't even started shaving yet.

Sunday, 15 September

Stage 21: Fuenlabrada–Madrid, 106 km
Winner: Fabio Jakobsen
Red jersey: Primož Roglič

Something that has hugely enhanced *The Cycling Podcast*'s coverage of this Vuelta has been the daily audio diaries by Nick Schultz of Mitchelton–Scott and James Knox of Deceuninck–Quick-Step. When we asked them to do this, a few days before the race started, we said we didn't expect one everyday. 'Just send us an audio file when you feel that you have something to say,' we told them.

Well, it turns out that they had something to say everyday. Their dedication has been impressive, as has been their determination to tell our listeners something interesting, taking them inside their race as much as possible. I guess one thing you can say about professional cyclists is that when they commit to something, they really do commit (see Willie Smit, above).

At the finish of today's final stage in Madrid I wait by the Deceuninck–Quick-Step bus, where Patrick Lefevere is holding court, celebrating yet another win – the final stage being taken by their young sprinter, Fabio Jakobsen.

Eventually Knox appears and embraces the Godfather of the team, Lefevere. Apart from finishing his first Grand Tour (having crashed out of the Giro earlier in the season) and riding a very good race, ending up 11th on GC, Knox embodies the ethos of the team, appearing to take as much satisfaction in his teammates' victories as in his own performance.

It is a team that has something special, of this there can be no doubt. It was in evidence the previous day when Knox, on course to finish in the top 10, struggled with injuries from a nasty crash on the road to Toledo. James's audio diaries over these last few days of the Vuelta have been honest, raw and unmissable.

Yesterday there was footage of him being literally pulled along by his teammate and roommate, none other than Philippe Gilbert, when it seemed that Knox was struggling to turn the pedals. I like to think that the outpouring of sympathy and support owed not only to the footage but also to Knox's daily dispatches on the podcast, and listeners' sense of having been on the journey with him.

Now that the journey has come to an end he can climb off the emotional rollercoaster. His final diary entry comes from a noisy, boisterous team bus where, he says, he is 'feeling a few drinks already'.

'When I think back to the start,' he continues, 'it's been such a long time, wow. Really, really happy to be finished. And to finish with a victory. Bit lost for words. All the ups and downs. Special team. We can be really proud of ourselves. I'm really proud of myself. Yeah, brilliant. Think I'll enjoy tonight…

'First Cumbrian to finish a Grand Tour. I'll take that. Yeah, I'll take that.'